THEURGY

SEVEN APPROACHES TO DIVINE CONNECTION

EDITED BY
JEAN-LOUIS DE BIASI

WITH CLIO AJANA • PATRICK DUNN • HERCULES INVICTUS
TONY MIERZWICKI • JOHN OPSOPAUS • BRANDY WILLIAMS

LLEWELLYN
WOODBURY, MINNESOTA

Theurgy: Seven Approaches to Divine Connection Copyright © 2025 Edited by Jean-Louis de Biasi with Clio Ajana, Patrick Dunn, Hercules Invictus, Tony Mierzwicki, John Opsopaus and Brandy Williams. All rights reserved. No part of this book may be used or reproduced in any manner whatsoever, including internet usage, without written permission from Llewellyn Worldwide Ltd., except in the case of brief quotations embodied in critical articles and reviews. No part of this book may be used or reproduced in any manner for the purpose of training artificial intelligence technologies or systems.

FIRST EDITION
First Printing, 2025

Book design by Christine Ha
Cover design by Kevin R. Brown
Interior illustrations by the Llewellyn Art Department

Llewellyn Publications is a registered trademark of Llewellyn Worldwide Ltd.

Library of Congress Cataloging-in-Publication Data (Pending)
ISBN: 978-0-7387-7633-0

Llewellyn Worldwide Ltd. does not participate in, endorse, or have any authority or responsibility concerning private business transactions between our authors and the public.

All mail addressed to the author is forwarded but the publisher cannot, unless specifically instructed by the author, give out an address or phone number.

Any internet references contained in this work are current at publication time, but the publisher cannot guarantee that a specific location will continue to be maintained. Please refer to the publisher's website for links to authors' websites and other sources.

Llewellyn Publications
A Division of Llewellyn Worldwide Ltd.
2143 Wooddale Drive
Woodbury, MN 55125-2989
www.llewellyn.com

Printed in the United States of America

GPSR Representation:
UPI-2M PLUS d.o.o., Medulićeva 20, 10000 Zagreb, Croatia,
matt.parsons@upi2mbooks.hr

THEURGY

Other Books by the Authors

Clio Ajana

Bringing Race to the Table: Exploring Racism in the Pagan Community (contributor)

Shades of Ritual: Minority Voices in Practice (contributor)

Jesus Girls: True Tales of Growing Up Female and Evangelical (contributor)

Jean-Louis de Biasi

Esoteric Freemasonry: Rituals & Practices for a Deeper Understanding

Secrets and Practices of the Freemasons: Sacred Mysteries, Rituals and Symbols Revealed

Hidden Mandala Coloring Book: Inspired by the Sacred Designs of Italy

Patrick Dunn

The Orphic Hymns: A New Translation for the Occult Practitioner

The Practical Art of Divine Magic: Contemporary & Ancient Techniques of Theurgy

Hercules Invictus

Ashtar's The Space Brothers Speak: Transmissions From the Solar Council (contributor)

Weird Time: Exploring the Mysteries of Time and Space (contributor)

Mimics—The Others Among Us (contributor)

Weird Winged Wonders: The Twilight World of Cryptid Creatures (contributor)

Olympian Ice: Elohim Hercules: Realm of Elemental Earth

Tony Mierzwicki

Hellenismos: Practicing Greek Polytheism Today

Graeco-Egyptian Magick: Everyday Empowerment

Magick on the Edge: Adventures in Experimental Magick (contributor)

Manifesting Prosperity: A Wealth Magic Anthology (contributor)

John Opsopaus
The Oracles of Apollo: Practical Ancient Greek Divination for Today

The Secret Texts of Hellenic Polytheism: A Practical Guide to the Restored Pagan Religion of George Gemistos Plethon

The Oracles of Homer and the Bones: Divination with the Ancient Homeromanteion and Astragalomanteion

Pythagorean Theology and the Esoteric Elements

The Pythagorean Tarot: An Interpretation Based on Pythagorean and Alchemical Principles

Brandy Williams
Practical Magic for Beginners: Techniques & Rituals to Focus Magical Energy

Cord Magic: Tapping into the Power of String, Yarn, Twists & Knots

Llewellyn's Complete Book of Ceremonial Magick: A Comprehensive Guide to the Western Mystery Tradition (contributor)

CONTENTS

Introduction   1
   The Theurgic Panel   2
   Main Principles of Theurgy   5

Practicing Theurgy in the Platonic Tradition by John Opsopaus, PhD   7
   History of Neoplatonic Theurgy   8
   Applying the Theory of Neoplatonic Theurgy Today   12
   Jungian Depth Psychology   18
   Theurgy: The Hieratic Art   19
   Conclusion   37
      Practice: Sustasis Ritual for Athena   38

I Was a Teenage Theurgist by Hercules Invictus   43
   How I Discovered Theurgy   43
   The Iconostasi   45
      Practice: Establishing Your Own Iconostasi   46

Contents

Seeking Guidance   47
   Practice: Receiving Guidance   49
Embodying and Expressing   50
   Practice: Embodiment and Expression 101   51
My Guided Journey   52
En Onomati Theou   53
   Practice: En Onomati Theou—What More Can I Do?   55
Tips on Living a More Olympian Life   57
A Call to Adventure   58
In Closing: Living Theurgy   59

Carrying Deity in Modern Magical Practice by Brandy Williams   61
Classical Theurgy   63
Assumption of Godform   67
Liber XV, the Gnostic Mass   75
Drawing Down the Moon   83
Pagan Aspecting   90
Practice   94
   Deity Practice   95
   Daily Sitting Practice   96
Learning from Each Other   100

The Practice of Theurgic Meditation and Contemplation by Patrick Dunn   103
Mindfulness   104
Meditation on Beauty   106
   Exercise: Meditation on Beauty   107
Plotinus and Contemplation   109
   Exercise: Plotinus's Contemplation   111

Contents

The View from Above 112
   Exercise: The View from Above 114
Meditation on Virtue 115
   Exercise: Rehearsal and Recapitulation 117
Dwelling in the Nous 117
   Exercise: Via Negativa 118
Henōsis 119
Conclusion 120

Immortal Theurgy by Jean-Louis de Biasi 121
   An Initiatory Tradition 122
   The Eightfold Theurgic Path 123
     Practice: Seeking the Hidden Self 125
     Practice: Rhythmic Breathing 131
     Practice: Sun Salutation 135
     A Kemetic Practice 138
     Practice: Magnetization and Energization 142
     Practice: Transformative Astrology 151
     Practice: Ascent to the Light 152
     Practice: Consecration of a Divine Statue 155
   Before You Go 162

Theurgy: An Intimate Path to the Gods by Clio Ajana 165
   The Birth of My Desire 165
   Brush with the Theurgic Path 168
   First Steps on the Path 169
   Constellation of the Worshipped 172
     Exercise 1: Daily Practice—Deity of the Day 173
     Exercise 2: Prayer Circle for the Deity of the Day 174

Contents

    Exercise 3: Magickal Journal Review with Deity During Ritual Circle 175
    Exercise 4: Remapping the Constellation 177
  Progress Becomes Evident 178
  Continuing the Theurgic Path 179
    Exercise 5: Crafting with Planetary Hours 180
    Exercise 6: Use of Numerological Calculations 181
  Theurgy Is Worth the Effort 182

A Qabalistic Approach to Theurgy by Tony Mierzwicki 185
  Ascension Processes in the Ancient World 186
  Qabalistic Tree of Life and Planetary Correspondences 190
    Sephirothic Energy Attunement Ritual 203
  Communicating with Deities 215
  Approaches to Planetary or Sephirothic Initiation 216

Appendix A: Proclus's "On the Hieratic Art of the Hellenes" by John Opsopaus, PhD 217

Appendix B: Proclus's Hymn IV: Common Hymn for the Gods by John Opsopaus, PhD 223

Appendix C: The Hermetic Theurgic Creed by Jean-Louis de Biasi 225

Bibliographies by Chapter 227
  John Opsopaus, PhD 227
  Hercules Invictus 229
  Brandy Williams 229
  Patrick Dunn 233
  Jean-Louis de Biasi 233
  Clio Ajana 234
  Tony Mierzwicki 235

About the Authors 239

INTRODUCTION

A few years ago, the word *theurgy* was almost unknown to the public. The terms *magic* or *high magic* were mostly used to refer to a field closely related to this spiritual path. Inspired by modern research, some initiates and practitioners began using this term more broadly, as it aligned more closely with their practices and beliefs.

In a few words, *theurgy* is a "divine work." It is a set of spiritual ritual practices revealing our inner abilities and aiming to invoke the presence of divine powers or deities to achieve personal transformation, spiritual ascent, and union with the Divine.

As you immediately notice, the theurgic path is a holistic system placing you as the main actor of your own salvation. This spiritual path was founded on the most sacred land of the Mediterranean world for philosophers and Western adepts: Egypt. Julian the Chaldean and his son are often credited as the founding figures of theurgy. They were the ones who received the Chaldean Oracles through theurgic rituals. These mystical texts provided rituals and doctrines for communicating with the Divine. They were foundational to theurgical practices. This tradition further developed within the context of Neoplatonism, a philosophical system that sought to reconcile Platonic thought with religious practices. A key figure of late antiquity is Iamblichus, who integrated theurgy with Neoplatonism, emphasizing rituals, invocations, and the use of divine symbols.

The spread of Christianity pushed adepts, initiates, and sometimes groups to hide their beliefs and practices. Some figures within this new religion incorporated a few theurgical concepts and practices, influencing Christian mystical traditions. It is evident that such pagan elements were twisted to make them palatable to this very different theology.

The Renaissance gradually ended these dark days, and theurgy experienced a resurgence through the works of scholars like Marsilio Ficino and his small Florentine group. Real lineages were reactivated at this time and continue to this day. Today, scholars are doing essential work in translating and commenting on the sources of this tradition. Individual specialists and initiates are maintaining, exploring, and sometimes adapting this fascinating ritual path. Books such as this anthology provide the essential keys to easily experiment with rituals and spiritual techniques of this path.

The Theurgic Panel

In 2016, a group of authors and specialists was invited by Hercules to create a panel about theurgy on his podcast, *Voice of Olympus*. I was part of it as an author and Grand Master of the theurgic Order of the Aurum Solis. (It is important to note that Carl Llewellyn, founder of Llewellyn Publications, was the seventh Grand Master of this Order.)

The title of the panel changed a few times over the years, but the conversation has continued until today. This anthology is one of the offspring of this regular discussion on various aspects of theurgy. It aims to provide a broad perspective on this tradition, making it accessible to anyone, both beginners and advanced readers. Within these pages, you will discover multiple layers of material and practices, inviting you to delve deeper and deeper into this fascinating subject. Each time you open this book, you will gain fresh insights into this world.

However, as with any long-lasting tradition, some differences and divergences have emerged. This was true in the past and remains true today. Fundamentally, the seven specialists who participated in this book agree on the same principles and share a strong emotional attachment to their common origin and history. However, you will find in this anthology what can be

Introduction

called various facets of the same path. This is normal, exciting, and useful. It is a unique opportunity to learn and experiment.

The Authors

When **John Opsopaus, PhD**, began practicing Hellenismos (worship of the ancient Greek gods) in the 1980s, he started by performing the everyday household and group religious rituals, but soon his practice expanded to include the shamanic and mystical practices of the Pythagoreans and Neoplatonists, including theurgy. This is now his principal spiritual practice, which he has taught in workshops and writings, online and in print, for many years.

In his chapter, John explains the principles of Neoplatonic theurgy and illustrates them by constructing a ritual to invoke Athena for a meeting. After reviewing the history of Neoplatonic theurgy and its theory and explaining how it uses symbols to connect with a deity or daimon, he uses material from an ancient theurgical hymn to illustrate constructing a complete ritual for a *sustasis*, or meeting.

Hercules Invictus is a Lemnian Greek who is openly Olympian in his spirituality and worldview, dedicated to living the mythic life and committed to sharing his Olympian odyssey with others.

In his chapter "I was a Teenage Theurgist," Hercules shares how he discovered theurgy, why it so powerfully resonated with him, and how, by using the cultural and spiritual tools he grew up with as a Greek American in the 1960s and 1970s, he started practicing it. These simple tools helped launch his journey, enlivened his theurgic practice, and still serve him well to this day. He sincerely hopes that they will prove useful to you as well!

Brandy Williams is a Witch, Golden Dawn magician, Thelemite, and Tantric practitioner, and in all of these spiritual practices, she is a theurgist in love with the gods.

In her chapter, Brandy connects ancient theurgy with the modern Witchcraft ritual of Drawing Down, the ceremonial magic rituals Assumption of God-Form and the Gnostic Mass, and contemporary Pagan aspecting of deity. The chapter includes detailed instructions for embodying deity through the daily practice of communing with the goddesses and gods.

Patrick Dunn is a Hellenic Pagan and an eclectic occultist, in addition to being a poet, linguist, and university English professor with a PhD in modern literature and language. He is the author of several works exploring theurgy, magic, semiotics, and cartomancy, as well as an updated translation of *The Orphic Hymns*.

Meditation and contemplation have a long tradition in classical theurgy. Ancient philosophers and theurgists devised many methods of contemplation, from something resembling mindfulness meditation to specific contemplations on beauty and virtue. In this essay, Patrick describes several of those methods, with instructions for how to pursue them and integrate them into your own theurgic or spiritual practice. Finally, he discusses how to use them to pursue one of the ultimate goals of theurgy: *henōsis*, an experience of oneness with the fundamental ground of being, or of unity with the Divine itself.

As for me, **Jean-Louis de Biasi**, I am a philosopher and a published author with more than thirty books translated into several languages. I am a certified yoga teacher with extensive expertise in ancient Mediterranean traditions, Eastern spiritual techniques, Western esoteric practices, and Freemasonry. I am a Master Mason (raised in 1992) and a Past Master. I have received all the degrees of the Egyptian Freemasonry (33°-95°-AA) and other allied degrees, including the 32 degrees of the American Scottish Rite and the Royal Arch. I was fortunate to spend a couple of months in Egypt in the '80s and to practice theurgic rituals during a full night in the Great Pyramid. I have traveled extensively in Italy, Greece, Turkey, Lebanon, and Syria to connect with the most sacred places of the theurgic tradition.

In the chapter I wrote for this anthology, I chose to present a holistic view of the theurgic path. It is important to see that, like yoga for the East, theurgy is one of the few paths that includes several spiritual and psychic practices. The main symbol of the Aurum Solis, the Glorious Star, has been used to highlight eight categories, also known as *rays*, that are components of this path. I prepared various practices associated with each ray to give you the opportunity to experiment directly. Based on my experience as Grand Master of initiatory orders, I also emphasize and explain the importance of initiations and the risk of delusion.

Clio Ajana's chapter reflects a personal journey toward creating a fuller and more complete relationship with the deities whom she serves, worships, and devotes herself to. Active theurgic practice results for her in a deeper and more profound bond with the Gods. It is never boring, as it permits an enrichment of one's faith through open and consistent practice. The level of communication and satisfaction with religious practice deepens with the use of "divine working."

Her chapter sets this personal journey against a chronological background from monotheistic religious practice with minimal understanding of and communication with deity to a pantheist polytheistic practice filled with a consistent two-way bond with the Gods. The goal of her chapter is to reflect how choosing a conscious working of theurgy in one's life allows the practitioner to delve into the message that the Divine often seeks to explore with those individuals who dare to accept the challenge to embrace a full union with deity.

Tony Mierzwicki is an international author and lecturer walking a number of parallel paths, but the one relevant to this book is that of communing with divine energies through a process of planetary attunement and ascension, primarily derived from the Greek Magical Papyri.

Tony's essay acknowledges that while readers are happy to work theurgy so as to effect union with the Divine by using magickal ceremonies and sacred formulae, they do not necessarily want to do so using rituals taken from the Greek Magical Papyri. Many readers would rather use techniques that they are already familiar with in keeping with their own paths. He offers advice on adapting his own path of attunement to the planetary deities and archetypal energies ruling the days of the week. He then goes on to outline that each of the planets/sephiroth is actually a stepping stone for the soul in its ascent to its heavenly home.

Main Principles of Theurgy

Students sometimes ask how we can summarize the main principles of this unique ritualistic path. The best way is to ask our past masters. I am thrilled to share with you a hymn written by Proclus, which is a wonderful synthesis of the theurgic path. (You will find in appendix C a second text presenting eight principles from a powerful figure in our history called Gemistos Plethon.) But as the ancient initiates would say during the initiation: "Now is the time to listen and stay silent while we invoke the immortal divinities."

Introduction

Hear me, O Gods, you who hold the rudder of sacred wisdom![1]

You, who light in our souls, the flame of return to lead us back among the Immortals.

By the secret initiations to the hymns, you give us the power to escape from the dark cave and purify ourselves. Grant my wishes, powerful liberators!

By the understanding of the divine books, and by dispersing darkness, grant me a pure and holy light giving me the power to really know the unchanging deity and the human I am.

May a malevolent genius bringing suffering over me never succeed to keep me endlessly jailed under the waters of forgetfulness, nor separate me from the Gods.

May a terrifying reparation never chain my soul in the jails of life and my soul in the icy surges of generation as she doesn't want to wander there anymore.

You, O Gods, sovereigns of the radiant wisdom, grant my wishes and reveal to the one who hastens on the ascending path of the return, the holy ecstasies and initiations present at the core of your sacred words![2]

Now is the time for you to go forward and explore theurgy. As you can already see, this is quite an endeavor!

---

1. The meaning of this word, "Gods," should be understood as "all Deities," either Gods or a Goddess.
2. Proclus, *Hymn to the Gods*. Translation by Jean-Louis de Biasi.

PRACTICING THEURGY IN THE PLATONIC TRADITION

BY JOHN OPSOPAUS, PhD

Theurgy—the ancient spiritual practice of interacting with gods, daimons, and other spirits—was developed into its most sophisticated form in the West by the Neoplatonists of late antiquity. This is the form of theurgy that I have practiced for some three decades, and in this chapter, I will explain the theory behind Neoplatonic theurgy and how to construct an effective Neoplatonic theurgical ritual and then to conduct it.

First, however, it is worthwhile to say a few words about the value of such a practice. Many people, of course, pray to the gods, but theurgy allows us to interact with them more directly—to converse or even to argue with them, to be shown things by them, and to undergo experiences with them. In this way, we can better understand ourselves and the rest of existence; in particular, we can discover our destinies and how best to fulfill them. We can obtain the aid of gods and daimons in dealing with our issues, both big and small. It is especially valuable to practice theurgy in midlife, when we have become established in the material world through family and career and are facing the second half of life and the inevitable end of this incarnation. The gods and daimons will guide us and reveal our task in this time of life, when our orientation should become more spiritual. Of course, theurgy is valuable for younger people too. Who would not benefit from the collaboration of gods and daimons?

Aside from its benefits for the individual, more widespread practice of theurgy would improve twenty-first-century society. Our world is out of balance, dominated by materialistic, rationalistic, and narrowly scientific modes of thinking, which lead to feelings of meaninglessness, depression, cynicism, callousness, superficiality, indulgence, and narcissism. While reason and science, along with our knowledge of material reality and the ability to control it, have contributed greatly to human life and prosperity, the spiritual side of our world is, for the most part, in shambles. To many, the mainstream religions seem superficial and do not speak to people's deep spiritual need for meaning. Therefore, many abandon religion entirely and are set adrift with a shallow, materialist worldview. Theurgy can bring about a revitalization of life's spiritual dimension, helping us to understand our place in the cosmos and to live more meaningful lives. If we don't consciously reclaim our spiritual nature, then these repressed forces will erupt ever more strongly in forms such as dogmatic and violent fundamentalisms, in prejudice and violence, in blatant, unapologetic irrationality, and ultimately in societal psychoses.

History of Neoplatonic Theurgy

The term *theurgy* (Greek *theourgia*) was apparently coined in the late second century CE by Julian the Chaldean and his son Julian the Theurgist, who might have been from Syria. Theurgical practices have existed in many cultures from prehistoric times and perhaps first entered the classical world in the seventh century BCE when Greek *iatromanteis* (healer-seers) learned the spiritual techniques of west-Asian shamans. Later Platonic theurgy builds on these practices and seems to be a philosophical systematization and refinement of Egyptian temple ritual, which was highly respected in the Platonic tradition.

Julian the Chaldean probably used his son as a medium to converse with the gods and also with the soul of Plato. As a result, they received the verses now known as the Chaldean Oracles, which were treated as revealed wisdom by Neoplatonists but now survive only in fragments. They were "the paradigmatic example of inspired, theurgic divination for the Neoplatonists."[3]

Neoplatonism (also called *Late Platonism*) is a recent term for the new direction of Platonic philosophy that began with Plotinus (204–270 CE), who learned his philosophy in Alexandria. It had an increased emphasis on the spiritual dimensions of Platonic philosophy and especially on practices leading to union with the first principle of everything, the Ineffable One, by means of contemplation or meditation. In a sense, this is the highest form of theurgy, for it does not rely on material substances and actions, and Plotinus does not seem to have used the more ritualistic procedures of the Julians or later theurgists, who adopted spiritual practices from Egyptian, Persian, and other Mediterranean cultures.

Porphyry (c.234–c.305 CE), from Roman Syria, was Plotinus's student and literary executer, who wrote his master's biography and assembled his writings into a collection he called *The Enneads*. Porphyry was an accomplished philosopher in his own right, but many of his works were lost or destroyed, or they survive only in fragments. He is commonly supposed to have favored the more contemplative methods of his master over the more ritualistic theurgy of his successor, Iamblichus (c.245–c.325 CE), but recent scholarship suggests this was more a difference of emphasis and a philosophical debate.[4] On the other hand, it has been argued that Iamblichus's theurgy is more effective precisely because we are fundamentally embodied beings, not disembodied spirits.[5] In fact, Iamblichus wrote *On the Mysteries*, the most comprehensive surviving text on theurgical theory, in response to a series of questions from Porphyry.[6] Iamblichus was born in Syria and, after

---

3. Crystal Addey, *Divination and Theurgy in Neoplatonism: Oracles of the Gods* (Ashgate, 2014), 10.
4. Addey, "Debating Oracles: Porphyry's *Letter to Anebo* and Iamblichus's *De Mysteriis*," chap. 4 in *Divination and Theurgy*.
5. Gregory Shaw, *Hellenic Tantra: The Theurgic Platonism of Iamblichus* (Angelico Press, 2024).
6. Its actual title is *The Reply of the Master Abamon to the Letter of Porphyry to Anebo, and the Solution to the Questions it Contains*, but Ficino titled his translation *On the Mysteries of the Egyptians, Chaldeans, and Assyrians*; Emma C. Clarke, John M. Dillon, and Jackson P. Hershbell, trans., *Iamblichus: On the Mysteries*, ed. Johan C. Thom. Writings of the Greco-Roman World, no. 4. (Society of Biblical Literature, 2003).

perhaps studying under Porphyry in Rome, returned to Syria to found his own school in Apamea. He believed that the Assyrians and Egyptians knew the true theurgical arts, which they had learned from the gods themselves, and he warned the Greeks against changing them.

Proclus (412–485 CE), who was born in Constantinople and studied in Alexandria before settling in Athens, headed the Platonic Academy for almost fifty years and was perhaps the last and greatest master of theurgy in late antiquity, at least the greatest of those whose works survive. In addition to works on philosophy and theology, we have his seven theurgical hymns (Hymn IV is appendix B in this book), and his short essay, "On the Hieratic Art," which is perhaps the shortest surviving summary of the principles of theurgy (appendix A). In addition, Proclus's commentaries on the Platonic dialogues often provide valuable insights pertinent to theurgy.

After the emperor Justinian closed all the pagan schools in 529 CE, seven leading philosophers from the Platonic Academy fled Athens to the east in search of a more tolerant environment, where pagan philosophy survived.[7] Although some Neoplatonic ideas and practices were absorbed into Christianity, and some Christians studied Neoplatonism, especially in Byzantium, they had to be careful because practicing it was punished with cruel torture and execution.[8] Especially in the eighth through the tenth centuries in the Middle East, many Neoplatonic texts were translated into Syriac and Arabic, and some survived only in these translations, but were brought back later to the West and translated into Latin. For the most part, theurgy went underground in the West until the Renaissance.

After Constantinople fell to the Ottoman Turks in 1453, many scholars fled to the West, bringing with them valuable Greek manuscripts that had been unavailable in Western Europe. Fifteen years previously, Cosimo de' Medici had heard the lectures on Plato given by the Neopagan Greek philosopher George Gemistos Plethon (c.1355–1452), who developed religious

---

7. For a nuanced discussion of these events and their evidential basis, see Edward Watts, "Justinian, Malalas, and the End of Athenian Philosophical Teaching in A.D. 529," *The Journal of Roman Studies* 94 (2004): 168–82, https://doi.org/10.2307/4135014.
8. Niketas Siniossoglou, *Radical Platonism in Byzantium: Illumination and Utopia in Gemistos Plethon* (Cambridge University Press, 2011), 134–48.

rites rooted in the Platonic tradition (presented in my book *Secret Texts of Hellenic Polytheism*), and so in 1462, Cosimo established a Platonic Academy in Florence and put the young scholar Marsilio Ficino (1433–1499) in charge. Ficino translated the works of Plato and the Neoplatonists into Latin so they could be read in the West. He was also practicing theurgy in the Platonic Academy, as we know from his *Three Books on Life* and other sources, and this led to a renaissance of theurgy in Europe.[9] Renaissance theurgy merged with medieval magical traditions to engender many systems of ceremonial magic as well as magical orders and esoteric associations that practiced some form of theurgy. Many are with us still, but their history is often difficult to document. (See Brandy Williams's chapter for the history of some more-recent theurgical practices.)

A less obvious form of Western theurgy is *spiritual alchemy*, in which material operations in the laboratory are used to effect a transmutation of the alchemist's soul (metaphorically, from lead into gold). This was the goal of some—but certainly not all—of the alchemists, but due to their symbolic language, it is often difficult to tell what the true purpose of their operations was. Central to the work of spiritual alchemists was a conjunction of opposites (*coniunctio oppositorum* in Jung's terms), especially of the material and the spiritual dimensions of reality. Recognizing the importance of gender balance in any work directed toward a complete and integrated psyche, some male alchemists worked with a *soror mystica* (mystic sister) in a practice akin to Tantra.

Another recent manifestation of theurgy is the practice of *active imagination* developed by C. G. Jung (1875–1961) and his colleagues in analytical, or depth, psychology. Although he initially developed the techniques in an ad hoc fashion, he later discovered their roots in ancient Neoplatonism and Gnosticism. These early (1913–1916) theurgical experiments provided the foundation of his entire psychological system and therapeutic technique. Jung devoted the last two decades of his life to spiritual alchemy and its potential for healing the ills of individuals and, therefore, of the modern world.

---

9. Marsilio Ficino, *Three Books on Life: A Critical Edition and Translation with Introduction and Notes*, ed. and trans. Carol V. Kaske and John R. Clark (Renaissance Society of America, 1989), 45–70.

Applying the Theory of Neoplatonic Theurgy Today

Although the theory of Neoplatonic theurgy is reasonably well documented, we do not have detailed descriptions of ritual practice. We do have theurgical rituals from other sources, such as the Graeco-Egyptian Magical Papyri, but we don't know how reliable these sources might be. We would like to have tried-and-tested rituals that have been preserved through the ages due to their effectiveness, but we do not have these in the Neoplatonic tradition. Most likely, they were passed down and taught orally, but the documented chain of transmission is broken. Therefore, we must reconstruct the practices from our understanding of the Neoplatonic theory and from other theurgical traditions grounded in a similar theoretical basis.

Although much has been lost and destroyed over the centuries, a substantial amount of Neoplatonic philosophy has survived, and much of it is helpful in understanding Neoplatonic theurgy. Most important is Iamblichus's work known as *On the Mysteries*, which provides the theoretical foundation for theurgy. The writings of Proclus are also very valuable, including his commentaries on various Platonic dialogues (which often address theurgical topics), his short essay "On the Hieratic Art" (translated appendix A), and his seven theurgical hymns (Hymn IV is appendix B). Later in this chapter, I will construct a theurgical ritual using some material from his hymns.

We can fill in many of the details of Neoplatonic theurgical ritual from scholarly studies of Pagan religion and magic in ancient Greece. From them, we can learn the general principles, which we then apply in our theurgical rites. Other sources are the surviving Graeco-Egyptian *Hermetica* and *Magical Papyri*, which contain several relatively complete theurgical rituals. They are not specifically Neoplatonic, but they follow similar principles and are good guides. In the theurgical ritual I develop later in this chapter, I adopt some ideas from these ancient magical spells. As I mentioned before, we cannot assume that these rituals are effective just because they are old; they have survived by luck, not necessarily because they work. So we must be experimental, using ideas that make sense based on our understanding of the general principles and then testing them to see how effective they are.

We can also learn from theurgy-like practices that have survived into modern times in the West, such as those in ceremonial magic, which borrows from spiritual alchemy and Renaissance magic. Analogous techniques such as active imagination in analytical, or depth, psychology (which has Neoplatonic and Gnostic roots) provide useful information. We can also learn from other cultures with living theurgical traditions. For example, I have found Tibetan "deity yoga" to be especially informative. Of course, we need to be sensitive to the cultural context of these religious and spiritual practices, but they have a universal core because humans are fundamentally the same. We then can see the similarities to Neoplatonic theurgy and use them to fill in the gaps.

The Neoplatonic Cosmos

I will turn now to some of the principles on which Neoplatonic theurgy is based. To understand them, it is necessary to say a few words about Neoplatonic cosmology, but I will be brief. Certainly, Platonist philosophers through the ages have differed on many points, but most of them are not too important for our purposes here, and we can use the relatively simple cosmology of Plotinus.

To explain the Neoplatonic worldview, I have found it helpful to use the *Tetractys*, the ancient Pythagorean sacred symbol (a sort of mandala, see figure). Look at the lowest row of four dots. This symbolizes the material world, which we know through sensation. You can think of the four elements, the four qualities (warm, moist, cool, dry), the four seasons, the four cardinal directions, etc. This is the world of Becoming, the realm of coming to be and passing away, of mortality, where everything is in flux.

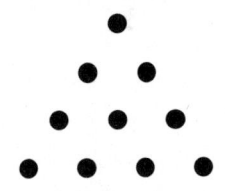

Moving up two levels, the row of two dots symbolizes the Platonic realm of Being, the realm of what *is* and what *is not*, that is, duality. The Platonic realm is outside of time and space; it is the realm of eternal Platonic Forms or Ideas. They are like numbers, for the relations among them, such as 2 + 3 = 5, did not come to be at some time, nor will they ever change. Together, these interrelated Ideas constitute a Cosmic *Nous*, or Mind.[10] Among the Ideas in the Platonic realm are also the eternal gods, who do not have physical bodies

---

10. In Neoplatonism, *nous* (νοῦς) refers to the mind that transcends the rational mind and is able to intuit directly the relations among the Ideas.

or reside in physical space. Plethon calls them the supercelestial gods because they reside outside of the heavens.[11]

Now, consider the row of three dots, which are between the row of four, representing the world of Becoming, and the row of two, representing Platonic Being. The material world exists in time and space, but the immaterial realm of Beings is outside of space and time. Now, it is a principle of Platonism that whenever opposite principles are united, as in the cosmos, there must be a mediating principle that shares some characteristics with each of the opposites, thus joining them together. The row of three dots represents this principle, the world soul (Latin, *anima mundi*), which mediates between Being and Becoming in that it is immaterial but exists in time and space. It projects the eternal Platonic Ideas into time as the laws that perpetually govern change in the material world. It is the soul of nature.

The world soul is the realm of the celestial gods, who reside in the heavens and animate the visible planets and stars. Although the supercelestial gods exist outside of time and are thus immortal, the celestial gods exist in time and move through the heavens. They are everlasting and therefore immortal because they have aetherial bodies. The celestial gods govern the processes of material nature, including mortal life. The world soul is also the realm where the *daimons* reside, who are mediators between the gods and mortals. Like the celestial gods, the daimons have aetherial bodies and exist in time but are everlasting and therefore immortal. They carry out the gods' laws in this realm of Becoming and serve as their agents in time and space. Therefore, in theurgy we often interact with daimons.

Finally, we come to the apex of the Tetractys, which symbolizes the highest principle in Neoplatonism, called the Ineffable One, the One Itself, etc. It is the highest principle of unity, the cause of anything being something. As such, it transcends all duality, including male and female, material and immaterial, existence and nonexistence, being and nonbeing. We cannot even say that it *is*. The One Itself therefore transcends our ability to understand it

---

11. Georgios Gemistos Plethon, *Plethon's Laws and Other Works (Translated)*, trans. John Opsopaus (Pythagorean Pentagram Pr., 2023), I.5.3, 23. See also John Opsopaus, *The Secret Texts of Hellenic Polytheism: A Practical Guide to the Restored Pagan Religion of George Gemistos Plethon* (Llewellyn, 2022), 259.

rationally or to speak about it comprehensibly. It can be grasped—as far as possible by humans—only through theurgical union with it.

Symbols

Symbols are essential in Neoplatonic theurgy, and so we must consider what they are. According to Platonists, the Ineffable One is the ultimate cause of everything: It is the cause of the Platonic Ideas, including the supercelestial gods. It is the cause of the images of the Ideas in the world soul, namely the celestial gods and daimons. And by means of them, it is the cause of everything in the material world. Therefore, everything is in lines of descent or causation from the One, which Neoplatonists call *seirai* ("lineages," "lines," "chords," "series"), sometimes translated as "chains." They are the paths or rays by which each specific divine *energeia* (activity, action, manifestation) descends into the world, and they are the means by which theurgists attune their minds and souls to specific deities and ascend toward them. Anything in which a particular god's energy is embodied may be used to engage that god through theurgy.

When things in a god's lineage are used in theurgy, they are known as *symbols* or *tokens* (*sumbola, sunthêmata*). Although the gods are omnipresent, symbols "tune" the theurgist's mind to a particular divine energy, analogous to tuning a radio to a particular frequency (or connecting a browser to a particular website). Symbols are activated in the imagination, which is the highest part of the human nonrational soul and the part through which deities usually communicate with us. Symbols come in a variety of forms, and because they are the principal tools of theurgy, we must learn to discover or create them.

The most obvious symbols are material objects. For example, we know from tradition that the owl and the olive tree are symbols of Athena and that the lyre, the laurel, the rooster, and a bow and arrows are symbols of Apollo. Material symbols include all sorts of animals, plants, stones, metals, and other substances (such as incense). We can learn them from tradition (but they should always be tested) or discover them by learning to perceive the *signatures* of particular gods in material things.

Among material objects, images (statues or pictures) are important symbols of a god. These include images of the god in a characteristic pose with their attributes, but also images of just the attributes (e.g., Apollo's lyre, Athena's owl). As discussed later, images may be consecrated ("animated") specifically for use in theurgical communication with a particular deity.

Theurgists also use more abstract signs or sigils, which might be drawn, painted, or engraved, to invoke gods. Such a symbol is called a *kharaktêr* ("character," "mark," "engraving") and may be familiar or esoteric. For example, for Athena we might use a simple drawing of her owl, spear, or the Gorgoneion on her aegis. These drawings do not have to be very artistic, and they can be quite simple, provided they connect you strongly to the god. The god's name, especially written in an ancient script, is an effective kharaktêr.

The foregoing examples are of material symbols (that is, physical objects), but nonmaterial symbols are also traditional and effective. Of course, we call the deity by their names and epithets, but theurgy also uses esoteric "barbarian names" (*onomata barbara*) such as we find in the Magical Papyri. Indeed, a Chaldean Oracle warns us, "do not change barbarian names."[12] Unfortunately, we don't know these esoteric names for many of the gods (Proclus avoided mentioning them), and there is no guarantee that those in the surviving papyri are correct, but we can test them. Ultimately, the gods tell us how they should be invoked, and sometimes they teach us secret names to use.

More generally, invocations, prayers, and hymns offered to the gods help us to connect with them, for they typically mention characteristics or attributes of the god. They are recited, chanted, or sung and may be traditional or newly composed; this is part of the theurgic art. For an example, you can read Proclus's short theurgic Hymn IV in appendix B of this book.

The myths associated with a deity are important symbols, for often they are part of the god's essence and describe their actions in the cosmos and connect us with their divine energy by means of its manifestation. For this purpose, we often have to understand the myth allegorically or symbolically, as sometimes revealed in the writings of the Neoplatonists and other philosophers, but frequently, we have to work it out for ourselves. In fact, the myth operates on our minds even if we don't understand its symbolic meaning, as

---

12. My translation of oracle 150 in Ruth Majercik, *The Chaldean Oracles: Text, Translation, and Commentary* (Brill, 1989), 106.

Iamblichus explained.[13] In a theurgical ritual it is not necessary to recount the whole myth; it is sufficient to allude to it, which activates its symbolic meaning in our minds and tunes our mind to the divine energy. Later, I will show how Proclus uses myths in his seventh theurgical hymn and how we can adapt them to invoke Athena.

The least material kind of symbol exists only in the mind of the theurgist: By visualizing symbols of the god and contemplating their nature, we tune our mind to the divine energy and connect with it. This places more demands on the concentration of the theurgist, and so it works best in conjunction with more tangible symbols.

Now you know the variety of symbols that may be employed in theurgy and how they work, but I've also mentioned the problem of finding effective symbols. We wish we knew all the symbols taught in the Neoplatonic schools, which were tested and passed down in the tradition through the centuries, but we do not. We have the symbols recorded in ancient sources such as the Graeco-Egyptian Magical Papyri, but just because they were written down once and survived the accidents of history does not prove they were effective in theurgy; we don't have the evidence of long-term use. So we must treat these sources critically and experimentally. On the other hand, theurgy was a continuous tradition down through at least the time when Iamblichus, Proclus, and other Neoplatonists were teaching, writing, and practicing (sixth century CE), and so we can presume they had access to effective symbols. Unfortunately, much of the instruction was oral, and if they had handbooks and tables, they have not survived.

Therefore, once again we must adopt an experimental approach (as did the first theurgists). Taking what we have in the ancient sources, and guided by Neoplatonic theory and our own experience and intuition, we try various symbols and discover which work best. This is, in any case, partly an individual matter, because the purpose of a symbol is to tune an individual's mind to a particular divine energy, and different symbols will work better for different individuals. (Similarly, an effective sacrifice must be appropriate to the sacrificer as well as to the god.[14])

---

13. Iamblichus, *On the Mysteries*, II.11, 114–17.
14. Gregory Shaw, *Theurgy and the Soul: The Neoplatonism of Iamblichus* (Pennsylvania State University Press, 1995), 153.

Finally, as mentioned before, once we are in conversation with a god, we can ask them how they should be invoked. They will often give personal "secret" means of invocation (signs, words, etc.) to be used by the individual theurgist. They may also reveal public symbols that any theurgist can use. In this way, we revitalize a living theurgical tradition.

Jungian Depth Psychology

Analytical, or depth, psychology, which C. G. Jung originated in the early twentieth century, provides an additional way to understand theurgy. Jung discovered that below the personal unconscious mind is a *collective unconscious* that is common to all humans. It contains the universal *archetypes*, which are unconscious patterns of thought and behavior that Jung compared to the Platonic Ideas. Because they are part of human nature and manifest in our imagination, the archetypes appear in the world's mythologies under various names in such figures as the great mother, the wise old man, the clever maiden, the trickster, the seductress, the wizard, the witch, and so forth. In other words, the archetypes are the dynamic images of the gods in the human psyche.

Archetypes are innate and evolved patterns of thought and behavior common to all people, but our brains adapt them to our individual circumstances. Jung called these unconscious adaptations *complexes*, but in depth psychology, the word does not have the negative connotation that it does in colloquial language. Certainly, they can be troublesome, for complexes can behave as autonomous beings or subpersonalities, and when they distort our thinking, we may behave badly. This is literal *possession*, and complexes are effectively daimons. On the other hand, daimons (complexes), as the offspring of gods (archetypes), have much to offer us, for they arise from our inherited potential as human beings. Sometimes indeed we invite possession by the daimons, for they can bring ideas, skills, and traits from the unconscious, which are otherwise inaccessible or underdeveloped. This is what the ancient poets, such as Homer and Hesiod, did when they invoked the Muses for inspiration. Daimons can be personal, familial, national, or cultural, for they develop in the context of an individual's experience and environment.

In the early twentieth century, while navigating his own midlife crisis, Jung discovered a method of conversing with the universal archetypes and his personal daimons. His method is now known as *active imagination*, but it was also called "trancing," "visioning," and several other names.[15] He remarked that he later realized its connections to Neoplatonism and Gnosticism.[16] Jung recorded the results of his early theurgical experiments in the Black Books (notebooks with black covers), which he revised and interpreted in his famous Red Book (so-called because it is bound in red leather), both of which have been recently published for the first time. He wrote that these experiments were the source of all his later ideas, which shows the potential value of theurgy and inspiration from the gods.[17] The experiences of Jung and other depth psychologists using active imagination are helpful in understanding and practicing theurgy today.

Theurgy: The Hieratic Art

Let us now turn to the practice of theurgy, also known as the *hieratic* ("priestly") art, and I'll begin with a brief overview of the kinds of theurgical operations.[18] The first is called *sustasis*, which means an introduction, meeting, or liaison, but specifically communication between a person and a god. That is, the theurgist invokes the god into their presence, and they engage with each other. This might also include visionary journeys and interactions with other beings experienced via the *true imagination*, which is the visionary and creative faculty of our minds (as contrasted with mere fantasy or daydreaming). I will present a sustasis ritual in detail later in this chapter. Another theurgical operation is called *telestikê*, which refers to the art of bringing something to fulfillment (*telos*), especially by a mystical rite. In the context of theurgy, it means the animation or ensoulment of a divine image, such as a statue or icon. To accomplish this, the image incorporates symbols in the line (*seira*) of the deity. Symbolic objects and substances can also

....
15. C. G. Jung, *Jung on Active Imagination*, ed. and introduction Joan Chodorow (Princeton University Press, 1997), 3; See also Barbara Hannah, *Encounters with the Soul* and Robert A. Johnson, *Inner Work*.
16. C. G. Jung, *Memories, Dreams, Reflections*, rev. ed., recorded and edited by Aniela Jaffé, trans. Richard Winston and Clara Winston (Random House, 1963), 200–201.
17. Jung, *Memories, Dreams, Reflections*, 199.
18. These are described in more detail in Opsopaus, *Pythagorean Theology and the Esoteric Elements*, part I, chap. 5.

be placed in a receptacle under the statue or behind the icon. These symbols, in effect, tune the image to a particular divine energy, and invoking the deity into it is like turning on the radio. This facilitates communication because, in effect, the deity resides in the image (although in fact the deity is everywhere). "Binding and release" is a similar operation that draws the divine energy into another person, traditionally a prepubescent child, who functions as a medium speaking for the god. Finally, theurgic ascent is an operation by which a theurgist ascends from their embodied state to union (*henôsis*) with a god, perhaps even the Ineffable One.

General Considerations

In this chapter I will only explain the sustasis, which is perhaps the easiest and most useful theurgical operation, but first I think I should discuss some important matters for the practicing theurgist. The first is obvious, I suppose. We should always treat the deity whom we invoke—whether god or daimon—with respect. Even when we disagree or argue with them, it should be done with respect. Theurgists do not treat deities as their servants, which would be the height of arrogance and folly, far from wisdom. Rather, humility is essential for the theurgist, because by practicing theurgy, we recognize that the ego is not all-knowing and all-powerful, and that we need divine aid. On the other hand, we should not suppose that we are wiser or better than other people because the gods have graced us with their presence. This *ego inflation* is a trap for all spiritual practitioners and ultimately undermines the humility needed for spiritual progress. Ancient philosophers learned theurgy after a program of preliminary spiritual practice and initiation intended to purify their minds and souls so as to better avoid these problems.[19]

Nevertheless, it is important to understand that gods have their own specific natures, functions, and agendas. As eternal beings, they might not be sensitive to contemporary ethics and societal norms. Therefore, it is appropriate and proper to treat what they say critically and to negotiate with them. Be respectful, but don't abandon your moral authority as a human who has an immortal *nous* (higher mind) akin to theirs, but is also living here and

---

19. See MacLennan, *The Wisdom of Hypatia* and Opsopaus, *Cebes' Path to Enlightenment* for more on these preliminary practices.

now. Plan to be completely honest in your interactions; dissimulation and evasion are pointless anyway, since the deities know your thoughts and intentions. Therefore, it is best to conduct a sustasis alone, with no observers or assistants, so that it is easier to be completely honest and unselfconscious.

Although we use our knowledge of mythology and philosophy to choose symbols for our theurgical operations, when we engage with the gods themselves, we must be prepared to abandon (or at least question) our preconceived ideas. We may learn from the gods that their nature, their attributes, their genealogies, and much else are different from what we learn from books. Finally, however, it is important to never forget that our interactions with the gods take place through the medium of our individual minds, which can color them. Moreover, the gods tell us what we need to hear, which is often different from what others need to hear. So while theurgy can be a very enlightening experience and improve your life in many ways, don't imagine that the insights you gain are the revelations of a new religion that you should give to the world. Your experiences are *unverified personal gnosis*— that is, they are true for you but perhaps not for others. To suppose they are is at very least a lack of humility, and probably excessive ego inflation. Sometimes personal gnosis can be verified—that is, it can be demonstrated to be public truth—but that is a different topic.

Performing a Sustasis

In the remainder of this chapter, I will show you how to design a Neoplatonic sustasis ritual for a meeting with Athena. A sustasis with a different god or daimon would be similar except for the invocation formulas and symbols, which depend on the deity invoked. I will explain how they are chosen for Athena so you see how to choose them for a different deity.

Temenos (Temple)

The ritual should be conducted in a *temenos*, or place set aside for ritual and magic. If you do not have a dedicated temenos, then any place can be consecrated temporarily for the operation. In either case, it should be a place where you will not be disturbed. It does not need to be indoors. You may find it helpful to conduct the operation in dim light, but I have performed *sustaseis* in bright sunlight. You will be taking notes during your operation, so you need a table or stand for a journal (sometimes called a *liber spirituum*, or book of spirits) and enough light to see what you are writing. (Some people record audio on their phone or another device.) You probably want a chair so you can sit during the operation, which might last for several hours.

Purifications

In Plato's *Sophist* the Stranger defines purification as a process of separation, especially of the sacred from the mundane.[20] Here we use it as a means of separating from mundane matters and entering into a time, space, and personal state that is receptive to divine energy. To shift our mental state, we can take a ritual bath and don something special. It does not have to be elaborate or traditional ritual robes; it might be no more than a pendant or wreath, so long as it signals to your mind that you are doing sacred rites. However, it can be helpful to wear some symbols appropriate to the deity.

If the sustasis is not conducted in a permanent temple, then a temporary temenos can be consecrated, typically by circumambulation. One traditional way is to carry a bowl of lustral water (*khernips*), which is sprinkled to purify the temenos (an operation called *perirransis*), but you can demarcate sacred space in whatever way you are accustomed. Just as sacred space is clearly defined, so also sacred time is defined by demarcating the beginning and end of the ritual. Circumambulation marks the beginning, as does lighting incense (if you use it) and perhaps a candle for illumination. It is also valuable to take a few moments to ground and center yourself, banishing mundane thoughts and orienting your mind toward the deity to be invoked. The end of the rite is defined by extinguishing the incense and candles, exiting the temenos, and removing any special garments.

Prayer

In this section, I explain how I formulate a prayer for a sustasis or meeting with a divine being. In general, it has three parts: an invocation, a narration

---

20. Plato, *Sophist* 226d. Classical authors, such as Plato and Homer, are cited using standard reference numbers (such as "226d"), which are the same in all editions and translations.

(or aretalogy), and a petition.[21] Typically, they occur in that order, but that's not required, and the parts can blend together. Of course, you are not literally calling the god to come from far away—the gods are omnipresent—even less are you commanding them to come. Rather, the invocation, narration, and petition are all means of progressively tuning your soul to the omnipresent energy of the god so they can communicate with you.

I will use a sustasis with Athena for my example, but you will see how to adapt it to other gods. I will be taking formulas more or less directly from Proclus's Seventh Hymn, a theurgical hymn to Athena.[22] You will find useful ideas in the other hymns of this master theurgist as well as in the Homeric and Orphic hymns and in other ancient literature.

Invocation

The purpose of the invocation is to get the deity's attention by calling them by name, by epithet, and by short descriptive phrases. Traditionally, the individual clauses begin with such phrases as "Hear me," "Attend," and "Hearken." The intention is that the god should hear you favorably, so it's not out of place to include a "please." Of course, the god is already present, and so the names activate *sumpatheia* (a hidden affinity or concord) in your soul, tuning it to the specific energy of the god. To accomplish this, we use the names of the god known from ancient ritual and mythology, but also esoteric names, which might have been received from gods or daimons in earlier theurgical operations. My invocation slightly adapts the first four verses of Proclus's hymn:[23]

> **Hear! Athena, child of aegis-bearing Zeus, who sprang**
> **from the paternal fount and summit of your line!**

---

21. A good discussion of the structure of ancient Graeco-Egyptian magical spells and prayers is Fritz Graf, "Prayer in Magical and Religious Ritual," in *Magika Hiera: Ancient Greek Magic and Religion*, eds. Christopher A. Faraone and Dirk Obbink (Oxford University Press, 1991), 188–213.
22. R. M. van den Berg, *Proclus' Hymns: Essays, Translations, Commentary* (Brill, 2001). This source provides a detailed analysis and interpretation of Hymn VII (pp. 274–314) as well as additional valuable information on the theurgical aspects of Proclus's hymns.
23. Van den Berg, *Proclus' Hymns*, 275–76. Translations are my own.

Hear me, thou with manly mind, shield-bearing, daughter of a mighty parent, Pallas, Tritogeneia, exceeding strong, lance-wielding, golden-helmed, attend!

The names "Athena," "Pallas," and "Tritogeneia" are familiar from Greek mythology, but here, they are esoteric symbols that connect us with the goddess. In Plato's *Timaeus*, Socrates says that Athena is a goddess of war and wisdom.[24] And Proclus explains that the names "Athena" and "Pallas" refer to her two powers: to perfect and to protect.[25] Athena, as goddess of wisdom, has the power to perfect—that is, to illuminate and to elevate us to the divine realm, which is my goal in this ritual.

As we know, she was born from the brow of Zeus, who had absorbed her mother, Mêtis (Cunning Wisdom). Athena sprang from this paternal fount, who is the highest source of her line or lineage (seira). As the wisdom born of Zeus, she has a manly mind.[26] Pallas, a goddess of war, according to Proclus, has the power to protect, that is, to preserve the soul pure and unaffected by mundane concerns.[27] This function is reinforced by her other attributes, for, as Iamblichus explains, her shield symbolizes the power that preserves the divine realms from mundane contamination, and her fiery lances symbolize her ability to project the Platonic Ideas on the lower levels of reality while remaining herself untouched and aloof.[28] "Tritogeneia" is more obscure, but Proclus says it symbolizes her ability to illuminate all the way down to the third order of gods, who are most responsible for earthly life.[29]

---

24. Plato, *Timaeus*, 24d.
25. Van den Berg, *Proclus' Hymns*, 282–83, citing Proclus, *Procli Diadochi in Platonis Cratylum commentaria*, ed., Giorgio Pasquali (In aedibus B. G. Teubneri, 1908), § 185, 111, 26ff.
26. The word *arsenothumos* is rare and occurs only twice in extant Greek literature, from *arseno-* ("male," "masculine," "manly") and *thumos* ("mind," "soul," "spirit," "heart").
27. Van den Berg, *Proclus' Hymns*, 282–83, citing Proclus, *In Crat. comm.*, § 185, 111, 26ff.
28. Van den Berg, *Proclus' Hymns*, 281–82, citing Proclus, *Procli Diadochi in Platonis Timaeum commentaria*, ed. Ernestus Diehl, 3 vols. (In aedibus B. G. Teubneri, 1903–1906), I, 156, 31ff.
29. Van den Berg, *Proclus' Hymns*, 283, citing Proclus, *In Tim. comm.*, I 166, 25–29.

Narration, or Aretalogy

The aretalogy narrates the excellences (*aretai*) of the deity. The purpose is not just to praise, but also to evoke in the theurgist's mind recollection of circumstances in which the god acted beneficially; in this way, one's mind is connected with these beneficial aspects of the god. These may be events from mythology or circumstances when the god has previously helped the theurgist personally. Therefore, many of the formulas begin with a phrase such as "you who" or "who"—for example, "you, who always stood beside Odysseus"—but of course this is not necessary.

My aretalogy begins with a brief prayer that the goddess accept our narration of her excellence and that our words be successful in connecting with her:

> *Welcome thou this prayer with gracious heart, O Mistress, and*
> *do not abandon ever my words to the winds,*

Now, the aretalogy proper begins, briefly stating circumstances when the goddess helped mortals in relevant ways, in particular as a goddess of wisdom. Wisdom is itself a symbol of the goddess, and by mentioning it, we ask her to unbar the path to her divine wisdom:

> *you, who opened wide god-trodden gates of wisdom, and*
> *subdued the earth-born Giants' tribe, who fought the gods;*

Thus, we recall the Gigantomachy in which Athena assisted Zeus and the other Olympian gods to overthrow the earthly Giants. Plato interpreted this war symbolically: Materialist philosophers were trying to drag the gods down to earth, but Athena (through her wisdom) and the other gods preserved and secured the gods' heavenly status.[30] This conflict occurs in our individual souls as well, and just as Zeus sought her aid, so too our individual highest principle seeks her aid. In this formula, we see her as both goddess of wisdom (perfection) and goddess of war (protection).

The next formula recalls another well-known myth: Hephaistos attempted to rape Athena, but she quickly turned aside, and his semen landed on her

---

30. Plato, *Sophist* 246a–c.

thigh. Disgusted, she wiped it off with a rag, and it fell to earth, engendering the Athenians.

> *you, who fleeing longing of lust-filled Hephaistos have*
> *preserved th' unyielding belt of your virginity;*

Proclus gives a Neoplatonic interpretation, explaining that Hephaistos tried to mimic Athena's production of the eternal Ideas by embodying them in the earthly bodies of mortals.[31] But ever-virgin Athena has preserved them in their immaterial purity; these eternal Ideas, not their mortal copies, are what we seek through her.

Reinforcing the same intention, the next formula recalls the Orphic myth of Dionysos: The Titans were jealous of Dionysos, the infant child of Zeus (and destined to be his successor), and so they enticed him with all sorts of playthings, and especially a mirror, with which he became fascinated by his own appearance. While thus distracted, they killed him, cut him up, and put him in a pot to cook. Athena, however, wisely saved his heart before it was cut up, and she took it to Zeus. He made a potion from it and gave it to Semele, a mortal woman, who later gave birth to a regenerated Dionysos. In the meantime, Zeus blasted the Titans, who by then had eaten the other parts and from the ash made mortal people. Thus, humans are made of Dionysian and Titanic stuff: We are divine and mortal. As Proclus summarizes in his hymn:

> *you, who saved the uncut heart of Bacchus, lord in vaults*
> *of aether, carved up by the Titan's hands, and brought*
> *and gave it to his father, so that by the sire's*
> *unspeakable designs, renewed from Semele,*
> *throughout the cosmos Dionysos was reborn;*

Proclus interprets the myth several ways, but the most relevant for us is that the "titanic" distractions, circumstances, and emotions of embodied life can fragment our psyches; we're roasted and consumed by earthly life. But

---

31. Van den Berg, *Proclus' Hymns*, 286–287, citing Proclus, *In Tim. comm.*, I 144, 8–18.

Athena can rescue our "heart"—that is, our nous, and elevate it to Zeus, who can alchemically transform it so that we are reborn as *Bacchi* (true initiates).[32]

The next formula from Proclus's hymn seems to allude to an otherwise unknown myth, and the text is ambiguous, but we can adapt it for our invocation:

> **you, whose ax cuts off at root the heads of beasts, travails**
> **of seeing-all Hekáte, putting us to sleep;**

For theurgists, Hekate was *Daimoniarkhês*, the ruler of daimons, and although daimons are not necessarily harmful, some, especially the material daimons who are responsible for bringing us into embodiment, can impede spiritual ascent. In the *Republic*, Plato said there is a many-headed animal in each of us: the nonrational part of the soul with its many emotions, which cause our travails.[33] They drug the soul and drag us down to earth, symbolized by the underworld, Hekate's realm, guarded by three-headed Kerberos. The beasts in this formula may correspond to the avenging daimons known as "the hounds of Hekate," for she sees everything and through these beasts will bring about the inevitable consequences of our irrational behavior. Like Herakles cutting off the Hydra's heads, Athena, through her wisdom, chops off the heads of these beasts at their roots so they don't grow back.

Hekate's many-headed beasts can put us to sleep, but Athena loves the virtues, the excellences (*aretai*), which have the power to wake us up:

> **you, who love the mortal-waking virtues' holy strength;**

There is a ladder of virtues in Neoplatonism in which the cardinal virtues (prudence, fortitude, justice, self-control) are reinterpreted at successively higher levels as the aspirant advances. The level of virtues that have the power to awaken us are the *contemplative virtues*, which come from the

---

32. See van den Berg, *Proclus' Hymns*, 288–90 for a discussion.
33. Plato, *Republic* 588c.

supra-rational wisdom of Athena.[34] In fact, Proclus calls Athena "Virtue" (*Aretê*).[35]

We can continue with another formula adapted from Hymn VII:

> ***you, who flash out from your face the pure and holy light;***

Athena's face flashes with pure, holy light because her nous contains the fiery eternal Ideas. (Neoplatonic sages, such as Plotinus and Proclus, were also reported to have shining faces or sparkling eyes, revealing their divinely inspired nous.[36])

Traditionally, Athena is a goddess of arts and crafts (*tekhnai*), but Proclus gives this an esoteric interpretation that facilitates our theurgic purpose:

> ***you, who order our whole life by arts of many forms,***
> ***implanting intellective craftsmanship in souls;***

The goddess, in her wisdom, weaves together the eternal Ideas and projects them into our souls, where they have their creative effect. By this "intellective craftsmanship" we imitate the creative powers of the Demiurge and bring the Ideas into manifestation. Thus, we live her wisdom.

> ***you, who the Acropolis on th' crested hill obtained,***
> ***a symbol, Mistress, of your great and highest line;***

The acropolis is the highest point of any city (*akro-polis*), but especially of Athens, whose Acropolis is dedicated to Athena and is an international emblem of Greek culture. Therefore, the Acropolis, as the summit and spiritual center of Athens, is a symbol for Athena herself, the apex of her lineage or line (*seira*), which includes all of us who seek wisdom through philosophy.

---

34. Bruce J. MacLennan, *The Wisdom of Hypatia* (Llewellyn Publications, 2013), 253.
35. Van den Berg, *Proclus' Hymns*, 295–96, citing Proclus, *In Tim. comm.*, I 166, 27; 170, 3–10.
36. Van den Berg, *Proclus' Hymns*, 302–3.

The next formula continues the theme of Athens as the home of philosophy (especially Platonism), symbolized by the myth of the contest of Athena and Poseidon for patronage of the city:

> *you, who love the mortal-feeding land, O Mother of*
> *the Books, who fought your uncle's holy love of it,*
> *and gave the town your name and noble mind to have;*

Athena is the Mother of the Books, and thus a patron of literature, but especially of philosophy. According to Proclus, her uncle, Poseidon—a god of the sea—represents the ever-changing flow of material reality, for water was a common symbol of physical things, which are continually in a state of flux, coming to be and passing away.[37] In this way, mortals are nourished and sustained by her eternal Ideas.

The rest of Hymn VII is not so relevant to sustasis, and so we will look to other sources for the remainder of the aretalogy. One useful idea, which Proclus uses in Hymn I (verse 41) and Hymn IV (verses 6–7) alludes to an incident in the *Iliad* (5.127–28) wherein Athena helps Diomedes by taking the "mist" from his eyes so that in the battle he can distinguish mortal men from gods disguised as mortals.[38] We can use it as follows:

> *you, who cleared the deadly mist from Diomedes' eyes,*
> *revealing who was human, who was deathless god,*
> *bestowing holy light from very sacred books;*

This discernment is an important ability in theurgy too so that we can distinguish gods and daimons from possibly irrelevant and deceptive manifestations of our mortal nature.

We can wrap up the aretalogy with an important incident from the *Odyssey*, when the hero arrived at the Cave of the Nymphs in Ithaca and Athena came to him to help him recover his sovereignty. Of course, the *Odyssey* was widely seen as an allegory of the soul's wanderings and final return to its true home, and Porphyry's symbolic explanation of the episode survives and is an

---

37. Van den Berg, *Proclus' Hymns*, 299.
38. Homer, *Iliad* 5.127.

important source of Neoplatonic interpretation.³⁹ I have drawn on the *Odyssey* for this formula:⁴⁰

> *you, who always stood beside Odysseus, guarding him,*
> *who joined your wit to his and kindly cheered his heart;*
> *transforming, you dispelled the mists, revealed his home,*
> *and hid his treasures in the Naiads' shady cave,*
> *then sat in counsel 'neath the long-leafed olive tree.*

We hereby put ourselves in Odysseus's place, for Athena was always ready to come to his aid. As goddess of war and wisdom, she is, like him, wise, wily, and courageous. Here again, she dispels the mists, clearing away the darkness and obscurity so he can recognize that he has arrived at his origin and home.

Let's look at this myth in more detail with Porphyry as our guide to see how it connects us to the goddess. The cave represents earth, the material world; it is cold and moist, symbolizing matter in flux and generation, and the Naiad nymphs who dwell in it are especially associated with the entry of souls into material existence.⁴¹ When Athena dispels the mists, Odysseus can see the material world for what it is, including the two gates through which souls enter and leave material embodiment. She reveals that he has finally come to the shores of his true home after his wandering on the stormy seas of material reality (pursued by their lord, Poseidon). He can reclaim his true home if he can succeed in these final struggles, but he will have to be resourceful and clever. She has always been with him, protecting and guiding him, even when she has adopted another form or been disguised. Now, she helps him hide the gifts that he has received from the wise and peaceful Phaeacians, who know how to navigate the seas of material reality. These gifts symbolize the eternal Ideas, which he hides in the dark depths of materiality,

---

39. See Akçay, *Porphyry's On the Cave of the Nymphs* and Porphyry, *On the Cave of the Nymphs*, trans. Robert Lamberton.
40. Homer, *Odyssey* 13.102–12 for the cave and 13.300–75 for the interaction of Athena and Odysseus.
41. Porphyry, *On the Cave of the Nymphs*, trans. Thomas Taylor (Phanes Press, 1991), chap. 2–6, 17 on pages 29–38, 55–56.

where he can recover them when needed; we can interpret this as esoteric knowledge hidden in material symbols. Homer describes the harbor:[42]

> **High at the head a branching olive grows,**
> **Beneath, a gloomy grotto's cool recess.**

The tree's position shows that the Cosmic Nous, which contains the Ideas, prevails over the material world, for the olive is especially Athena's gift (by which she beat Poseidon in the contest for Athens) and symbolizes wisdom. The world was produced and is governed by divine wisdom, which is why the olive grows above the cave; it is evergreen, which signifies that wisdom is eternal. Because Athena sprang from the head of Zeus, the tree is placed at the head of the harbor. Here, Athena and Odysseus sit together by the tree's trunk to converse; that is, they have a sustasis. They consider together how best to conquer the indulgent, irrational, and violent powers (the suitors) that stand in the way of him reclaiming his rightful kingdom and reuniting with his wife (i.e., his soul).[43]

You should keep all the preceding symbolic meanings in mind as you recite the aretalogy so that your soul will be attuned closely to Athena's divine energy and she will hear your prayer.

The previous formulas deal with the nature of the goddess—her names, powers, and actions—and implicitly why it is her nature to help us. You can also mention your own characteristics or qualifications that strengthen your connection to the goddess. For example, if you have learned any secret names of the goddess, either passed down in tradition or learned in previous theurgical operations, now is a good time to use them:

> **Hear me, for I know and speak thy secret name: [NN]!**

---

42. Homer, *Odyssey*, 13.102–3; translation by Thomas Taylor in Porphyry's *Cave of the Nymphs*, 52.
43. Porphyry, *Cave of the Nymphs*, chap. 15–16, 52–54.

Of course, you replace [NN] with the name. Likewise, if you have any symbolic *kharaktêres*, either passed down in tradition or previously given to you by the goddess herself, you can use them at any point in the invocation:[44]

Look upon thy sacred symbols and thy secret signs!

When you recite this, either draw the characters in the air, visualize them vividly in your mind, or focus your attention on a talisman bearing them. If you don't have an alternative, you may want to try the name "Athena" in Linear B characters, which is the oldest written form of her name that we have (see figure). The owl (for perfection) and Gorgoneion (for protection) are also good symbols.

Finally, you can also strengthen your connection to the goddess through offerings, such as incense, at any time or now as you transition to the petition:

Come to me, fair goddess, for I burn for thee sweet spice!

The Orphic Hymns recommend aromatic herbs for Athena; myrrh is also a good choice.[45] You can also ask the goddess what incense she would prefer for any future sustasis.

Petition

Having obtained the goddess's attention, we begin to make our requests. Although our goal is a sustasis, and so we are asking that the goddess come and meet with us, we can ask for other things as well. This petition begins with a formula from the Seventh Hymn:[46]

---

44. See for examples PGM III.495–500; IV.945–49 in Hans Dieter Betz, ed., *The Greek Magical Papyri in Translation, Including the Demotic Spells, Volume 1: The Texts*, 2nd ed (University of Chicago Press, 1992), 31, 57. These texts are cited by papyrus number (e.g., III or IV) and range of line numbers (e.g., 495–500), which are indicated in Betz, the most accessible English translations of these authentic ancient magical texts.
45. Apostolos N. Athanassakis and Benjamin M. Wolkow, trans., *The Orphic Hymns* (Johns Hopkins, 2013), 28.
46. Greek text in van den Berg, *Proclus' Hymns*, 275–76. My translation.

> *Hearken, hearken, Mistress! Praying much, I come to thee*
> *by force of need; but thou, attend with gentle ear.*

Another verse from Hymn VII recalls Odysseus's homecoming with a common symbol of philosophical salvation:

> *Give me blessèd mooring, for I wander o'er the earth.*

Thus, we seek blessed tranquility, peace, and stability amidst the storms of earthly existence. Continuing, we ask the goddess to inspire us with the love and longing that will draw us up to the divine realms:

> *Grant my soul the holy light from your own sacred myths,*
> *your wisdom, and your love; inspire my love with strength*
> *in quantity and kind to rise from earthly depths*
> *toward Olympus in the noble sire's abodes.*

Next, we get more to the point, requesting that the goddess come to us. The Seventh Hymn does not pray for the arrival of the goddess, but we can turn to the *Greek Magical Papyri* for models:[47]

> *Leave thy high acropolis, O glorious child of Zeus!*

Of course, as previously discussed, the deity is not coming from somewhere else, for she is omnipresent (and certainly is not being commanded or compelled to come), but we are conditioning our mind and aetherial body to engage with the divine energy. (The following formulas are not specific to Athena and may be used for any deity.)

> *Come thou, come to me from thine abodes, O blessèd one!*

---

47. E.g., PGM I.2–4, 298–300; III.494–500; IV.945–9, 1029–30; V.414–21; VI.24–28; PDM xiv.131–34; Suppl. 130–35, in Betz, *Greek Magical Papyri*, 3, 11, 31, 57–58, 108–9, 111, 202–3, 328.

We ask the deity (or daimon) to appear in a familiar form, which they do for our benefit:

Come in joy, thou goddess, and appear in thine own form.

In the following formulas, we are explicit that we are invoking the deity for a conversation or other interaction:

Enter, goddess, and give answer with thy holy voice
 so I hear clearly and can comprehend your words.
I beseech thee, gracious one, to grant the truth to me.
Nod assent, I pray, that you will guide and counsel me.

Formulas such as the following (which we find in invocations in the *Greek Magical Papyri*) may be repeated *ad libitum* until the deity arrives:

Hither come! Hither! Come hither! Appear!
Quickly quickly, hurry hurry!
Come to me! Come to me! Hither hither!
Now now! Quickly quickly!

The foregoing demonstrates, I hope, how to construct a theurgical invocation for a *sustasis*. Formulas can be added, deleted, and moved around, provided you keep their purpose in mind: As theurgist, you are leading your mind through a series of stages so that in the end it is receptive to the deity's specific energy. You can do the same for other gods and goddesses, but you will need to formulate the symbols that engage the relevant divine energies.

Manifestation

After you have recited the invocation, you wait for the deity's arrival with a calm, attentive, expectant mind; maintain a soft focus on the image of the god or the candle.

Alternatively, you can visualize yourself passing through a portal for your audience with the god. Close your eyes and visualize yourself entering step by step a deep, sacred grotto or descending a long stairway into a subterranean crypt or—more appropriately for Athena—ascending the steps of a magnificent temple. Step through the doors without expectations, and observe what arises in your imagination. Open your eyes and await the god.

When they have come, you may perceive subtle signs of animation in your environment: a change in the temperature, odd lights or shadows, whispers, a feeling of presence. Or you may experience none of these things but see or hear the deity in your imagination or even with your senses. According to Iamblichus, gods and daimons communicate with us by means of our aetherial bodies, and in particular by means of the imagination (*phantasia*), the highest part of the lower soul, which resides in the aetherial body.[48] Therefore, we perceive these deities with our imagination or with our senses, whose perceptions are processed through the imagination. The god may speak with your own mouth or write with your own hand.

It is appropriate to greet the deity politely, to thank them for meeting with you, and to ask how they prefer to be addressed. I should note that who shows up is not always whom you invoked. This is not necessarily a problem. You should ask who they are and why they have come. They almost always have something important to discuss with you. After all, the gods know better than you do! In fact, it is sometimes useful to invoke an unknown god—for example, when there is some issue in your life and you are not sure who is involved or who can help. In this case, you use symbols for the issue, with the intention that they will tune your mind to the relevant deity.

It is also worth mentioning here that when we invoke a god or goddess, often one of the daimons in their lineage arrives instead. One reason is, as Plutarch explains, daimons are often known by the same name as the deity they serve, and Proclus says these daimons gladly manifest instead of the invoked god.[49] Moreover, daimons are better able to interact with us, for they exist in time and space with us, whereas the supercelestial gods exist outside of time and space and are by nature less equipped to deal with us as individuals. Don't feel slighted!

....
48. Iamblichus, *On the Mysteries*, III.14 [132–33], 152–54.
49. Plutarch, *The Obsolescence of Oracles*, in Plutarch, *Moralia*, vol. 5, trans. Frank Cole Babbitt, Loeb Classical Library 306, ed. Jeffrey Henderson (Harvard University Press, 1936), 412–13; Hans Lewy, *Chaldaean Oracles and Theurgy: Mysticism, Magic and Plantonism in the Later Roman Empire*, Nouvelle édition per Michel Tardieu (Études Augustiniennes, 1978), 245.

Meeting

You are now engaged in your meeting with the deity; there is no script, for you are face-to-face with a god or daimon. Although you are interacting with a being that may be known from mythology, you are not in a role-playing game. Be yourself; don't pretend. In addition to discussion, the deity may lead you on journeys, introduce you to other beings, transform you (though you remain yourself inside), subject you to trials—anything at all! But be yourself; if you don't want to do something, negotiate about it. The choice is ultimately yours. As part of your negotiation, you may make an agreement with the deity, but think carefully about your pacts; they're real!

Beginning theurgists sometimes worry that they are "just making it up," but unless you are consciously scripting the interactions and events or have planned them in advance, you can trust that they are not coming from your ego. They arise in the unconscious mind, where the images of the eternal gods and daimons reside and behave independently of your ego, and from there they appear in your imagination.

Eventually, your meeting will come to an end. The deity may call an end to it, or you might find that your concentration is waning. Tell the deity that you are tired and need to return to the mundane world; the gods know our limitations well! Politely ask—or insist if necessary!—that the meeting come to an end.

Release

In the release, you politely ask the deity to depart. Again, of course, the goddess is not going anywhere; rather, you are turning your attention to other matters, essentially tuning the radio of your mind to a different station. For this purpose, the *Greek Magical Papyri* provide models that can be adapted to any deity.[50] Expressing gratitude is important in theurgy:

> *I give thanks to you, Athena, for your presence here,*
> *for I rejoice that you have come to me today.*

---

50. E.g., PGM I.342–47; II.176–83; III.259–62, 598–600; IV.1057–68; V.41–9; VII.334 in Betz, *Greek Magical Papyri*, 12, 18, 26, 33–34, 59, 102, 126.

You ask the goddess to return to the divine realms in order to dissolve the sympathetic connection to her, to ensure that you return to mundane reality, and to avoid any lingering possession:

> *Hasten now, O Lady, hasten to your throne; return*
> *to your acropolis, the heavens where you dwell;*
> *depart, thou beautiful and holy light, depart!*

Nevertheless, we pray for well-being and the opportunity for future meetings:

> *Go in joy, farewell, but be forever kind to me,*
> *and grant me strength, well-being, luck, and health,*
> *but most of all the right to meet with you again.*

As remarked previously, the rite is completed by extinguishing the incense and candles, exiting the temenos, and removing any special garments. It is a good idea to ensure you have returned to mundane, embodied reality by clapping, stamping your feet, or eating some food and drinking some water. If you feel some lingering spaciness, then do a banishing, insisting that the deity return to their realm and restore you to mundane reality.

Enactment

In order to bring the results of your sustasis into manifestation in ordinary reality, it is useful to enact them in some concrete way. Of course, if you have made some vow in the course of your meeting, you should carry it out. In addition, it is valuable to recopy the notes you made during the sustasis, correcting obvious errors and filling in the blanks, but keep to a fair and accurate account of the operation. Copying it neatly into a nice journal acknowledges the sacred character of your interaction. You can add additional insights, reflection, and interpretation in following days, weeks, and even years.

Conclusion

I will summarize what you have learned in this chapter. First, you have seen that theurgy in the Platonic tradition was developed most fully by the

Neoplatonists from Graeco-Egyptian spiritual traditions, but with roots in ancient shamanism. You have also learned the basics of Neoplatonic cosmology and theology, which define the framework in which theurgy takes place, and the philosophical principles on which it operates. These are important, because the scarcity of reliable ancient theurgical rituals requires us to design our own. Nevertheless, we can learn effective techniques from what survives and from parallel sources. You have seen how to perform a sustasis, or meeting with a god or daimon, which I've illustrated by composing a Neoplatonic sustasis with Athena. On this basis you can compose your own sustasis with any deity.

The complete Athena sustasis ritual follows; see also the appendices to this book for Proclus's brief summary of theurgy, which you are now prepared to understand, and his short, fourth theurgical hymn, in which you can see some of the principles applied.

Practice: Sustasis Ritual for Athena

So that you can see it as a whole, I've gathered together here the parts of the sustasis ritual for Athena that we have developed in this chapter, together with some other practical details. Of course, you can adapt it to your personal practice.

Temenos
- Your temenos should have a table and chair so you can record the meeting in your spirit journal.

Equipment
- Spirit journal and pen
- Image of Athena
- *Optional:* incense (e.g., myrrh), candle, olive sprig or wand, olive wreath, or other symbols of Athena (e.g., owl, kharaktêres)

Purifications
- Take a ritual bath.
- Don ritual garb and symbolic accessories (e.g., Athena pendant).
- Unless you have a permanently consecrated temple, purify the *temenos* (e.g., by circumambulation).

Prayer
- Light candles (if using).
- Light incense (if using).
- If you have an olive wreath, place it on your head now.
- If you have an olive sprig or wand, pick it up in your right hand.
- Recite the invocatory prayer:

> *Hear! Athena, child of aegis-bearing Zeus, who sprang*
>   *from the paternal fount and summit of your line!*
> *Hear me, thou with manly mind, shield-bearing, daughter of*
>   *a mighty parent, Pallas, Tritogeneia,*
>   *exceeding strong, lance-wielding, golden-helmed, attend!*
> *Welcome thou this prayer with gracious heart, O mistress, and*
>   *do not abandon ever my words to the winds,*
> *you, who opened wide god-trodden gates of wisdom, and*
>   *subdued the earth-born Giants' tribe, who fought the gods;*
> *you, who fleeing longing of lust-filled Hephaistos have*
>   *preserved th' unyielding belt of your virginity;*
> *you, who saved the uncut heart of Bacchus, lord in vaults*
>   *of aether, carved up by the Titan's hands, and brought*
>   *and gave it to his father, so that by the sire's*
>   *unspeakable designs, renewed from Semele,*
>   *throughout the cosmos Dionysos was reborn;*
> *you, whose ax cuts off at root the heads of beasts, travails*
>   *of seeing-all Hekáte, putting us to sleep;*
> *you, who love the mortal-waking virtues' holy strength;*
> *you, who flash out from your face the pure and holy light;*
> *you, who order our whole life by arts of many forms,*
>   *implanting intellective craftsmanship in souls;*

you, who the Acropolis on th' crested hill obtained,
    a symbol, Mistress, of your great and highest line;
you, who love the mortal-feeding land, O Mother of
    the Books, who fought your uncle's holy love of it,
    and gave the town your name and noble mind to have;
you, who cleared the deadly mist from Diomedes' eyes,
    revealing who was human, who was deathless god,
    bestowing holy light from very sacred books;
you, who always stood beside Odysseus, guarding him,
    who joined your wit to his and kindly cheered his heart;
    transforming, you dispelled the mists, revealed his home,
    and hid his treasures in the Naiads' shady cave,
    then sat in counsel 'neath the long-leafed olive tree.

- Recite any of the following three verses as appropriate:

    Hear me, for I know and speak thy secret name: [NN]!
    Look upon thy sacred symbols and thy secret signs!
    Come to me, fair goddess, for I burn for thee sweet spice!

- Continue by praying for the goddess's arrival:

*Hearken, hearken, Mistress! Praying much, I come to thee
    by force of need; but thou, attend with gentle ear.
Give me blesséd mooring, for I wander o'er the earth.
Grant my soul the holy light from your own sacred myths,
    your wisdom, and your love; inspire my love with strength
    in quantity and kind to rise from earthly depths
    toward Olympus in the noble sire's abodes.
Leave thy high acropolis, O glorious child of Zeus!
Come thou, come to me from thine abodes, O blesséd one!
Come in joy, thou goddess, and appear in thine own form.
Enter, goddess, and give answer with thy holy voice
    so I hear clearly and can comprehend your words.
I beseech thee, gracious one, to grant the truth to me.
Nod assent, I pray, that you will guide and counsel me.*

- Repeat the following ad libitum:

  Hither come! Hither! Come hither! Appear!
  Quickly quickly, hurry hurry!
  Come to me! Come to me! Hither hither!
  Now now! Quickly quickly!

- Wait with a quiet, attentive, and expectant mind; maintain a soft focus on the image or candle. Optionally, visualize yourself passing through a portal. When you discern the arrival of the goddess, greet her politely. If you are holding an olive sprig or wand, put it down.

Meeting
- Meet with the goddess, discussing matters of mutual interest and perhaps accompanying her in various experiences.

Release
- When the meeting has come to an end, thank the goddess and ask her to depart.
- Remove the olive wreath if used.
- If you are using an olive sprig or wand, pick it up in your left hand.
- You may close your eyes, if you choose, but recite the dismissal:

  I give thanks to you, Athena, for your presence here,
    for I rejoice that you have come to me today.
  Hasten now, O Lady, hasten to your throne; return
    to your acropolis, the heavens where you dwell;
    depart, thou beautiful and holy light, depart!
  Go in joy, farewell, but be forever kind to me,
    and grant me strength, well-being, luck, and health,
    but most of all the right to meet with you again.

- Extinguish the incense and candle.
- Exit the *temenos* and remove ritual garb.
- Ensure that you are firmly grounded again in mundane reality.

I WAS A TEENAGE THEURGIST
HERCULES INVICTUS

I first learned about theurgy while attending Greek parochial school in the late 1960s, early 1970s. What captivated my imagination the most was the theurgic belief that the essence of the Divine could be housed in items, statues, people, and even oneself. And that once properly localized in this world, the Divine could powerfully establish its presence and take direct action in worldly affairs.

How I Discovered Theurgy

Accounts of blessed items, living statuary, and god-influenced individuals are plentiful in the Greek mythology and folklore I grew up with. Though I was (and still am) fascinated by this lore, I remained more firmly fixated on discovering how to become a living repository of divine Olympian energies and a conscious channel for their application toward noble and heroic ends.

Specifically, I wanted to embody and express my highest understanding of the Olympian Herakles, better known as Hercules. He was the mightiest and most accomplished of the ancient Greek heroes, an actual demigod. And he earned his way to Mount Olympus after a long life of service and adventure. Aside from his memorable presence in the myths and folklore, Hercules is still alive in a sense and still actively adventures in our modern imagination throughout our popular culture. His exploits can be experienced through toys, books, comics, TV shows, cartoons, games, and films. Through these I sought a more complete understanding and experience of my chosen deity.

Theurgia (as we Greeks call it) was never presented to me as a viable choice for future soul evolution by my schooling. Theurgy was introduced as a spiritual practice of the Hellenistic era that evolved during, and survived into, the Christian era. As it was part of our much-valued Greek cultural heritage, it was worthy of preservation and study, nothing more. I was not encouraged to pursue this path or even to learn more about it.

But nonetheless, I decided to follow this knowledge trail, see where it would lead me, learn what I could, and apply whatever I discovered to the best of my ability.

I continued with my independent studies and my immersion into all things Olympian through pop culture. In his *Histories*, Herodotus demonstrated that Hercules could be better understood by widening the focus of one's inquiries to extend beyond Greece and Rome, so I did this as well.[51] Nonetheless, my explorations always led me back to the Greco-Roman Hercules and the neo-Theosophical Herculean Path revealed by Alice A. Bailey in *The Labours of Hercules: An Astrological Interpretation* (1957), which depicted our hero as a solar initiate, magically evolving as he learned the spiritual lessons imparted by the signs of the zodiac, represented by iconic episodes in his famous labors.

Having experimented with honoring other heroic exemplars (such as Theseus, the Greek folk hero Koutalianos, and Alexander the Great), I determined that Hercules was indeed my best candidate for a personal deity. Before my eleventh birthday, I decided to invite Hercules to come and live with me in my family's small apartment in the Bronx. Because I am Greek, as is Hercules, and Hellenes have traditional hospitality customs and related practices, I believed that I knew the best possible way: I would set up an *iconostasi*.

---

51. Herodotus, *The Histories*, Everyman's Library, trans. George Rawlinson, intro Hugh Bowden (J. M. Dent / Tuttle, 1992), 140–42.

The Iconostasi

Most Greek households of my youth boasted an iconostasi, or icon stand. Paintings of the divine family of Greek Orthodox Christianity (Jesus and Mary, mostly), popular well-known religious personages (such as saints and angels), as well as more obscure holy folk were housed in this frame-like structure with shelves. Photos of loved ones who had passed or were otherwise away could sometimes be found there. And occasionally there were statues (or other representations) of personages from ancient Greek mythology, philosophy (such as Socrates), and history (like Pericles and the emperor Constantine).

Sometimes the iconostasi spilled over onto other surfaces, especially the tops of furniture with drawers. Usually, when that happened, the very personal, or very pagan, items would be found on surfaces rather than in the icon stand. Some households allowed their iconostasi to spill over into their porches or yards, whether front, side, or back.

The iconostasi was the home of the personages who were represented on the shelves. The structure and its residents were kept clean and well fed. Items such as holy water and palm crucifixes (from Palm Sunday celebrations) were kept there as well. Some families occasionally lit a candle and placed it before the structure.

When one is no longer living on Gaia, having passed into the realms beyond, their icons, *agalmata* (statuary), and other iconostasi items are usually passed on to other family members for their own household shrines. Sometimes they are stolen, and there is actually a lot of cautionary lore meant to discourage one from doing that.

My first personal iconostasi was simple and, as you might guess, dedicated to Hercules. It was established when I was eleven and I invited Hercules into my heart and into my home. It consisted of a representation of Hercules and some books that told of his exploits. These items were temporary and often upgraded as I acquired better ones.

As Greeks are proud of their pagan past and habituated to having homes full of ancient images, my possessing and displaying these items separately and in a place of honor was no big deal in our household. At first, my parents were a bit taken aback by my actual devotion to the Olympians but in time took it in stride. My mother joked that Olympus would surely have a place for me when I died, but that I would also be welcome to visit with them in the Greek Orthodox heaven whenever I wished…because we're Greek!

In addition to Hercules, my current iconostasi also houses representations (mostly statuary) of the Dodekatheon (the council of twelve Olympians) and other mythic personages, mostly but not exclusively Olympian. It spills over onto almost every raised flat surface in our home. All of these altars are themed and always evolving and moving around. One of my favorites is our shrine to the Golden Fleece.

Aside from items I've personally added, I have a few from my close circle of loved ones as well as statues of Hermes, Aphrodite, Adonis, and Diogenes from kin that are no longer with us. Alas, an old Athena statue that was meant for me was swiped by parties unidentified for reasons unknown.

Practice: Establishing Your Own Iconostasi

Please note: You will get more out of these exercises if you keep a journal and revisit your entries often. This is so important that I will occasionally reinforce it throughout this chapter.

To begin, choose (or get chosen by) a divine personage who resonates with you most powerfully. Study everything you can about the deity of your choice. Get to know them to the best of your ability. Selecting more than one power, or even an entire pantheon, to work with is fine.

If you would like the Olympians to be a bigger part of your life, invite them to your home as guests. Lighting a candle and talking to your statue (or other representation) is a great first step. This practice can continue until you feel a sense of presence. If you'd like to offer them a place in your daily life, consider using an iconostasi.

To create one, obtain an appealing display case with shelves. Candles, though atmospheric and traditional, are optional. If anyone you share space with is allergic to scents or fire is a potential hazard, these can be skipped or replaced with electric candles.

Before hanging your future iconostasi on a wall, make sure that it will be accessible and, ideally, at eye level. Otherwise, follow your inner guidance and find a place that feels right to you.

Gather representations (statuary, figurines, images, items, symbols) of your deific Guest(s) and arrange them on the shelves. Ancestors, people you admire (heroes and mentors), and VIPs in your personal life are also welcome to join them.

To communicate with your Guest(s), you simply choose the representation(s) you wish to address, light a candle (or turn on an electric one), place it before them, and speak your mind. Answers often come through synchronicities, or you can use divinatory tools if you wish.

Theurgic tip: Spend time with your iconostasi residents. Get to know them well, as you would a friend or family member. Remain sensitive to impressions of their likes and dislikes.

Seeking Guidance

Your icon stand can function on that level indefinitely, if you so desire. The iconostasi is a great way to get to know, build trust with, and establish rapport with your unseen roomies. Use the tools that work best for you to communicate (mine are synchronicities and experiences in altered states). Remember that building a solid relationship takes time.

Onward!

During my eleventh and twelfth years, I shot up in size. I became stronger and bulkier. The hair atop my head was now a long and shaggy mane. And I grew a beard and moustache. By the time I was thirteen, my personal practices had moved far beyond my bookshelf iconostasi and its ancillary household shrines.

Initially, it began with me dressing like the Sword-and-Sandal Hercules from my favorite movies as often as I could get away with. I wrote plays and cast myself as my favorite hero-god (one of them was performed in my high school English class). I also started placing myself in the mythic tales directly, experiencing them in my imagination as deeply and realistically as I could, then relating what I'd felt in story form from the perspective of the mythic legend.

Though I enjoyed the process of exploration and discovery, my intent from childhood was, in essence, to theurgically merge with the Divine, so I occasionally requested help with that.

My answer finally came in the form of a waking dream. I call it my Primal Vision.

I am floating, alone and without form, near the peak of a mountain. I can see the ruins of an abandoned Grecian city with an acropolis below me.

In time, a powerfully built man clad in the pelt of a lion, having completed his long and lonely climb, makes his way toward the acropolis. He locates then enters the temple that is located within. Though his brown mane and beard are streaked with white and gray, he appears both healthy and powerful. His sky-blue eyes are sharp and alert.

As I observe him, I gradually merge with and become him.

I know, without doubt, that I am Hercules, son of Zeus. I remove my knobby olive club from its harness and cautiously proceed.

Entering the naos *(temple), which I somehow know is dedicated to the Highest, I move through it unerringly until I reach a large stone altar upon which rests an antique horn. I then recall that I have been here many times before and that I know exactly what to do.*

The horn is of monstrous size, and I know that it is from a Heavenly Bull. It is etched with arcane glyphs, some of them inlaid with a silvery metal. I put down my club, lift the artifact to my lips, then blow into the smaller end.

The bellowing call reverberates throughout the heavens, and echoes of it reach Gaia.

With the Horn of Summoning still in hand, I then exit the temple and gaze into the skies where I once hovered. In time, I can detect other presences, entities both incarnate and discarnate, human and definitely not, who responded to my call. I know that they are here to help me with my Olympian mission.

And with this realization, the vision slowly starts to fade.

This vision has served me well throughout my life's journey, and I treasure it greatly. Whenever I need assistance, I simply place myself mentally inside the temple and blow the horn. I welcome and am grateful for all who find their way to me, knowing that in some way, they will assist me with my Olympian mission.

Among other things, my Primal Vision inspired this Olympian blessing, which I have extensively used in public ceremonies:

> *I call upon heaven*
> *and the benevolent powers*
> *that shaped us in the dawn of time*
> *and guide us still*
> *to bless this world, its people,*
> *and all that they hold dear.*
> *May all be blessed*
> *with optimal wellness,*
> *with abundance and prosperity,*
> *with love and peace,*
> *with joy and fulfillment!*
> *In the name of the Highest,*
> *I dedicate myself toward this becoming so.*
> *And from the altar high atop Mount Olympus,*
> *my soul's true home,*
> *I sound the Horn of Summoning*
> *and welcome all who heed the call.*

Practice: Receiving Guidance

Before attempting to receive guidance from an external source, ask yourself the question(s) first and see what you come up with on your own. Really think things through. What do you really want (to be, to know, to have)? Why? What type(s) of guidance or assistance are you expecting from the higher realms to help you attain or obtain your objective?

Know, accept, and acknowledge that the answer(s) may not come right away or in a form you're expecting, but trust that you will be provided with helpful insights when they are most needed.

Read up on how seeking oracles and prophecies plays out (and works out) in Greco-Roman mythology and history. The myths of Oedipus and Perseus are good places to start, as is the Roman classic *De Divinatione* by Cicero.

The Oracles of Apollo by fellow theurgist John Opsopaus, PhD, is an invaluable modern resource that I highly recommend.

Once you've reviewed the stories and asked yourself the questions, it's now time to ask the Divine.

1. Place yourself in a meditative state using your favorite technique.
2. Imagine yourself in a temple dedicated to your chosen deity.
3. Visualize a light suffusing the temple and radiating outward toward you.
4. Bask in the light until you feel the presence of the deity.
5. Ask your question(s).
6. Remain receptive to receiving a response. It may come in words, images, symbols, or feelings.
7. Express gratitude.

As soon as possible, record as much of the experience as you can recall in your journal. Meditate upon the details often and make note of any thoughts or insights that occur to you. For instance: What color light suffused the temple during your meditation? What does that color mean to you?

I personally treat all divinatory messages as advice based on opinions, no matter their origin. I will be thankful to the source of the advice given and seriously consider what I've been told or shown, but the decision on what to do always remains mine to make. And I take full responsibility for my actions.

Theurgic tip: If some time has passed and you do not feel that your query has been addressed, you may repeat the process. I have oftentimes found that reframing the question, asking another familial or household deity, or requesting the wisdom to better recognize an answer when it comes often does the trick.

Embodying and Expressing

Insofar as becoming a living expression of my Olympian ideal, the solution was, fortunately, crystal clear from the start. The muscle men in the Hercules movies I loved were mostly bodybuilders. And bodybuilders, at the time, were focused on replicating the classical athletic physiques immortalized in

Greco-Roman statuary. By following their path, I, too, could become a living statue!

Hercules was always associated with strength and bodybuilding, gymnasiums, spas, and health in general. He was said to have brought us the Olympic and Nemean games, and he was well known for utilizing hot-water therapy. He was known as *Alexikakos*, the averter of ills, including plagues.

My first exemplar was a man who was inspired by a statue of Hercules in the Brooklyn Museum and was taught the secrets of strength by lions in the Brooklyn Zoo. He became a legend in his own lifetime and remains one of the most recognizable icons of the early physical culture movement. I speak of Angelo Siciliano, better known as Charles Atlas. I first discovered him in comic book ads during my childhood. A smiling man, muscular and strong, he promised me that I, too, could be like him with a minimal investment of my time. The living icon still walked the earth during this period, and, though a bit older than he appeared in the ads, he still looked very strong and supremely healthy. I decided to take him up on his word and enroll.

My dad, a large and powerful man, occasionally worked out at home, and I thereby had access to his equipment (when he wasn't around).

Throughout my own life I've explored many states of physical being. I've been in shape and out of shape, healthy and ill, heavy and lean. I always feel best when building strength and striving for optimal wellness, so I work out as often as I can.

Practice: Embodiment and Expression 101

Aside from welcoming deities into your home and increasingly involving them with your personal life, you can strive to be more like them in ways great and small, as I did above by increasing my personal strength and musculature.

A technique I developed as a child, which I mentioned briefly above, is to place yourself in the stories of your chosen deity in an effort to better understand them.

1. Choose a myth that resonates or allow one to choose you.
2. Quest for lore about this myth and consume it.
3. When you feel full, stop.

4. Formulate a guided journey—a short, scripted imaginary scenario that sets the stage, or opens the door, for an open and unstructured spontaneous inner experience (an example follows below).
5. Place yourself in the mythic figure and experience events through their eyes.
6. Allow the myth to become sensory. Immerse yourself in it.
7. Revisit the experience in your imagination as often as you desire.

Theurgic tip: Experiment with different myths and remain open to the insights they offer. Record your experiences as best you can and add your subsequent thoughts and insights.

My Guided Journey

I will now share part of a long-ago preparation for an Underworld journey to serve as an example of how I've personally used some of the steps above to enter and experience myths directly:

> *For my ultimate Labor, King Eurystheus charged me with retrieving Hades's fierce hound, the triple-headed Kerberos.*
>
> *It is said that no one who is impure can safely interact with the Powers Below. To aid me in my current quest, one of my aunts, the goddess Demeter, directed her initiates at Eleusis to institute a new purification rite to honor her daughter Persephone. By participating in this ceremony, I will be cleansed of any and all accrued miasma. I would be rendered pure and worthy to travel through the Underworld.*
>
> *I am indeed grateful for this opportunity and appreciate all who have assisted me thus far. Theseus, the king of Athens, proclaimed me an honorary citizen of Athena's city to facilitate the process of my initiation, as Eumolpus, the Hierophant, is a staunch traditionalist and refuses to initiate foreigners.*
>
> *It also helps that Musaeos, the son of my fellow Argonaut Orpheus, is one of the mystae in attendance on this day. He has prepared me as thoroughly as his order allows.*

I have fasted; I have bathed in the River Ilisos.

Freed from my sandals and with my eyes downcast, I patiently wait to be summoned by the white-robed officiants, who are still chanting.

In my right hand, I hold a small piglet by its back legs. In my left hand are some round and sticky cakes.

The sweet smell of poppies both living and dried, the latter offered as incense, permeates the air.

I know that by undergoing this process I will learn many things that I can never share with the profane, for the secrets of Eleusis are sacrosanct.

En Onomati Theou

I believe that my daily actions are my prayer, offering, and sacrifice to Hercules and his Olympian family. I consecrate all my actions *en onomati theou*, which in Greek means "in the name of the Divine."

Though I've used the moniker since childhood, I legally changed my birth name to my deity's name about two decades ago to demonstrate my lifelong devotion to the practice of *en onomati theou*.

When your deeds are dedicated to the Divine and you operate as a conduit for the divinities, you experience a sense of oneness and harmony that is hard to describe. Rather than lose yourself, it feels like you have finally discovered who you truly are. You become the divine presence alive and active in our world.

Hercules is the mightiest son of the most powerful deity in the Hellenic pantheon, yet he found the lessons of mortality challenging. This taught me to grant others, and myself, plenty of slack as we wend our way through life. And though he made many mistakes, Hercules still accomplished great things during his mortal sojourn, and he now dwells among the Olympians. This taught me the importance of taking action and doing the best you can, even if you're still "far from perfect."

My attention and energies are currently focused on attending to Hercules's divine spheres of activity to the best of my ability. Hercules, for instance, is concerned (in part) with strength building and application, fitness, optimal wellness, commerce, vocation, choice, adherence to principle, and heroic endeavor. He also stands for personal responsibility, community service, and growth through challenge.

As well as striving to embody and express my Highest understanding of my deity, I have attempted to involve myself in Hercules's spheres of activity as much as possible through my work and hobbies. I've worked in the fitness industry (including with and for Charles Atlas Ltd.) and have used exercise as a therapeutic tool as an activity therapist and recreation director. I've helped people to the best of my ability throughout my decades-long career in human services, especially through vocational rehabilitation and workforce development. You get the idea. However, I'll share one more example, as it ultimately led to the existence of this book:

Hercules shares several traits with Hermes. He is a crosser of boundaries and has been portrayed as a herm. He is involved with commerce and bold ventures. To honor and better understand that aspect of deity, I started a mythology-based company and became involved with my local chamber of commerce. As communication is also a trait they both share, I got involved with producing media (mostly fringe media).

One of my shows is a podcast, *Voice of Olympus*, which premiered on the Spiritual Unity Radio Station over a decade ago.

Reviewing a theurgic book by Brandy Williams (*For the Love of the Gods: The History and Modern Practice of Theurgy*) in late 2016 led to an interview on *Voice of Olympus*. Whilst speaking to Brandy, I shared my desire to focus on theurgy for a series of episodes, and Brandy suggested the names of several Llewellyn authors. She also suggested a panel format.

I knew of Brandy from her prior works and thought very highly of her. It turned out that I was familiar with the others as well. They had all already contributed much to my understanding and had published recent and very relevant works. Reviews of books soon led to interviews, and the monthly panel–format show evolved as we proceeded.

Jean-Louis de Biasi (*Rediscover the Magick of the Gods and Goddesses: Revealing the Mysteries of Theurgy*); Apollonius, aka Bruce MacLennan, aka John Opsopaus (*The Oracles of Apollo: Practical Ancient Greek Divination for Today* and *The Wisdom of Hypatia: Ancient Spiritual Practices for a More*

Meaningful Life); and Tony Mierzwicki (*Hellenismos: Practicing Greek Polytheism Today*) stayed on as regular panelists. Patrick Dunn (*The Practical Art of Divine Magic: Contemporary & Ancient Techniques of Theurgy* and *The Orphic Hymns: A New Translation for the Occult Practitioner*) has been on as a special guest. Recently, we opened our doors to new voices, and we are honored to have been joined by Clio Ajana.

The title of the panel changed a few times during the course of our mutual journey, but the conversation has continued uninterrupted for over seven years and has now flowered into the writing of this book.

We wanted to share our love of theurgy with an even wider circle of folks. It was also hoped that folks could use the tools we developed in our own theurgic practices to make their own lives more mythical, mystical, or magickal. Individual theurgists, though they embrace certain commonalities, often practice their theurgy in unique and personal ways.

And here we are!

Practice: En Onomati Theou—What More Can I Do?

Earlier on in my journey, over two decades ago, I penned the following words to give voice to my best understanding of theurgic practice at the time and provide a more focused direction to my personal Olympian odyssey:

> *Life is a mythic journey.*
>
> *I am a mythic hero, the central character of my own unique saga.*
>
> *I am the gods that call me, the gods I seek, the gods I serve, the gods whose myths I live.*
>
> *My challenges are here, before me, in the eternal now. My adventure never ends.*
>
> *I assume full responsibility for all my choices and actions.*
>
> *I am a multidimensional being and can never, in truth, be fettered or restrained without my consent.*
>
> *The realms of myth, magic, and legend are here around me and within me. To experience them, I need only shift my perspective… slightly.*

These declarations served me well and took me far for much of my spiritual life. I am not presenting them here as beliefs to be accepted or adopted, but as notions to be entertained and contemplated. The following prompts will help you do so, but they require much soul-searching and deep self-reflection. As always, record everything and revisit your entries from time to time in a quest for fresh insights.

1. Ask yourself if your life is about something. If so, what is it about?
2. Ask yourself where and how you fit into the life you are living. What is your primary role? What other roles do you play?
3. Ask yourself what you are actually striving for. How will you know when or if you've attained it?
4. Ask yourself what the tales of your chosen deity say about you or how they inform your own life story. Does your divine choice serve as a path to becoming godlier yourself?
5. Ask yourself who and what is helping you or holding you back as you follow your chosen path to greater insights and understandings.
6. Ask yourself if you are living or being lived.
7. Ask yourself how you know the answers to these questions as well as any others you've asked yourself while on this wonderful mythic adventure we call mortal life!

Theurgic tip: Though it may seem so after a casual or first cautious read-through, I don't believe that theurgy leads to a loss of self. The *henōsis* (oneness, union) you seek as a theurgist ultimately leads back to you! An expanded, open, and more mythic you! "Know thyself," sayeth the Delphic maxim! Always ask yourself difficult questions and work out your own answers as best you can. Accept them as temporary and test both their truth and their usefulness. Compare them to the answers of others on the same or similar paths. Dialogue with the gods! Learn, expand your knowledge, grow, evolve, have fun!

Tips on Living a More Olympian Life

Immersing oneself in Olympian antiquity will greatly enhance your theurgic practice. Fortunately, there are numerous threads of Hellenic influence woven into the tapestry of Western civilization.

A classical education was valued for many centuries, and thus much information about classical antiquity survives to this day. Thanks to the efforts of countless scholars and practitioners, this vast body of knowledge is still being explored, debated, and applied. It is also readily available. Rare and out-of-print material can often be found online inexpensively if not for free. There is more than enough factual and speculative material available to inform and guide you (as well as occupy your time) throughout this current lifetime.

Our popular culture also preserves (and constantly reinvents) Greco-Roman myths and themes. There are plenty of books, comic books, graphic novels, pick-a-path books, TV shows, cartoons, movies, plays, board games, card games, RPGs, video and computer games, toys, action figures, and other fun ways to fill your life with Olympian themes and imagery.

Words (especially in the sciences), concepts (such as philosophy and higher learning), plus institutions (such as democracy, republics, and tyranny) from Mediterranean antiquity still thrive in our modern world as well. There are countless paintings and statues as well as Greco-Roman architecture in our civic centers.

The myths, thanks to transpersonal psychologists and mythologists, have come to reside in our psyches. We follow their timeless tales through our diversions or act them out in our daily lives.

Hermeticism, *mageia*, and Neopaganism have also taken root in our culture. New esoteric material is continually being added to the corpus of literature. For decades I have also dialogued, interacted, and collaborated with diverse occult individuals and groups. I learned a great deal, and it's helped me develop broader perspectives on a wide range of topics.

Be creative in your seeking! And, as you can see, living an Olympus-focused life in an Olympian-rich world is not actually much of a problem.

A Call to Adventure

The ever-evolving conversation focused on theurgy will continue, grow, and evolve. It outlived the two e-radio channels that hosted it and continues in this book as well as on our YouTube channel. Thank you for being a part of this journey!

Other conversations are also taking place as well. I am currently in the autumn of my years and live in the shadow of a winter that is fast approaching. Although I could find no surviving tales that explain them, on ancient pottery, there are several depictions of Hercules's encounter with Geras, best known to us as Old Age. In Greek mythology, Geras is a child of Nyx, the primordial goddess of night. Erebos, the god of eternal darkness, is sometimes credited with being his father.

In some images, our hero is aggressively staving off, or fiercely fighting, Old Age. Geras, shriveled and small, does not seem to stand a chance of winning. In other depictions, the encounter between Hercules and Geras seems remarkably free of conflict, almost friendly. They are reaching out to each other, seemingly striving to embrace.

How do we make sense of these contradictory images? Do they occur at different points in a greater tale? Do they depict different incidents altogether? Alas, we may never actually know. But now that I am in my late sixties, with more days behind me than ahead of me, perhaps I could venture a guess:

At my age, the impulse to mitigate or forestall the effects of aging, which can no longer be ignored, is quite strong. New exercises, supplements, and diets are studied and attempted. Cosmetic, emotional, mental, and spiritual techniques are then gradually added to our arsenal of weapons until Geras is kept at bay. Some fight old age even harder with drugs, surgery, and fringe (or cutting-edge) sciences.

Through this struggle, acceptance ultimately emerges, and with it, a sense of peace. Embracing Old Age and facing the finality of all mortal life allows you to appreciate the preciousness of each and every passing moment.

When I personally found myself there, I made a promise: Until I die, I resolve to fully immerse myself in, and enjoy, the process of living.

And then I started a public conversation with others who are also, each in their own way, currently engaged in wrestling with Geras. Currently, I am experimenting with diet, supplements, and exercise with a healthy dose of mental and spiritual techniques. Though it's true that we are all seeking answers, more importantly, we are sharing the journey with each other and with the world at large.

If you are on the theurgic path, or simply getting older as a mortal Olympian, and would like to join the conversation, please feel free to contact me through Llewellyn Publishing. I have climbed the mountain, I have located the horn, and I have sounded the call.

In Closing: Living Theurgy

My lifelong theurgic journey, though extremely unconventional, has enhanced and enriched my personal life on all levels in countless ways. At this point in time, being over sixty-five years of age and a senior theurgist rather than a teenage one, I can honestly say that my decision to pursue these studies from a very early age was well worth the time and energy expended.

I wish you great joy and success in *your* theurgic exploration and adventures!

Joyous Journeys!

CARRYING DEITY IN MODERN MAGICAL PRACTICE
BRANDY WILLIAMS

"Inanna…Inanna…Inanna…"

The sound drifted through the trees. I stood alone in the clearing, surrounded by cedar trees, decked out in silk and turquoise jewelry. The jewels had been worn by other priestesses at this three-day ritual and carried a heavy charge from the Goddess. I could feel her settle around me, waiting. There in the dark alone I felt a thrill of uncertainty: Would it work? Was I ready?

The sound suddenly welled up in front of me.

"Inanna…Inanna…Inanna!"

A wall of men stepped into the clearing chanting her name and calling her down on me, knocking consciousness right to the back of my brain. She was here, she was me, and she exulted in the dance. I exulted in the dance. I loved them all and wanted to touch them all. All! While the men circled me, weaving around me, three men put themselves between me and the rest of the group, warriors who had chosen to protect the priestess while she carried me, to keep her person safe and my touch in reserve.

The three men beckoned to me, leading me away, while the other men circled around us and followed. They led me to the circle where the women were chanting, "Dumuzi! Dumuzi! Dumuzi!" There he was, my beloved, dressed in silk and jewels, dancing with the crowd. Then he looked up and saw me and everything else fell away.

The women and men together led us to the tent. There, they made their petitions, asking us for the gifts the group had chosen to request. Then at last we were alone. While the people danced around the tent, singing and banging on drums, we loved one another as we had done for thousands of years, remembering to spare a thought to grant them what they had asked.

In the morning when she had gone and I was myself again, one of the men said to me, "You were so beautiful!"

"It wasn't me," I said immediately. "It was her."

How did I come to the place where I represented Goddess for a hundred people? Since I was a teenager, I have felt a very strong call to honor the gods. In my young adulthood, I discovered it was possible to carry them. I have carried more deities than I can count in my four decades as a Pagan Witch and ceremonial magician.

When we talk about theurgy, we often start with ancient history. In fact, people in the magical communities practice theurgy today; we just call it by different names: Drawing Down the Moon, Assumption of Godform, Pagan aspecting. When I discovered the website of John Opsopaus in the late 1990s, I read through his descriptions of theurgy with avid fascination. It was a revelation to discover that the ancients had practiced this too.

Once I understood what was meant by theurgy, I ran into the word everywhere. Writers in the magical communities use the word but often don't stop to explain the term. It stands in for a whole worldview and a specific methodology for interacting with the Divine.

Even today with the proliferation of books on magical practice, only a few talk about the process of carrying the gods. Each of them discusses the practice from within their tradition with only a few references to other magical traditions. However, we can trace the transmission of this ritual directly from ancient theurgy to the Golden Dawn, Thelema, Witchcraft, and into the Pagan communities. Learning about these connections gives us a more complete picture of what we are doing and opens new possibilities in what we can do.

Tracing this development, we will look at each of the forms of this ritual in turn, examining how they developed, how they are done, and how they are changing. We can start with a brief survey of classical theurgy. What did the ancients do, and how does it map onto what we do today?

Classical Theurgy

Theurgy is the term Hellenistic pagans used for various practices, including carrying deity. The word itself translates as "god-work," which is a great capsule definition.

How It Developed

In this volume, John Opsopaus gives a detailed description of the development of theurgy in "Practicing Theurgy in the Platonic Tradition." Here, I want to draw attention to a few aspects of that development.

- **Theurgy arose in Africa:** The earliest theurgists met at the great library in Alexandria, the city in Kemet (Egypt) where the peoples of the ancient European and Asian worlds came together. They continued the work of Plato, who had himself studied for many years in the great temples of Kemet.
- **Theurgy is inclusive:** While the ancient cultures had inequalities just as ours do, theurgy was developed by women as well as men, black people as well as white, living all over the Roman empire in Egypt, Greece, Italy, Spain, and Syria.
- **Theurgy is Pagan spirituality:** The lofty theological structures built by the Neoplatonists rested on a solid foundation of Hellenistic religion. Theurgists honored the gods in the temples and festivals and in their homes.

Theurgists understand the human soul to be made of the same spiritual energy as the gods. The divine force is a single unity that manifests in an infinite number of names and faces. Today, we call this idea the one and the many. This divine force creates the world through a flow of energy, which spills over from the remotest regions of the universe into daimons, human souls, and animals, plants, and stones. There is no distinction between spirit and matter; everything is alive and sacred.

Our language today assumes a separation of the human soul from the deity we are invoking. When we practice theurgy, we might more accurately think of what we are doing as moving our consciousness from awareness of our limited and separate self to a place on the chain of being closer to the wellhead itself.

How It's Done

The ancient theurgists developed a technical language to describe what they experienced as they called and carried deity. John Opsopaus details the ancient practice of theurgic ritual in "A Summary of Pythagorean Theology."[52] This is one of the earliest contemporary writings on practical theurgy and remains an indispensable guide.

The Method: Desmos kai Eklusis

The term the ancients used to describe carrying is *desmos kai eklusis*. This is translated as "binding and releasing." We can also think of this as calling and receiving—the theurgist calls deity into a receiver.

Both the statue and the person who will receive deity must be prepared to carry the divine presence. The statue is prepared with substances like herbs and stones that have a particular resonance with the specific deity. The person can also hold stones and herbs but also prepares to receive deity by praying. John Opsopaus makes the important point that calling deity into a person treats the person like the statue, as a vessel for the spirit.[53] In both cases, the power of the deity is brought into the physical world so the theurgist can have a direct relationship with that deity.

The great advantage of calling a deity into a person is that the caller can ask questions and the spirit speaking through the receiver can answer. When

---

52. John Opsopaus, "A Summary of Pythagorean Theology, Part V: Theurgy," Biblioteca Arcana, updated January 26, 2010, wisdomofhypatia.com/OM/BA/ETP/V.html.
53. John Opsopaus, "Practicing Theurgy in the Platonic Tradition," in *Theurgy: Seven Approaches to Divine Connection* (Llewellyn Publications, 2025), 19.

we call deity into ourselves, this requires a dual consciousness to both ask the question and be receptive to the answer.

The Result: Sustasis

Calling a deity into a statue or another person establishes a relationship with the deity. The ancients called this relationship *sustasis*. This is translated as "liaison" or "conjunction" but can also be thought of as "alliance." Once an alliance has been established, the theurgist can go even deeper into the relationship. The theurgist may make offerings, including vows to do particular actions on behalf of the deity.

Much as the ancients did, Witches, magicians, and Pagans call deity today. Our practices are forms of *desmos kai eklusis*, binding and releasing, calling and receiving. The specific rituals are:

- Assumption of Godform
- The Gnostic Mass
- Drawing Down the Moon
- Pagan aspecting

In some cases one person calls while another receives. In other cases the same person makes the call and receives the deity. In all these cases the practitioner forms an alliance with the deity.

There are two main reasons these rituals are performed, and they also map onto the reasons the ancients engaged in theurgy.

Being deity for others: The receiver carries the deity to allow other people to interact with the deity. There are two main forms of interaction:

- The deity answers questions.
- The deity confers initiation.

Becoming deity: The practitioner interacts with deity in solitary practice for the purpose of spiritual growth. The theurgist seeks to move consciousness along the thread that connects the human soul to deity. The ultimate goal is to allow consciousness to be absorbed into the deity.

Stages of Carrying

There are levels of carrying deity in classic theurgy. The Neoplatonic theurgist Iamblichus describes three distinct stages:[54]

- **Participation:** The theurgist acts in common with the god.
- **Communion:** The deity possesses the theurgist.
- **Union:** The theurgist becomes the deity.

This list describes the quality of the trance. Each of these stages also corresponds with a level of relationship:

- **Participation:** Establishes a friendship or alliance between the theurgist and the specific deity.
- **Communion:** Allows the deity and the theurgist to accomplish the work of the deity in the world together.
- **Union:** The fulfillment of the human soul in the divine fire or power.[55]

Contemporary writers offer experiences with deity in similar graded lists. Some of these lists identify many more stages. I like the simplicity of the list of Iamblichus. It marks the major milestones as the human soul moves from its separate particularity into full absorption into the divine presence.

How It's Changing

Contemporary practitioners study the writings of the ancient theurgists directly. Some are able to read them in the original Greek, and several of the contributors to this volume do so. Many of us study English translations. These writings explain the worldview of the ancient practitioners, which is complex and comprehensive and rivals the theology of the great world religions. We've only begun to assimilate their understandings in the development of contemporary Pagan theology.

---

54. Gregory Shaw, "Containing Ecstasy: Strategies of Iamblichean Theory," *Dionysius* 21 (2003): 60.
55. Shaw, "Containing Ecstasy," 60.

Public performance of pagan ritual was suppressed in antiquity. Consequently, the writings describing the results of these rituals were separated from the ritual instructions. However, in 1986, a translation of Greek and Kemetic rituals was published by Hans Dieter Betz as *The Greek Magical Papyri in Translation*. Since that publication, magicians and academics have been reconnecting these rituals with the Neoplatonic descriptions of their results.[56]

Today, Hellenic reconstructionists revive theurgy as practiced by ancient magicians and philosophers. Theurgy has also been a wellspring of magical practice for the last century and a half. We'll look at that next.

Assumption of Godform

Golden Dawn magicians practice a theurgic ritual called Assumption of Godform. It was created consciously as a modern form of *desmos kai eklusis*, binding and releasing, calling and receiving.

To talk about Assumption of Godform, we also need to talk about the Neophyte initiation. This is an extraordinary leap forward in ceremonial ritual. Renaissance magicians prayed to God, invoked angels, and commanded demons—magick that leaned heavily on monotheistic theology and imagery. The Neophyte initiation on the other hand bursts forth in an entirely new magical structure. The candidate is guided through a psychic transformation by officers who perform Assumption of Godform to take on the aspect of Kemetic (Egyptian) deities. Tracing the development of the Neophyte ritual connects the Golden Dawn to the ancient practice of theurgy.

How It Developed

In 1888, William Wynn Westcott and Samuel Liddell MacGregor Mathers, along with others, founded the Hermetic Order of the Golden Dawn. This was the first modern magical group, and it has had an enormous influence on every group since.

---

56. Brandy Williams, "The Survival of Theurgic Ritual," chap. 13 in *For the Love of the Gods: The History and Modern Practice of Theurgy*, 2nd ed. (Mnemosyne Press, 2022), ebook.

Westcott had a document with mysterious origins called the Cipher Manuscript, a jumble of ritual fragments and texts. Westcott hired Mathers to take the manuscript and turn it into usable ritual. Mathers used the Cipher Manuscript to frame the Neophyte initiation, which brought new members into the Golden Dawn.

Alex Owen points to an additional source that Mathers used to create the Neophyte initiation.[57] Charles Wycliffe Goodwin's *Fragment of a Graeco-Egyptian Work Upon Magic: From a Papyrus in the British Museum* was published for the Cambridge Antiquarian Society in 1852. While the ancient text that Goodwin translated clearly informs the Neophyte ritual, the full impact of Goodwin's work is much more fundamental to the development of the Golden Dawn. Goodwin quotes from Iamblichus and summarizes descriptions of theurgic rites. He notes that Iamblichus presented his descriptions as rites that were performed by Egyptian priests. Goodwin then says, "Our fragment affords several illustrations of these passages."[58] *Fragment of a Graeco-Egyptian Work* is one of the earliest works to explicitly link Neoplatonic theurgy with the Magical Papyri.

Samuel Liddell MacGregor Mathers and spouse Moina Mathers later constructed Rites of Isis in which ritualists posing as statues of Osiris and Isis came alive. They presented these rites as Graeco-Egyptian theurgy. A journalist who attended one of these rites interviewed Mathers, who said:

> *We believe as our predecessors did… that divine force can be made to appear in statues. No we are not monotheists, and for that reason we have sometimes been called idolators. But is not the universe, God manifest in matter, a great eidolon? We are pantheists; we believe that each force of the universe is regulated by a god. Gods are, therefore, innumerable and infinite.*[59]

....

57. Alex Owen, *The Place of Enchantment: British Occultism and the Culture of the Modern* (University of Chicago Press, 2004), 271.
58. Charles Wycliffe Goodwin, ed., *Fragment of a Graeco-Egyptian Work Upon Magic: From a Papyrus in the British Museum* (Deighton; Macmillan, 1852), vii–viii.
59. Frederic Lees, "Isis Worship in Paris: Conversations with the Hierophant Rameses and the High Priestess Anari," *The Humanitarian* 16, no. 2 (1900), 82–87, (site discontinued), quoted in Alison Butler, *Victorian Occultism and the Making of Modern Magic: Invoking Tradition* (Palgrave Macmillan, 2011), 58.

Like the practitioners of theurgy today, the Golden Dawn consciously resurrected theurgy by reading about rituals, linking them to theurgic writings, and creating new rituals that bring practitioners an awareness of the divine nature of the human soul.

How It's Done

We've talked about the two main reasons people engage in *desmos kai eklusis*, binding and releasing, calling and receiving. People carry deity to allow other people to interact with the deity. Also, people invoke deity for the purpose of their own spiritual growth.

Assumption of Godform is performed for both of these reasons. The original Isis-Urania Golden Dawn Temple taught Assumption of Godform to magicians who had gone through all the initiations of the First Order and had been invited to the Second Order. These magicians would then engage in the ritual in their own private magical work. However, in the initiation rituals, the officers assuming Godforms weren't interacting with the deity for their own benefit but instead holding the energy so the initiate could be exposed to it.

Assumption of Godform in Personal Work

The first person to publish a version of the Assumption of Godform was a member of the original temple. Aleister Crowley printed his version in 1909 in his magazine *The Equinox*. At the time of publication, he had already left the Golden Dawn and established his own branch of ceremonial magick called Thelema. Because this is the earliest publication and it is now in the public domain, this version gets quoted extensively.

Crowley's description appears in the text "Liber O Vel Manus Et Sagittae," section III. He starts with "Assumption of God-forms." He instructs the magician to study images of "the Gods of Egypt" by visiting museums or viewing them in books.[60] He suggests painting these images. Next, the magician sits in the "characteristic attitude of the God desired."[61] The magician

---

60. Aleister Crowley, "Liber O Vel Manus Et Sagittae," *The Equinox* 1, no. 2 (1909): 16–17.
61. Crowley, "Liber O," 16–17.

imagines the Godform enveloping their own body. Crowley notes, "This must be practiced until mastery of the image is attained, and an identity with it and with the God experienced."[62]

Crowley names the second step in the process "Vibrations of Divine Names."[63] This is done in a standing position. The practitioner takes a deep breath and inhales the name of the deity. The name descends through the body to the feet. At that point, the magician steps forward, throws their hands forward, and vibrates the name. The magician steps back again and places one finger on their lips, closing the gesture.[64]

Crowley wrote another, more detailed work describing the theurgic operation of calling the gods: "Liber Astarte vel Berylli"—a dense but relatively complete description of how to engage in sustasis. It includes more detail about how to choose the deity, ways to approach the deity, and what the experience will be like. It's an essential companion piece to "Liber O Vel Manus Et Sagittae."

Crowley's works are compact and need expanding and explaining. Fortunately, subsequent generations of Golden Dawn magicians have written extensively about the system in general and theurgy in particular. Israel Regardie was Crowley's secretary and student and traveled with him for a few years before they parted company. Regardie subsequently took an initiation into a successor to the Isis-Urania Temple, the Stella Matutina, and dedicated himself to Golden Dawn magick. Then, as a great boon to all ceremonial magicians, he collected the rituals and knowledge papers in a massive tome called *The Golden Dawn*. This was first published in 1937 and reissued by Llewellyn in 2016 with a long-needed index compiled by John Michael Greer.

Regardie's book *The Tree of Life* is an indispensable companion to *The Golden Dawn*. He consciously presents the Golden Dawn system as a form of Neoplatonic theurgy—in fact, he quotes from the Neoplatonic teacher Iamblichus in the epigraph of the book.[65] While Regardie mentions Assumption of Godform in passing in *The Golden Dawn*, he devotes an entire chapter to

---

62. Crowley, "Liber O," 16–17.
63. Crowley, "Liber O," 16–17.
64. Crowley, "Liber O," 17–18.
65. Israel Regardie, *The Tree of Life: An Illustrated Study in Magic*, ed. and annotated Chic Cicero and Sandra Tabatha Cicero (Llewellyn Publications, 2003).

the operation (chapter eleven, "The Assumption of Godforms") in *The Tree of Life*. He suggests support practices to engage with the chosen deity before attempting the actual operation. For the actual operation, he expands on Crowley's methodology. Regardie instructs the practitioner to:

- Visit museums to study the deity[66]
- Study the deity's physical form, especially headdress[67]
- Learn the deity's stories[68]
- Learn and speak or sing hymns of the deity[69]

When these preparations are complete, the magician can engage in the operation. In this two-step process, the magician:

- Builds up an image of the deity in front[70]
- Imagines the deity enveloping the magician's body[71]

Regardie explains:

> *This Astral effigy of the God, previously but an image external to the body of the Theurgist, should now be arranged as a divine figure around his own astral form until they coincide, his own Body of Light being changed and transmuted into the Body of the God.*[72]

Regardie not only preserved the rituals and knowledge of the Golden Dawn but brought the order forward in time, resurrecting the Hermetic Order of the Golden Dawn in the US in the 1980s. His close friend and confidant Chic Cicero was one of the people who assisted him in this work. Following in Regardie's footsteps, Chic Cicero and Sandra Tabatha Cicero have dedicated their lives to Golden Dawn magick. They have written a number of books together that make the system accessible to contemporary

....
66. Regardie, *Tree of Life*, 141.
67. Regardie, *Tree of Life*, 255.
68. Regardie, *Tree of Life*, 255
69. Regardie, *Tree of Life*, 258–59.
70. Regardie, *Tree of Life*, 257
71. Regardie, *Tree of Life*, 258.
72. Regardie, *Tree of Life*, 258.

practitioners. Their book *Golden Dawn Magic* describes Assumption of Godform. Their version outlines four steps:

- Preparation
- Building the Astral Form
- Assuming the Godform
- Taking Off and Dissolving the Godform[73]

The preparation section directs the practitioner to study the image and the name of the chosen deity as usual. It is noteworthy that this version of the ritual includes the specific step of stepping out of the Godform and dissolving it.[74]

Assumption of Godform in Initiation

In the Neophyte and other initiation rituals of the Golden Dawn, the officers also practice Assumption of Godform. In this case, though, they don't engage in a lengthy invocation. Instead, they take up positions in the ritual that correspond to deity forms.

The officers construct a temple, which they imagine as the Hall of Maat from the Egyptian *Book of the Dead*. The seven officers who conduct the initiations assume the forms of Osiris, Horus, Maat, Anubis, Mut, Neith, and Opowet. In addition, there are officers of the temple who don't have active roles in the initiation but sit on a dais overlooking the ritual, and they assume the forms of Nephthys, Isis, and Thoth.[75]

The Hierophant is the main officer in the ritual. Before the ritual starts, the Hierophant sets or activates the godforms in their physical positions in the hall. Officers center themselves in those forces, then perform the actions and speak the words specified in the ritual script.

---

73. Chic Cicero and Sandra Tabatha Cicero, *Golden Dawn Magic: A Complete Guide to the High Magical Arts* (Llewellyn Publications, 2019), 324, Kindle.
74. Cicero and Cicero, *Golden Dawn Magic*, 326.
75. Chic Cicero and Sandra Tabatha Cicero, *The Essential Golden Dawn: An Introduction to High Magic* (Llewellyn Publications, 2003), 102–7, Kindle.

In the initiations, the candidate identifies with a character on a journey in order to experience a personal transformation. It is the presence of the deities that affects that transformation. Regardie explains:

> *When an officer in the Temple rehearses the part of a God, if he be acquainted with magical technical methods, he will assume the Form of that God so perfectly that the magnetic emanations from the God in him flow forth into the innermost soul of the Neophyte.*[76]

Regardie implies that officers carrying deity in initiations should have engaged in Assumption of Godform on their own before taking a role in the initiation ritual.

Stages of Carrying

Assumption of Godform was the first theurgic ritual to be published in the modern age and the first modern ritual to link Neoplatonic theurgy with Egyptian deities. From their descriptions, it's clear that the magicians inventing the ritual were pioneers feeling their way forward with the ancient texts to guide them. One of the ways this shows up is in the description of the results. The expected outcome of the ritual was an on-off switch; either you had the deity or you didn't. The versions of the ritual studied here don't include a graded list of trance states such as we find in Iamblichus and in contemporary Witchcraft and Pagan practice.

In Assumption of Godform as an individual practice, the early teachers reported an ecstatic and transformative experience. In "Liber O Vel Manus et Sagittae," after describing "Assumption of God-forms" and "Vibrations of Divine Names," Crowley says:

> *In both the above practices all consciousness of anything but the God-form and name should be absolutely blotted out; and the longer it takes for normal perception to return, the better.*[77]

....
76. Regardie, *Tree of Life*, 339.
77. Crowley, "Liber O," 17–18.

In the initiation rituals, on the other hand, the officer was expected to follow a script. There was no opportunity to speak for the deity as in classic *desmos kai eklusis*. The deity wasn't expected to interact with the initiate through words but instead through affecting the energy of the initiate simply by being carried by the officer.

Regardie specifically warned against engaging in mediumship. He believed that the medium centers awareness below normal consciousness susceptible to subconscious impulses, while the magician remains above normal consciousness open to the higher self.[78] It's helpful to remember that when he wrote, Spiritualism was a widely practiced form of spirituality. It's not clear whether Regardie meant Spiritualist mediumship, the kind practiced by the ancient theurgists, or both. At any rate, it appears that carrying deity to allow them to speak is not the intent of Assumption of Godform.

What It's Like

Assumption of Godform is my baseline theurgic practice. It was the first one that I learned, and its discipline has patterned my magical life—in particular its insistence on knowledge of the particular deity and clarity in handling energy.

John Opsopaus comments that a person performing *desmos kai eklusis* on their own acts as both caller and receiver, and these require different states of consciousness.[79] When I practice Assumption of Godform on my own, I am noting my own responses, so I remain conscious, and I don't experience the swooning trance that Crowley describes. I experience deeper trance in other forms of theurgy when I am the receiver and someone else is the caller.

When I act as officer in initiation, I experience a much lighter sense of presence. The deity doesn't step on my consciousness as in other forms of theurgy. *Godform* is a good description of the presence; it's a structured frame surrounding me and directed toward the initiate.

I can also speak to the experience of the Hierophant. I've acted as Hierophant in Golden Dawn initiations, and I founded a Golden Dawn–style order called Sisters of Seshat and manage the founding Isis-Nephthys temple.

---

78. Regardie, *The Tree of Life*, 31–32.
79. Opsopaus, "A Summary of Pythagorean Theology."

As a Hierophant, I don't bring the deities into my own subtle body when I invoke them. Instead, I set the godforms as an outline in the places where the officers will sit. The Isis-Nephthys temple uses a set of lamens (magical pendants), which include the image of deity on one side and the cartouche of the deity's name on the other. This is helpful to me as I set the godforms and helpful to the officers who step into them to embody them for the initiate.

How It's Changing

The Golden Dawn not only left a rich legacy but is also a living and still-developing system. The Hermetic Order of the Golden Dawn continues its work today. New lodges inspired by the original work have sprung up, and new forms of the initiation rituals have emerged.

Recognizing the importance of Pagan theurgy to the initiation rituals suggests new avenues to explore in the continued development of this form of magick. Here are some ideas: The Golden Dawn had access to the first English translations of the Graeco-Egyptian Magical Papyri and early translations of the *Chaldean Oracles*. Today, we have a much more complete collection of papyri: *The Greek Magical Papyri in Translation*. We also have Ruth Majercik's definitive edition of *The Chaldean Oracles*. Contemporary theurgists study this material and bring new techniques and new insights into our current practice. These ideas include using substances like stones and herbs and chanting vowels and singing hymns. We can also work directly with the Kemetic deities; Richard Reidy's two books *Eternal Egypt* and *Everlasting Egypt* give a number of rituals, including a complete methodology to invoke a deity into a statue.

Aleister Crowley developed his versions of theurgic ritual in a different direction, and we'll look at those next.

Liber XV, the Gnostic Mass

There is a theurgic ritual that is performed today in public all over the world. The formal name for the ritual is "Liber XV, the Gnostic Mass." It was written by Aleister Crowley, the Golden Dawn magician who first published Assumption of Godform as "Liber O Vel Manus et Sagittae."

The Gnostic Mass is arguably the most famous and most widely performed ritual Crowley wrote. It has a number of theurgic elements. In particular, I'm interested in exploring a moment in the Mass in which the priest invokes Nuit and the priestess responds as Nuit. I'm being careful about my descriptions here. As a Pagan, I would say that the priest invokes the goddess Nuit on the priestess, but these are not terms that are normally used by Thelemites to describe the ritual act.

How It Developed

After Crowley left the Golden Dawn, he had a revelation that had elements of theurgy. He received a channeled work, which he called *Liber AL vel Legis* (*The Book of the Law*). This book focuses on the spiritual entities Nuit, Hadit, and Ra-Hoor-Khuit. This revelation led Crowley to found a new branch of magick, Thelema. As Crowley developed the magick of Thelema, Nuit and Hadit evolved into a cosmic pair relating to each other through love in general and sexual love in particular.

Crowley joined the Ordo Templi Orientis in 1912 and learned the Supreme Secret of the order. Crowley described magicians who hold this secret as practicing both *thaumaturgy*, magick with a specific result, and *theurgy*, the recognition of the soul's essential divinity.[80] Although the idea of a secret of thaumaturgy gets a lot of attention, the essence of this magick is described by initiates as a personal theurgic revelation, which can ultimately not be conferred but only experienced.

Theodor Reuss, cofounder and head of the O.T.O., tasked Crowley with writing rituals for the order.[81] When Crowley attended a Russian Orthodox Mass in 1913, he was inspired to create his own Thelemic version for the order's use. Crowley's version of the Mass patterns the Christian Mass in consecration of a host and wine. The Thelemic priest engages in nearly the same actions with nearly the same words as the Christian priest. However, in the Gnostic Mass, a priestess assists the priest with the consecration,

---

80. Aleister Crowley, "Liber CXCIV, O.T.O., An Intimation with Reference to the Constitution of the Order," accessed June 8, 2025, line 23, lib.oto-usa.org/libri/liber0194.html.
81. Richard Kaczynski, *Perdurabo: The Life of Aleister Crowley* (New Falcon Publications, 2002), 204.

and there are overtly sexual metaphors in the actions. Lon Milo DuQuette explains that the Mass "is the central ceremony (both public and private) of the O.T.O. and is the ritualized celebration of the Order's supreme secret of magick."[82]

With this in mind, we can investigate one of the theurgic moments in the ritual.

How It's Done

The Gnostic Mass is performed by a five-person team, which includes a priest and a priestess. There are eight sections in the script. The final three sections closely pattern the consecration of the wine and host in the Christian Mass. This is not a Christian communion but a Thelemic one; while the Christian Mass is conducted by a priest alone, the Gnostic Mass communion is conducted by the priest and priestess together.

The ritual contains several acts of theurgy. Most notably, at the conclusion, the priest and the congregants who take communion make the declaration, "There is no part of me that is not of the Gods."[83] The Gnostic Mass is a passion play in which the priest acts out a story and the congregation in turn models the priest. It's an extraordinary ritual, layered and complex, and requires much more space than we have to explore. Our focus here is the section of the ritual that directly relates to *desmos kai eklusis*, binding and loosing, calling and receiving. The priest and priestess act as the pair in the operation, with the priest making an invocation and the priestess responding.

The priest invocation and priestess response occur in the middle of the ritual. Crowley titled the fourth section of the Mass "Of the Ceremony of the Opening of the Veil."[84] The Mass temple includes an altar with a "veil" (a curtain) stretched across the front. At this point in the ritual, the priestess is sitting on the altar. The priest closes the veil and circumambulates the temple

---

82. Lon Milo DuQuette, introduction to *The Best of the Equinox, Sex Magick*, vol. 3 by Aleister Crowley (Weiser Books, 2013).
83. Aleister Crowley, "Liber XV: O. T. O. Ecclesiae Gnosticae Catholicae Canon Missae." O. T. O. U.S.A. Library, accessed May 2, 2025, lib.oto-usa.org/libri/liber0015.html.
84. Crowley, "Liber XV," 254.

while the priestess steps down from the altar and unrobes. Then the priest stands in front of the veil and delivers a speech:

> *O circle of Stars whereof our Father is but the younger brother, marvel beyond imagination, soul of infinite space, before whom Time is Ashamed, the mind bewildered, and the understanding dark, not unto Thee may we attain, unless Thine image be Love. Therefore by seed and root and stem and bud and leaf and flower and fruit do we invoke Thee.*[85]

Thus far the priest is speaking in his own voice. The speech then shifts to a narrative voice drawn from *The Book of the Law*:

> *Then the priest answered & said unto the Queen of Space, kissing her lovely brows, and the dew of her light bathing his whole body in a sweet-smelling perfume of sweat: O Nuit, continuous one of Heaven, let it be ever thus; that men speak not of thee as One but as None; and let them speak not of thee at all, since thou art continuous.*[86]

The priest invokes Nuit, the circle of stars, and the Queen of Space. He also makes the invocation "by seed and root" with imagery specific to plant life on earth. Earlier in the Mass, the earth is identified as Babalon, "the Mother."[87] She's not named here, but there is an implication that the divine female force is both space and earth.

While the priest is making this invocation, the naked priestess stands hidden behind the veil. She responds with a speech that is primarily drawn from the first section of *The Book of the Law*, beginning, "But to love me is better than all things…" and ending:

> *Pale or purple, veiled or voluptuous, I who am all pleasure and purple, and drunkenness of the innermost sense, desire you. Put on the wings, and arouse the coiled splendour within you: come*

---

85. Crowley, "Liber XV," 256.
86. Crowley, "Liber XV," 256.
87. Crowley, "Liber XV," 251.

> *unto me! To me! To me! Sing the rapturous love-song unto me! Burn to me perfumes! Wear to me jewels! Drink to me, for I love you! I love you. I am the blue-lidded daughter of sunset; I am the naked brilliance of the voluptuous night-sky. To me! To me!*[88]

Once the priestess has completed this speech, she gets back on the altar and may re-robe or remain unclothed at her preference. For the rest of the Mass, she assists the priest with his subsequent ritual actions at the altar. She speaks again only once, to say a word simultaneously with the priest in the final section of the Mass.

This seems a clear example of *desmos kai eklusis*. However, this theurgic moment has many unique characteristics. It differs from Assumption of Godform, where the magician is both caller and receiver. In this case, the priest calls and the priestess receives. This ritual also differs from ancient theurgy in that the caller does not question the receiver, and the receiver does not answer extemporaneously. The priestess reads a fixed speech in which she speaks the words Nuit had already given in *The Book of the Law*. One way to look at it is that the priestess is acting more like a statue, a vessel for the presence, so the priest can interact with Nuit.

The priest also undergoes a theurgic transformation during the Mass. It is not, however, the same transformation that the priestess makes. Nuit is paired with Hadit, and some of the priest's orations indicate that he has identified with Hadit, but the priestess has not invoked Hadit on the priest in the same way that the priest has invoked Nuit on the priestess. One possibility is that he brings Hadit on himself. It's also possible to read the entire journey of the priest as a form of theurgic ascent, cognate with the Golden Dawn operation of Rising on the Planes. Space prevents us from continuing this thought, but it remains an interesting idea to explore.

Stages of Carrying

Crowley did not describe the work of the priestess as theurgy. I have not heard O.T.O. leadership use the terms *desmos kai eklusis* or *theurgic invocation* to describe "Of the Ceremony of the Opening of the Veil." Since the

---

88. Crowley, "Liber XV," 257.

Mass displays the Supreme Secret, there's not a whole lot of discussion about it from the handful of people who actually hold the secret. The stages of trance that priestesses experience have not yet been documented.

I can report on my experience and conversations I've had over nearly twenty years as a priestess performing the Mass. One interesting phenomenon is that both priestesses and priests report that sometimes they forget themselves in the Mass altogether and only come to consciousness when the ritual is concluded. I theorize that the roles of priestess and priest seem to have evolved into magical personalities. Individuals can step into the roles, but the magical personalities themselves carry the energies.

The work Crowley actually labeled as theurgy, "Liber DCCXI, Energized Enthusiasm, A Note on Theurgy," doesn't address *desmos kai eklusis*, focusing instead on three methods to induce ecstatic trance: listening to music, drinking wine, and having sex ("wine, woman and song").[89] Here, Crowley is using the word *theurgy* to describe the magician's realization of himself as IAO, the son of God.[90]

What It's Like

The curtain is drawn, the veil is closed, I am secluded and naked. I make myself receptive. The priest begins the invocation, and I listen intently. As he completes his speeches, I feel a presence settle around me and in me. I say, "But to love me is better than all things…"

The priestess who trained me as a novice instructed me to read the priestess speech from a copy of the script. As the weeks and months went on, I memorized the speech but continued to remain fairly conscious and mostly myself until saying the words became completely automatic. Then Nuit began to come through more strongly. Although I'm saying the same words each time, the emphasis on the words is different depending on how she comes through in the channel. Her speech is an invitation, and her love comes through so strongly that it can be overwhelming. When the speech is over, her

---

89. Aleister Crowley, "Liber DCCXI, Energized Enthusiasm, A Note on Theurgy," *The Equinox* 1, no. 9 (1913): 23.
90. Theodor Reuss and Aleister Crowley, *O.T.O. Rituals and Sex Magick*, ed. A. R. Naylor (I-H-O Books, 1999), 372.

presence steps to the background, and when the veil is opened for the next part of the Mass, I experience a change in the flow of energy.

The fact that the script does not permit the priestess to speak extemporaneously doesn't mean that Nuit herself doesn't have anything to say. Sometimes I hear Nuit at the back of my head talking to the congregants. Other Gnostic priestesses, both Witches and non-Witches, have also reported to me that Nuit is talking in their minds to the communicants. My practice has been to approach the communicants when the ritual is done and pass on the messages she had for them.

I manage my energy carefully when I perform the role. I spend some time before the ritual meditating and reciting a small prayer I wrote for the occasion. I also make sure to spend a few moments on my own recentering myself into waking consciousness. I have a bit of something to eat or drink; food is always grounding.

I experience similarities and differences between the priestess role in the Mass and the priestess role in Drawing Down the Moon, which I'll discuss below.

How It's Changing

The Gnostic Mass as written in *Liber XV* is a fixed ritual, and the O.T.O. protects and preserves it. In that sense, the Mass is not open to change. What does change is the understanding of those who experience it as congregants and Mass team members. It also inspires new rituals in the Thelemic magical system.

The official commentary on the Mass from the church hierarchy focuses on performance rather than meaning. It's a ritual that is experienced rather than explained; each person who engages with the Mass comes to their own understanding, which develops over time. However, some of us do talk about our own experiences and understanding in an unofficial capacity. These explanations by and large focus on Qabalah as an underlying principle to explain the magick. Applying the lens of theurgy to the ritual offers a new source of insight.

The Mass is gendered, and the experience of the priest and priestess are different. While the priest enacts the journey of consciousness, the priestess enacts surrender to presence. There are physical and energic consequences to each. Viewing these experiences as a form of theurgy can help us to understand how to process those experiences ourselves and how to support the clergy who engage in them on behalf of the congregation.

Thinking about the difference in the priest's journey and the experience of the priestess also helps to illuminate a gender discussion. Some people drawn to the Mass have expressed a desire to choose a role in the Mass based on something other than their gender assignment. Looking at the Mass as a form of *desmos kai eklusis* is one way to understand this. The priest acts as an active magician and conducts the binding or calling part of *desmos kai eklusis*. Taking the active role interests people of all genders. The priestess, on the other hand, has the extraordinary opportunity to experience the invocation of Nuit and carry her presence. It's not surprising that people might be drawn to that theurgic experience whether or not they identify as a woman.

Theurgy teaches how to manage an invoked presence. This involves preparation before the ritual itself. It's also helpful to think about how to transition from the channel back to normal consciousness. When the Mass ends, the presence can also end with a rather abrupt transition. (I once saw a ninth-degree priestess actually fall forward at that moment.) People who want to support clergy performing the Mass can offer a period of privacy before and after the ritual and make sure that refreshment is on hand.

Ancient theurgists invoked presence into people to be able to ask them questions. The priestess in the Mass has no opportunity to speak during the ritual itself. Her work in the ritual is to support the journey of the priest, who in turn is demonstrating to the congregants how they can engage in the journey themselves. However, when you put a presence in front of people, they will respond. In the final section of the Mass, each member of the congregation approaches the altar to take communion. Some look away from the priestess, but some look into her eyes. Some priestesses lock their energy and direct it toward the priest only, while others report that they make their energy available to the congregants individually or in general.

It might seem obvious to suggest creating an open-form ritual to invoke Nuit in which the person carrying the presence could then speak to the congregation. However, this ritual doesn't need to be written because it already exists. Witches call this Drawing Down the Moon, and we'll look at that next.

Drawing Down the Moon

Everyone present is silent with anticipation as the priest approaches the priestess. Strongly and with reverence, he invokes the presence: "By seed and root and stem and bud and leaf and flower and fruit." She answers, "Come unto me!" The priest touches her on the chest between her breasts and on her womb. He kisses her body in five places and kneels to adore her.

This is a description of the Gnostic Mass in Section VI, "Of the Consecration of the Elements." It is also a description of the Witchcraft ritual Drawing Down the Moon. This trance possession in Witchcraft has a direct connection with the theurgic tradition and is a living version of *desmos kai eklusis*, binding and loosing, calling and receiving.

How It Developed

Sorita d'Este and David Rankine explore the origin of the term "drawing down the moon" in *Wicca: Magickal Beginnings*. Writings in late antiquity reference Thessalian Witches who captured the reflection of the moon in a bowl of water for use in spells.[91] Janet Farrar and Gavin Bone theorize that these Witches were not only performing spells but were also engaging in shamanic trance work.[92]

D'Este and Rankine connect the contemporary practice of Drawing Down the Moon with the Golden Dawn's Assumption of Godform and Crowley's Gnostic Mass, linking the Witchcraft version with its ceremonial magical predecessors.[93] Gardnerian priest and historian Don Frew goes further and sees a direct connection between Witchcraft and theurgy: "It is my belief and contention that the texts and traditions of Gardnerian Craft can best be understood in the context of its roots in the Neoplatonic/Hermetic syncretism of late antiquity."[94]

---

91. Sorita d'Este and David Rankine, *Wicca: Magickal Beginnings* (Avalonia, 2008), 127, Kindle.
92. Janet Farrar and Gavin Bone, *Lifting the Veil: A Witches' Guide to Trance-Prophecy, Drawing Down the Moon, and Ecstatic Ritual* (Acorn Guild Press, 2016), 93–96, ebook.
93. D'Este and Rankine, *Wicca*, 132, Kindle.
94. Don Frew, "Gardnerian Wica as Theurgic Ascent," Theurgicon, August 28, 2010, theurgicon.com/gardnerian.pdf.

Drawing Down the Moon is one of the rituals in Gerald Gardner's *Book of Shadows*. Gardner was already familiar with Aleister Crowley's work when the two men met in 1947, the last year of Crowley's life. Crowley was seventy-one and worried about the survival of the O.T.O. When Crowley met Gardner, he identified the fellow Freemason as a candidate to bring the order forward and gave him an O.T.O. charter.[95] However, Gardner ultimately did not choose to create an O.T.O. group, instead dedicating himself to Witchcraft.[96]

Gardner reported that he was initiated into a group of Witches in 1939 who swore him to secrecy. Gardner wrote the rituals they gave him into his Book of Shadows. It's his most famous book, but he didn't publish it himself.

Versions of the book passed privately from one initiate to another until 1971. In that year, Jessie Wicker Bell, writing as Lady Sheba, published *The Book of Shadows*, although she did not identify it as Gardner's work. Gardnerian Michael Howard reports that he provided Bell with his own copy of Gardner's book. When Bell informed Howard that she was going to publish her own version, he reminded her that this would break her oaths, but she felt she had been instructed by the Goddess to do it.[97]

Some of the rituals were published before Lady Sheba's version, but her book made a full collection of rituals publicly accessible. Since then, several other versions of Gardnerian books have been published. When we talk about Gardner's Book of Shadows, it's important to note our exact sources since they are multiple.

How It's Done

Lady Sheba's book contains initiations, sabbats, esbats, and other rites. The ritual of Drawing Down the Moon has its own entry. The coven performs

---

95. Kaczynski, *Perdurabo*, 447–48; Philip Heselton, *Gerald Gardner and the Cauldron of Inspiration: An Investigation into the Sources of Gardnerian Witchcraft* (Capall Bann Publishing, 2003), 179–97.
96. American serviceman Grady McMurtry activated the charter Crowley gave him at a similar visit and continued the work of the O.T.O.
97. Michael Howard, *Modern Wicca: A History from Gerald Gardner to the Present* (Llewellyn Publications, 2009), 222–23.

the ritual during a full moon or waxing moon esbat. Either the high priest or high priestess casts the circle. The high priest says:

> *I invoke Thee and call upon Thee O'Mighty [sic] Mother of us all. Bringer of Fruitfulness by seed and by root. I invoke Thee, by stem and by bud. I invoke Thee, by life and by love and call upon Thee to descend into the body of this Thy Priestess and Servant. Hear with her ears, speak with her tongue, touch with her hands, kiss with her lips, that thy servants may be fulfilled.*[98]

Lady Sheba explains, "The High Priest draws down the power by the force of his concentration and prayer, touching her on the breast and womb with the Wand. He then kneels at her feet and adores while concentrating."[99]

The ritual then calls for the priestess to recite a prayer called the "Charge of the Goddess." This was compiled by Gerald Gardner and Doreen Valiente from various sources, including Leland's *Aradia* and Crowley's *Book of the Law*. Jason Mankey has assembled an excellent description and history of this poem.[100] The Charge gives voice to the Goddess, who describes herself and imparts instructions to her worshippers.

A decade later, after Lady Sheba published *The Book of Shadows*, Janet and Stewart Farrar published another version of Drawing Down the Moon in their 1981 books *A Witch's Bible* and *Eight Sabbats for Witches*. They received their initiations from Alex and Maxine Sanders.[101] Alex, in turn, had reportedly received a Gardnerian third-degree initiation. However, he did not identify as Gardnerian, insisting that he had been initiated by his grandmother, and called his line of Witchcraft Alexandrian.[102]

The Farrars give a bit more instruction about how to perform Drawing Down the Moon. In their version, the priestess stands with her arms crossed in front of her chest, then opens her arms as the priest makes the invocation.

---

98. Lady Sheba, *The Book of Shadows* (Llewellyn Publications, 1971), 77.
99. Lady Sheba, *Book of Shadows*, 77.
100. Jason Mankey, "The Charge of the Goddess: A History," *Raise the Horns* (blog), Patheos, updated April 7, 2015, https://www.patheos.com/blogs/panmankey/2015/04/the-charge-of-the-goddess-a-history/.
101. Howard, *Modern Wicca*, 265.
102. Howard, *Modern Wicca*, 171–77, 221–22.

They also give additional direction to the high priest. He makes a gesture called the five-fold kiss, kissing the high priestess in five places on the body. While he does this, he recites a prayer, which begins: "Hail, Aradia! From the Amalthean Horn / Pour forth thy store of love..."[103] This poem is copied from a poem of Aleister Crowley's written for the goddess Tyche.[104]

For several decades, these simple descriptions were all that we had to go on. Jason Mankey comments, "Bell's published version of the drawing down ritual is exceedingly short and lacking in any sort of context or instruction in just how to draw down a deity."[105] Priestesses and priests tried the ritual out with varying results. The priestess carrying the Goddess might speak to the coveners, answering their questions and giving advice. Some people who were able to meet the Goddess face-to-face called this the most moving spiritual experience of their lives.

Priestesses feeling their way into this experience had varying levels of success. The Goddess came easily for some; others only felt her presence occasionally. I've encountered coveners who swore off the procedure because the priestess had a hard time grounding after the possession or because the priestess took the liberty of lecturing the coven in the persona of the Goddess.

Jessie Wicker Bell wrote a few books and then retired from public sight to escape criticism of her work.[106] However, Janet Farrar has continued to write, first with Stewart, then after his death with Gavin Bone. Her book with Gavin Bone, *The Inner Mysteries: Progressive Witchcraft and Connection with the Divine,* published in 2003 and revised in 2012, expanded on her own experience and gave a much more detailed description of what was happening. In 2016, the pair wrote an entire book dedicated to this subject: *Lifting the Veil: A Witches' Guide to Trance-Prophesy, Drawing Down the Moon and Ecstatic Ritual.*

In his 2019 book *Transformative Witchcraft*, Gardnerian priest and historian Jason Mankey provides more detail about what the priest and priestess

---

103. Janet Farrar and Stewart Farrar, *Eight Sabbats* (Phoenix Publishing, 1981), 41.
104. D'Este and Rankine, *Wicca*, 134.
105. Jason Mankey, *Transformative Witchcraft: The Greater Mysteries* (Llewellyn Publications, 2019), 265.
106. Howard, *Modern Wicca*, 276.

actually do, including anecdotes from his own experience and circles he has attended. He offers this description:

> *Drawing down the moon is the opening up of oneself to deity so that deity speaks with your tongue, sees with your eyes, and experiences with your body. It's a willful surrendering of consciousness in order to become one with deity so that others around you may experience that deity.*[107]

This is one of the two main reasons people engage in *desmos kai eklusis*, to allow other people to interact with deity.

Mankey has practical instructions for the person carrying deity that incorporate the advice from the ceremonial texts and expand on them in the context of Witchcraft: First, learn about the deity you're calling. Research them, then talk to them. Ask them to visit in dreams or guided meditation. Next, do devotions for them, decorate an altar for them with objects they like, consume foods that they like. Finally, when you're ready to share your body with the deity, make a clear image of the deity in your mind, then let go and welcome them in. Mankey also discusses what happens when the Goddess doesn't show up, noting that the Charge is included in the ritual so the priestess has a fallback communication in that case. Finally, he covers how to help the priestess release the deity and return to normal consciousness.[108]

Stages of Carrying

Janet Farrar and Gavin Bone note three ways the priestess may experience the deity:

- She may feel the deity enter her body and speak as the deity but remain conscious.
- She may lose control of her body and lose memory of the process.
- She may "meet the deity in a trance state in another…reality."[109]

---

107. Mankey, *Transformative Witchcraft*, 228.
108. Mankey, *Transformative Witchcraft*, 260–64.
109. Janet Farrar and Gavin Bone, *The Inner Mysteries: Progressive Witchcraft and Connection with the Divine*, 2nd ed. (Acorn Guilde Press, 2012), 178.

What It's Like

When I engage in Drawing Down the Moon, I reach for the goddess Aradia. The priest who calls the Goddess is my working partner. I always carry her when I conduct an initiation; like many Witches, I feel strongly that it is the Goddess who initiates—the power flows from her. At times, she does speak to the coveners, especially during initiation where she might give instructions about how to connect with her. I experience her presence as coexisting with my own consciousness. This is a choice I make as a Witch, a magician, and a theurgist.

As a priestess who has performed the Gnostic Mass for nearly twenty years and Drawing Down the Moon for more than thirty, I experience similarities and differences in the rituals. They're similar during the invocation. In both cases, the priest calls the presence and I hold myself receptive, and I use the same gesture to welcome the presence, opening my arms. They're a bit different in my experience of the presence. In the Gnostic Mass, I carry Nuit, while in Drawing Down the Moon, I carry Aradia (although there is something of Nuit in the "Charge of the Goddess"). In both cases, the priest makes gestures on my body, which I understand to acknowledge and valorize the womb as the Holy Grail that regenerates life.

From there, the rituals diverge. In the Gnostic Mass, the priest makes five crosses on the body of the priestess and then five crosses on the cup. My experience is that an energy moves from my body to the cup at that point; however, I am still left with presence. The priest consecrates and consumes a cake of light and a goblet of wine as the body and blood of God.

Drawing Down the Moon also consecrates wine and cakes. The priest dips the athame into the cup, but this does not replicate the movement of energy from the priestess into the cup as in the Gnostic Mass. In Drawing Down the Moon, the Goddess is then free to speak to whoever else is present.

Here's my take on the differences between the rituals: In the Gnostic Mass, the priest invokes a presence and then manages that energy to accomplish the ritual. In Drawing Down the Moon, the Goddess is free to interact with all the participants; in that case, she and the priestess are in charge of the energy, not the priest.

How It's Changing

The original version of Drawing Down the Moon called for a priest to invoke a goddess onto a priestess. The next development was a ritual in which a priestess invokes a god onto a priest. Janet Farrar and Stewart Farrar invented the ritual of Drawing Down the Sun in which a priestess invokes the god onto a priest as a counterpart to Drawing Down the Moon.[110] Janet Farrar and Gavin Bone note that Doreen Valiente produced a "Charge of the God" to match the "Charge of the Goddess."[111]

Drawing Down the Sun was adopted by Gardnerian covens. In *Transformative Witchcraft*, Jason Mankey says, "In my coven, drawing down the God is just as important as spending time with our Lady."[112] Jason shares his experience as a priest of Drawing Down the Moon on a priestess and also as a priest who carries deity himself.

In these early versions of the ritual, the roles were still gender restricted. Drawing Down the Moon calls for the priestess to carry the Goddess and the priest to carry the God, and for the invocation to be cross-gender. This practice has evolved over the decades. Jason Mankey tells us that his coven works with two priests or two priestesses, and that men can draw down the Goddess and women can draw down the God.[113] I also know an experienced practitioner who invokes the deity onto themselves directly without the need for another person to invoke onto them; this practice is helpful where a group is led by a single person rather than a couple.

These developing practices call for a term to describe them. Janet Farrar and Gavin Bone use "deity assumption."[114] Others use "possession," although Jason Mankey finds the term troubling since Christians use it to describe involuntary demonic possession, while the Witchcraft ritual is a willed invitation to deity. Mankey notes the alternative word "aspecting," which can be used either as a synonym for possession or to describe a partial possession.[115]

---

110. Janet Farrar and Stewart Farrar, *A Witches' Bible, The Complete Witches' Handbook, Part 2, Principles, Rituals and Beliefs of Modern Witchcraft* (Phoenix Publishing, 1984), 68.
111. Farrar and Bone, *Lifting the Veil*, 15.
112. Mankey, *Transformative Witchcraft*, 283.
113. Mankey, *Transformative Witchcraft*, 6, 265.
114. Farrar and Bone, *Lifting the Veil*, 454.
115. Mankey, *Transformative Witchcraft*, 236.

Because I engage in all the practices described here, and because I am committed to gender inclusion, I use *carrying deity* as the general term.

So far, we've traced the ritual of *desmos kai eklusis* from Assumption of Godform and the Gnostic Mass to Drawing Down the Moon. The next movement takes carrying deity out into a much broader community.

Pagan Aspecting

I learned Drawing Down the Moon as an initiated Witch. In the late 1980s and early 1990s, my Wiccan friends and I set about using the ritual to call the gods on a grand scale. We re-created the Eleusinian Mysteries, the Dionysian Mysteries, and the Sumerian sacred marriage, holding these rituals in state parks with hundreds of participants. At all these rituals, we invoked the gods to presence on ourselves and each other.

At that time, I was active in the national Witch and Pagan communities and traded notes with other people leading major events. We were all inventing a new practice. There weren't any published manuals then about how to do what we were doing. We developed processes from our own experiments and mistakes and from the instructions of the deities themselves.

We described what we were doing as *aspecting*, a term used by the Reclaiming Tradition of Witchcraft. Jason Mankey comments that the term is used by different communities today to mean different things. Some use it as a synonym for Drawing Down; others use it to describe a partial connection with deity "to signify that a portion (an aspect) of a greater power is present."[116]

How It Developed

Throughout the 1980s and '90s, people were invoking deities to presence at small and large gatherings all over the country. Early Pagan festivals were mostly organized by Witches and Wiccans but attracted Norse and Hellenic reconstructionists and Afro-Caribbean groups. This mix of traditions brought an infusion of energy to the Pagan communities. Afro-Caribbean

---

116. Mankey, *Transformative Witchcraft*, 234–35.

traditions had a well-developed methodology and a tradition of support, and Witches and Pagans were able to learn from exposure to these activities.

Like my friends and me, Pagan groups in this time period reconstructed past Pagan practices in which the gods came through and gave instructions that allowed for deeper trance connections. Diana Paxson describes her experience in her 2015 book *The Essential Guide to Trance Possession*. A reconstructed Heathen ritual, which called for a priest to act as Odin, turned into a surprise loss-of-consciousness possession.[117] Paxson researched trance traditions and developed a methodology to use in her own groups and to teach others.

There is another Witchcraft tradition that engages in possession. It's called Faery, or Feri, and was initially developed by Victor Anderson and Cora Anderson. Victor reported being initiated by a pre-Gardnerian coven of Witches in eastern Oregon called Harpy Coven.[118] Victor and Cora combined Witchcraft with Southern folk magick along with Afro-Caribbean practices and Hawaiian *Huna* as well as their own original work.

Faery initiate Storm Faerywolf includes a ritual for Drawing Down the Moon in his work *Betwixt & Between*. In Faerywolf's version, the practitioner visualizes a line of energy reaching up to the moon and returning to the heart. He describes this as a preparation for possession by the Goddess.[119]

While some of the rituals of Pagan aspecting developed from Gardnerian and Alexandrian Witchcraft and some Pagans connect their practices to ancient theurgy, others do not. In particular, Afro-Caribbean ritual did not evolve from the rituals we are tracing here but instead influenced modern Pagan practice. The Afro-Caribbean traditions may have also shaped ancient practice. Remember, theurgy developed in Alexandria and is rooted in the temple culture of Kemet. Theurgy and spirit possession are not identical, but they are also not foreign to each other. They are in the same family.

....
117. Diana L. Paxson, *The Essential Guide to Possession, Depossession & Divine Relationships* (Weiser Books, 2015), xv–xvii.
118. Cordelia Benavidez, *Victor Anderson: An American Shaman* (Immanion Press, 2017), 121.
119. Storm Faerywolf, *Betwixt & Between: Exploring the Faery Tradition of Witchcraft* (Llewellyn Publications, 2017), 289–90.

Diana Paxson notes a difference between Afro-Caribbean traditions and European-based traditions. Traditions like the Golden Dawn and Thelema expect the practitioner to retain some control, while the African-based traditions expect spirit possession to erase consciousness.[120] Ivo Dominguez Jr. uses the term "Divine Possession" to describe the Afro-Caribbean methodology.[121] He explains, "In Voudoun, the Great Ones, the Loa, and the Orishas, are seen as Divine Horsemen, and the priestess or priest is mounted by them."[122] In this methodology, the practitioner, called the horse, "often has little or no control over her actions and often a very unclear recollection of the experience."[123]

How It's Done

Carrying deity occurs at Pagan gatherings large and small, public and private. The word *Pagan* covers a large territory, and there are a number of approaches to the practice. Pagan pioneers like Diana Paxson and Ivo Dominguez Jr. develop methodologies to teach within their traditions. Afro-Caribbean groups have their own well-honed methodologies, which include making altars, drawing symbols, drumming, and dancing. Each of these traditions has their own presentations of their methodologies in books and in personal teaching.

When my friends and I mounted reproductions of the ancient mysteries in the late 1980s and early 1990s, we approached these as Pagan reconstructions with a devotional methodology. We called what we did the *temple-research feedback loop*. We'd learn about the deity, invoke the deity, then do more research to investigate what we learned. When we had established a connection with deity, we would then carry them in public ritual.

Stages of Carrying

Ivo Dominguez Jr. created what he calls "a protocol for Divine Embodiment" combining elements of Drawing Down, Assumption of Godform, and the

---

120. Paxson, *Essential Guide*, 182–83.
121. Ivo Dominguez Jr., *Spirit Speak: Knowing and Understanding Spirit Guides, Ancestors, Ghosts, Angels, and the Divine* (New Page Books, 2008), 114.
122. Dominguez Jr., *Spirit Speak*, 115.
123. Dominguez Jr., *Spirit Speak*, 115.

kind of possession practiced in Afro-Caribbean traditions such as Yoruba.[124] He uses the term "Aspecting" to describe the methodology he created.[125] In his system, there are four levels corresponding to the four worlds of Qabbalah and the four elements.

- In the first level, the practitioner's voice and gestures change.
- In the second level, the practitioner looks physically different and radiates power.
- In the third level, the practitioner feels disconnected from their own body, and their memories of the aspecting experience may be unclear.
- In the fourth level, the practitioner's consciousness is "profoundly coupled" with the presence they are aspecting.[126]

This description captures the experience of the practitioner as their energies are overlaid and intertwined with the energies of the presence they are carrying. As the experience becomes more intense, it is more difficult to hang on to the memory of what has happened, and participants who are interacting with the practitioner can often detect the depth of the trance by the appearance of the practitioner and the energy they are giving out.

What It's Like

In the story I told earlier of the reconstruction of the Sumerian sacred marriage, the women at the gathering invoked Dumuzi on the priest (Alex), and the men at the gathering invoked Inanna on the priestess (me). Carrying Inanna at a public festival and consummating her marriage to Dumuzi was the most powerful ritual I've ever done. It was exhilarating, intoxicating, and exhausting.

In particular, I could see how receiving the adulation of the participants would be addictive. About that time, stories circulated about people who carried deity in those settings who overidentified with the deity and demanded the same adulation for their personal selves. This was what prompted me to

---
124. Dominguez Jr., *Spirit Speak*, 117.
125. Dominguez Jr., *Spirit Speak*, 120–22.
126. Dominguez Jr., *Spirit Speak*, 120–22.

step out of the field of Inanna at the end of the ritual and redirect the focus of the participants away from me and back to her.

How It's Changing

Forty years of Pagan gatherings have built up a pool of information and experience among practitioners. There's more awareness that the people standing in front of us as deities aren't putting on a play but instead actually are those deities. We're learning to honor and respect the dedication and commitment of the people who have agreed to carry those presences so that we can see, hear, and talk to them.

The most mature methodology I've seen at a festival was at the pan-Thelemic gathering Babalon Rising in 2016. An entire area of the campground was turned into small, private ritual spaces. In those tents, women and men carrying Babalon received visitors who wished to interact with that presence. Participants received a list of rules that included respecting the boundaries of the person carrying deity. Also, each receiver had a personal protector, called a *temple dog*, to make sure that those limits were respected. What happened between the person carrying Babalon and the participant was negotiated between the two of them and remained private to them.

In my group work, I continue to practice Assumption of Godform and Drawing Down the Moon. I also engage in a personal practice of carrying deity. Anyone can learn this practice, and we'll explore that next.

Practice

Every form of carrying deity begins with a private relationship between the practitioner and the deity. Assumption of Godform, the Gnostic Mass, Drawing Down the Moon, and Pagan aspecting all emphasize the personal connection between the practitioner and the presence. One way to establish and stabilize this connection is by sitting with deity. We set aside a space and time, call the deity, and remain receptive to the response.

People new to the theurgic path can start with sitting practice right away. Practitioners in the Golden Dawn, Thelemic, Witchcraft, and Pagan reconstructionist traditions can add sitting practice to our methodologies. It isn't different in kind than what we already do; it's really more of a suggestion to do it every day. Assumption of Godform is actually a form of sitting practice if we do it consistently.

Deity Practice
Here's a set of steps to establish a deity practice.

Choose a Deity
This can be a deity you already know and work with or one that you have been interested in exploring. The Neoplatonists worked with the Greek Olympian deities, and their teachers in Kemet worked with Egyptian deities. Either pantheon is a good choice to start with if this is your first time sitting with deity. With living traditions like the Afro-Caribbean and Hindu and Buddhist Tantric traditions, it is respectful and prudent to consult with those practitioners before working with the spirits. We don't have to invent those practices; we can learn them from an experienced teacher.

Research the Deity
- **Names:** What are their names and epithets? Make a list.
- **Images:** Are they female, male, another form of gender, or not gendered? Are they young or mature? Do they have human or animal faces? What color are they? What do they wear?
- **Historical context:** Where were they worshipped? In what time periods? Who worshipped them—women or men, elites or commoners or enslaved people? How did this change over time?
- **Timing:** What times (of day, month, year) were they invoked?
- **Chants and hymns:** Did the people who worshipped the deity have a hymn? Did they have a chant they recited to the deity?
- **Current context:** Who is working with them today? What have they learned that will help build our own practice?

Choose Offerings
- **Scent:** Almost every deity accepts incense. If the deity has a flower or tree association, this could be the incense to offer.

- **Flowers:** This is another offering almost every deity appreciates. This is a great opportunity to use colors associated with the deity.
- **Drink:** This can get very specific. Some deities want only milk, some want wine, some definitely do not want alcohol. This is where research pays off.
- **Food:** Meat is another highly charged offering. Some deities prefer meat; some definitely do not want it. Natural food like fruits and vegetables, honey, unleavened bread, and cheese made up offerings in antiquity.
- **Chant and hymn:** If research hasn't turned up a chant or hymn, you can repeat their name.

Build an Altar

This can be a shelf or a small table. There should be a chair or rug in front of it so you can spend time with the deity.

- **Find an image or statue of the deity:** You can make a color print of an image you like and put it in a document frame.
- **Surround this image with objects that connect to the deity:** For example, an altar to Athena might include a statue of an owl.
- **Make offerings at the altar:** The offerings can be physically placed and removed each day. That's a big commitment, though, so you can make physical offerings on special occasions and make your sitting practice itself your daily offering.

Daily Sitting Practice

Here are the steps:

- Sit at the altar.
- Ground, center, imagine a circle around you in the space.
- Visualize the deity.
- Say or chant one of their names.
- Hold yourself receptive.
- Imagine the deity settling over your body.
- See, hear, feel, experience.

- Make offerings (optional).
- Imagine the deity energy dissipating into the air or grounding beneath your feet.
- Record impressions. What knowledge did the deity impart? Especially track assignments from the deity (go to a particular place, make a particular offering, do a particular magical exercise) and track when they are completed.

Considerations in Practice

- **Consistency:** Pick a time of day to do the practice and stick with it. If you're not used to doing this kind of practice, you might sit for five minutes at first until you build up stamina. It's more important to do it every day than to do it for lengthy periods but skip days.
- **Duration:** You can try sitting practice with a given deity for a week or a month. After that, you can stop to evaluate the practice.
- **Evaluate:** Reread impressions. Have you completed your assignments? Has the sense of the deity changed over time—gotten stronger, gotten lighter, shifted in quality? Is your time with the deity making your life better? This doesn't have to mean that it makes you happier immediately; deities sometimes work to clear out difficult emotions and blockages, which is not a pleasant process but results in a release that frees energy.

Moving Forward

Once you've completed the evaluation, you can make a choice about how to continue.

- Decide to recommit to the practice for a period of time.
- End the practice, investigate a new deity, work with that deity for another week or month.
- Keep the current practice and add practice with a new deity.
- Engage in sitting practice with a pantheon of deities, such as the twelve Olympians or the nine Kemetic *netjer* (deities) of the Ennead. The ancient theurgists sought to be "spherical," which I

conceptualize as "well rounded."[127] One of the ways we can become more well rounded is by doing theurgic sitting practice with a set of deities.

Deepening practice: You may feel called to enter more fully into alliance with the specific deity. Here are some ways to deepen the practice.

- Upgrade the altar image. Obtain a nice statue and offer it to the deity.
- Visit places sacred to the deity, like temples and natural landscapes.
- Wear items that the deity likes. You can wear a stone associated with the deity in a pendant, necklace, bracelet, or ring.
- Grow plants that the deity likes.
- Celebrate a festival dedicated to the deity.
- Dedicate food to the deity before eating.
- Check in with the deity before going to sleep and on waking up.
- Write a poem to the deity.
- Compile information about the deity and distribute it as an offering to the deity.

Daily sitting practice allows us the opportunity to move consciousness from our limited personal focus into the larger and more universal field of the deity. This can be experienced as a blissful union. The goal of the ancient theurgists was essentially the same as the goal of contemporary ceremonial and Tantric practice—we aim to unite ourselves with the Divine.

It is important to end sitting practice and return to normal consciousness. All the practices warn that identifying ourselves as deity while we're walking around in the world leads to ego-inflation ("You think you're God!"), which is the exact opposite of what we're meaning to achieve. We can instead continue our devotion to the deity by making humble offerings to them. Wash dishes, do the shopping, change the diaper, do the work while remaining aware of the deity's presence in the world. We are the talisman that is prepared for the

---

127. Gregory Shaw, "The Role of Aesthesis in Theurgy," in *Iamblichus and the Foundations of Late Platonism*, Eugene Afonasin, John Dillon, and John F. Finamore, eds. (Brill, 2012), 97.

presence of the deity—daily in our practice and for our community when we are called to carry them.

Practice Support System

Daily sitting practice is intended to be done by an individual alone. People in East Asian traditions routinely sit with deity by themselves, but this is a relatively new practice in the Western Magical Tradition, and we haven't yet built up a cultural context for it. We don't know exactly what to expect from our deities and how they will affect us. For that reason, it's a good idea to make connections with people who can support the practice and who can be your meditation auditor. Witches in covens, magicians in lodges, and Pagans in groups have built-in support. You can also look for people who are working with the same deity or pantheon that you choose. The first time you sit with deity, you can set up a check-in time with one of your practice support friends to discuss your experience and make sure you have re-grounded in your normal consciousness.

When you do establish connection with the deity, I recommend setting boundaries and communicating with them before agreeing to a relationship. The first rush of contact can and should open your heart to the presence of the Divine. However, I've collected many stories of people who have been asked by deities to perform duties for them, from limited one-time requests all the way up to dedicating their lives to the deity. The open heart wants to say "yes!" but a lifetime commitment deserves some thought. This is another way your friends can help you. You can decide that you will check with your practice support people before you agree to a contract with a deity. This is especially true if you choose to work with a deity whose original culture has faded; they may have requests that don't match with your values.

Your meditation auditor can also alert you to a result that doesn't seem right. The ancient theurgists warned that mischievous or hostile spirits sometimes present themselves as deities, and contemporary magicians confirm this report. Theurgists and magicians learn how to identify various kinds of spirits and to defend ourselves from those who don't mean us well.

Learning from Each Other

We've traced the development of one ritual from the ancient theurgists to modern magical practice. The connection between *desmos kai eklusis*, Assumption of Godform, the Gnostic Mass, Drawing Down the Moon, and some forms of Pagan aspecting are clear. It is also clear that Faery Witchcraft, heathen practice, and Afro-Caribbean traditions developed practices for carrying deity independently.

There are connections, similarities, and differences in our practices. It's equally important to recognize all of these. Some of us embrace the similarities and engage with each other in dialogue; others reject contact outside of their specific traditions, which are represented as complete, self-contained, and superior to all others. It seems to me that insisting on purity of practice is limiting, while diversity helps us to be well rounded. Today, every practitioner has access to books that describe all the practices we've discussed here as well as opportunities to experience these rituals as witnesses or participants. I've learned something from every one of these methodologies, and my performance of each of these rituals benefits from that cross education.

As I've surveyed these practices, some insights have emerged. First, there's a tendency to mix descriptions of the techniques with descriptions of the results. *Desmos kai eklusis*, binding and loosing, calling and receiving, is the technique. Sustasis, alliance, is the result. Singing a hymn is a technique, not a stage of trance. It may induce a sense of presence for the singer or for the audience, which is the result.

Carrying deity is more than an on-off switch. It isn't just that you have deity or you don't. There are stages of trance. However, the depth of the trance is not the measure of success. It's more helpful to think in terms of the purpose of the rite. Are you invoking deity to initiate someone, to let someone talk to deity through you, or to interact with the deity yourself? What's most important is not how conscious you are; it's how well your state of trance matches the intended goal within the community norm. In Golden Dawn initiations the officer assuming a Godform remains conscious, in Afro-Caribbean traditions the horse surrenders consciousness altogether, and both are successful forms of carrying deity within the context of their rites.

What seems to me to be the most important distinction is how you frame your relationship to divinity. Do you understand yourself as separate from or contiguous with deity? The language that people use to describe carrying deity reflects this. Some traditions frame the gods as larger than humans and the people who carry them as serving the gods; the deity chooses the person who will carry them and remains in control of the process, while the receiver cedes consciousness and control of the body. Theurgy, on the other hand, frames the human soul as one consciousness stop on the divine continuity. Gods and humans are made of the same stuff, and the purpose of carrying deity is to elevate or expand the human soul to accept more of the divine presence and our own divine nature.

Inanna is a big presence. Carrying her taught me how to negotiate cohabitation of my person with an overwhelming deity. I learned how luminous she is by looking into the awestruck eyes of her worshippers. I also learned how important it is to separate myself from her. She had a particular lesson for my daily life: Inhabiting her sovereign authority taught me to carry myself in the world as a sovereign person and claim my own spiritual authority. It is extremely important to me that I remember what it was like to carry her so that I bring her presence forward in the world.

Although recent scholastic conversation has called this into question, it has long been thought that a Sumerian priestess taking the part of Inanna and the king taking the part of Dumuzi enacted the sacred marriage. The king asked the blessing of Inanna on the kingdom for protection and for the fertility of the crops. This is the original sacred marriage echoed in the Gnostic Mass. Reenacting that sacred marriage teaches me that the love of human for human affirms the mutual love between the human and the Divine. Love is the force that animates creation all along the chain of being.

Recognizing theurgy as foundational to ceremonial magick, Witchcraft, and some forms of Paganism offers a worldview to explore. The ancients taught a sophisticated cosmology and spiritual technology, which contextualize our practices and offer ways to improve them. As an example, the stages of carrying deity and the expected results that Iamblichus listed remain for me the clearest articulation of the practice. Every time I reread Iamblichus's *On The Mysteries*, I gain another layer of understanding. More than a hundred years after the magical world rediscovered the theurgy of the ancients, we have only just begun to rearticulate their knowledge, their methodologies, and their worldview. Anyone who carries deity can benefit from learning about them as well as learning from each other.

THE PRACTICE OF THEURGIC MEDITATION AND CONTEMPLATION
PATRICK DUNN

The ancient Greek word for "meditation" is μελέτη (*meletē*) from the verb μελετάω (*meletaō*). As is often the case in ancient Greek, the word *meletē* covers quite a bit of semantic space: It can mean "attention," "care," or even "worry." It can also mean "exercise" or "pursuit," which gives some sense of how the theurgists perceived meditation. Meditation was not just sitting and clearing one's mind of thoughts, but a spiritual exercise or pursuit. It was a way to grow stronger mentally and eventually unite with the fundamental ground, or origin, of being itself: the One.

The list of misconceptions of what constitutes meditation is long. You will hear people saying that one must only meditate in a certain posture or for a very long time or with one's tongue in this position or one's fingers in that position. While some traditions do have some strict forms, theurgic meditation can be done in any posture, even walking or doing physical exercise. And you can receive the benefits of this spiritual exercise in even short bursts of five or ten minutes.

Every section of this essay contains an exercise that I would urge you to try. Choose what fits your needs and circumstances, and use this essay as a springboard to developing your own approaches and methods.

Mindfulness

One of the fundamental practices of meditation across most traditions is that of mindfulness. In Buddhism, one form of mindfulness meditation is called Vipassanā, from the Pali meaning "clear seeing," and involves sitting and observing the mind. I recommend this practice as a good warm-up, as it were, though it can actually be one's entire meditation practice. We have no idea if this practice was common in antiquity in the West, but it certainly has benefits and is a good foundational practice for those who wish to pursue meditation as a part of their theurgic work.

One method of mindfulness is to observe each thought as it arises without clinging to any of them. Sometimes people use a visualization for this, imagining the thoughts as leaves on a river drifting by, cars on a road, or turning pages in a book. Here, you sit (or stand, or lie down) and let thoughts arise. When they do, you watch them go. In your mind, this might look like:

I need to call the insurance company today. See it drift by on a leaf.

My nose itches. Watch it go by.

Ugh, I have that song stuck in my head. There it goes, down the river.

My nose still itches. Watch it float by. Maybe notice if the itch is different than the last time.

I hate calling my insurance company. Watch it float by.

And so on.

It is important to point out that the goal is not to stop thoughts or clear one's mind. That is a misconception. The goal is simply to clearly see one's thoughts without attaching to or identifying with them.

Another popular method is to count your breaths from one to ten, and each time you find yourself following a thought instead of focusing on your breath, start again at one. You very well may have periods where you're thinking one, two, one, two, one, two, three. But it doesn't matter. If you get to ten, you start over again at one anyway, so it really doesn't matter if you never get there.

You can also label the thoughts as they arise or have a phrase that you use to dismiss them. I like to just think "I can think about that later" and let the thought go. But you can also just label them "thinking."

Sometimes people will say things like, "I can't meditate. My mind keeps wandering." That is, in fact, the point. This statement is like a person proclaiming, "I can't work out; whenever I do, my muscles get tired." That is part of the process. When you work out, your muscles start to shake and give out at the end of the set; that's why you have a spotter so you don't strangle yourself with the barbell. When you meditate, your mind wanders. When you *don't* meditate, for that matter, your mind wanders, but you're just not as aware of it. The practice of moving your mind back to the present, away from your discursive thoughts, *is* meditation. Learning to do this is to build a sort of mental "muscle," helping you shift the focus from the various thoughts that flit through our heads like birds to the sky behind the birds.

The goal of mindfulness meditation isn't to shut off the mind or stop thought. It's to let the thoughts go, to pass by, without identifying with them. Like waves on an ocean, the thoughts are not the self; the ocean is. The thoughts are just froth. Often, when a thought arises for us, we cling to it. For myself, I try to problem solve, which involves stirring the thought back and forth, again and again, as if by dwelling on it I can somehow change it. Mindfulness lets us see that these thoughts are, essentially, simply constructs of words, no more solid than a song, which is sung and done.

In some branches of Buddhism, the state of mind called *samādhi* is the "goal" of meditation. Early writers in English erroneously regarded this as an "empty" mind. The concept is actually more complex than that, but we don't need to go into it in depth, because in theurgic meditation, this is not the goal. The goal in theurgic meditation is *henōsis* (ἕνωσις), or oneness with the divine ground, or origin, of being. I will have more to say about that state later in this essay.

Mindfulness meditation lays a good foundation for the other meditations described in the rest of this essay, because it gives us a chance to look at our mind as it is—and *accept* it as it is. If I only have time for a few minutes of meditation, this is the method I fall back on, and when I have more time, I usually start with it as a sort of warm-up to other contemplative methods.

Tips

- Sit comfortably and don't worry about advanced mudras and postures unless you want to.
- Focus on your breath, and when thoughts arise, simply let them go. You can also use a visualization, such as leaves on a river or pages in a book, to let go of thoughts.
- If you get stuck, label a thought and move on. Don't beat yourself up. Doing meditation "badly" *is* doing it right.
- The only goal is to let your mind do what minds do without being carried away with it.

Meditation on Beauty

Theurgic meditation, like some of the more esoteric branches of Buddhism and Hinduism, relies more on visualization as a means of contemplation. These are guided contemplations on a single idea instead of your breath or the current state of your mind. But again, when the mind wanders (and it will), you simply bring it back to the subject of contemplation. That ability to just let thoughts happen without being derailed by them is a central skill of meditation.

One of the oldest accounts we have of this kind of contemplation occurs in Plato. We often think of Plato—especially if we were only introduced to him in high school or college—as a rather stuffy and extremely logical philosopher. But actually Plato had a mystical bent, and many contemporary philosophers simply gloss over that mysticism. In the *Symposium*, for example, he describes a detailed, step-by-step meditation designed to lead the meditator to henōsis.

The *Symposium* is an account of a drinking party, a custom in ancient Athens. These parties involved the sharing of wine but also usually had a theme, often a philosophical one. The participants were expected to converse intelligently on the theme. Plato describes a specific symposium (the word itself means "drinking together"), where his teacher, Socrates, interacts with a number of other participants. The topic of the party is "love," and each participant gives an account of love. Some are philosophical, some fanciful. The dialogue veers from serious philosophy to comedy and back again, especially as each participant gets drunk in turn. At the end, Socrates gives his account of love, one that he learned from the philosopher Diotima. She teaches Socrates that love is an intermediary between humans and the gods, triggered by the appreciation of Beauty, which is itself a reflection of the Good (one common word for "good" in Greek is the same as the word for "beauty"), which is the One. Thus, by following the contemplation of Diotima, we can experience this essential oneness, this henōsis.[128]

Diotima instructs us, first of all, to perceive beauty in the physical world, even in one particular beautiful person. But then, from that, recognize that the beauty of one person is reflected in others and that beauty is general. From that generality, then, of physical beauty, she instructs that we move on to perceive beauty of laws and customs, and from laws and customs to branches of knowledge, and from there to a full understanding of beauty.[129]

Exercise: Meditation on Beauty

How this might work in practice is simple.

1. Select any beautiful person or object to contemplate. This can literally be anyone or anything that strikes you with their beauty. I have done it when walking in the woods and seeing a beautiful flower, or in the museum in front of a beautiful painting. And, of course, that beauty can be rather "profane": It can be a person to whom you are attracted physically. This physical beauty is, indeed, where Diotima suggests starting.

2. Spend some moments contemplating the beauty of that person or thing. Focus your mind on it without analyzing it or thinking about it. Just hold it in mind, and when your mind inevitably wanders, bring it back. One of the strengths of this method, in my opinion, is that we have a natural magnetism toward beauty: It's not difficult to concentrate on lovely things. But your mind will still wander; gently bring it back each time. You may also find yourself trying to analyze the beauty. Resist that urge—gently,

---

128. Plato, *Symposium*, trans. Benjamin Jowett, accessed January 7, 2023, https://www.gutenberg.org/files/1600/1600-h/1600-h.htm.
129. Plato, *Symposium*.

though—as well. Simply hold the object or person in its beauty in your mind.
3. Recognize how the beauty of that object or person appears in other objects and people. If, for example, you are attracted to a handsome man, recognize that other men are also handsome. If you contemplate a beautiful flower, let your mind begin to recognize how that beauty is reflected in other flowers, not just of that type, but of many others. Try to hold the entire population of all such beautiful things in your mind at the same time. Again, when your mind inevitably wanders, bring it back.
4. Now do the same, but this time, focus on a beautiful custom or law. For example, people are often polite: focus on that politeness and recognize its beauty without analyzing it. Or perhaps you witness an act of charity: again, focus on that act, holding it in mind without analyzing it. Just let it rest there. Again, extrapolate out to the general population: Someone is kind to you at the grocery store. Kindness to strangers is a beautiful custom. Hold that incident in mind, then spread it out to recognize all kindness to all strangers as a general beauty, not limited, but spread throughout the population.

   I should mention that the more cynical among my readers might balk here. Beautiful laws? They might say. The laws of my country are unjust! Our customs are entwined with injustice and cruelty. That may be, but we are not focused on ugliness right now, but beauty. You can decry the unjustness of cruel laws and customs while still finding things that are beautiful in the way people treat each other. We are not denying injustice: We are focusing, for a moment, on the beauty of justice when we see it.
5. Finally, we begin to think of the beauty of intellectual pursuits. When struck by a well-honed argument, we hold it in mind the same way. Not arguing with it, not analyzing it, but recognizing it as well constructed and beautiful. Or perhaps we feel struck to awe by some new discovery of nature. We hold that awe in mind, then, again, as we have done before, extrapolate it to all of human knowledge.

I won't tell you what you'll find when you pursue this path, but one thing I noticed is that all these beauties seem to resonate into a sort of chord, composed of virtues that are all themselves notes of the same essence. When you begin to see that the beauty in your girlfriend, the beauty in just laws, and the beauty in human curiosity and knowledge are all manifestations of wisdom, justice, self-control, and courage, then you begin to approach an apprehension of the One.

Plotinus and Contemplation

One word used for both meditation and contemplation in ancient Greek is θεωρία, *theōria*, which means "beholding" or "looking at" and comes from the roots for "sight" and "to see." Contemplation, for the ancient Greeks, was a process of seeing a sight. The same roots give rise to θεωρός, *theōros*, a "spectator," but originally one sent by a king or other important person to go consult an oracle.

For Plotinus, the entire world engages in *theōria*: everything contemplates. In the *Enneads*, he suggests that, as "a joke," we might even say that plants contemplate.[130] And then he goes on to say,

> We might even say that a joking child, as well as a meditating man both aim at reaching contemplation when the former jokes, and the latter meditates. Indeed, there is not a single action that does not tend towards contemplation; more or less externalizing it according as it is carried out strictly or freely.[131]

By making this joke—that plants contemplate—Plotinus is actually *demonstrating* contemplation. He is the joking child.

Plotinus never lays out a detailed method of contemplation because that would to some degree be contrary to his point: The method of contemplation

---

130. Plotinus, "A. Of Nature," in *Third Ennead, Book Eight*, in *Plotinos Complete Works*, vol. 2, trans. Kenneth Sylvan Guthrie, accessed January 7, 2023, https://www.gutenberg.org/files/42931/42931-h/42931-h.htm#iii_8.
131. Plotinus, "A. Of Nature," in *Third Ennead, Book Eight*.

is the method of the One, the underlying principle that makes unity possible. It does not require instruction because it's something that all nature is already doing: Your mind, as it is right now, is contemplating. He does, however, in the third tractate suggest some contemplations of the One, which I think are meant to be exercises for the student rather than merely explanatory metaphors.

The first of these is to imagine the supreme essence of the universe, the One, as a spring of fresh, clear water always replenishing itself. Out of this spring flow streams, which flow into rivers, which flow into the sea. Each stream has a name and an identity but is always simply the movement of water coming from this one spring. When you contemplate each stream and trace it back to the source, you find that there's no point at which you can draw a line through the water and say "Here's the spring" and "Here's the stream." They appear different but are one, just as people appear different from each other or turnips appear to be different from tigers.[132]

The second of his contemplations is to imagine the One as a tree. It sends out roots deep into the soul and branches high overhead. On those branches, there are innumerable leaves. Each leaf is an individual, but they depend upon the tree: They are not, themselves, the tree. When a leaf falls, the tree doesn't cease to exist.[133]

Both of these are concrete visualizations, almost guided meditations. But they lead to a more philosophical contemplation. If the spring were to flow out completely into the streams, all the streams and rivers would dry up. If the tree were to give itself over to a single leaf, when that leaf fell, the tree would die. The universe is manifold, but the unity of it abides.

The method he's recommending here, again, is much like the meditation on beauty from Plato (which is no surprise, since Plotinus considered himself a Platonist, though we now generally classify him as a Neoplatonist). We perceive the world as manifold because it is. But that manifold nature of the world exists only because of its underlying beauty and unity. Again, I think of music: Each note is separated from the other notes in a song by time and duration and volume. If they weren't, every song would be perfectly unified:

---

132. Plotinus, "C. Of Unity," in *Third Ennead, Book Eight*.
133. Plotinus, "C. Of Unity," in *Third Ennead, Book Eight*.

an incoherent crash on the piano like someone laying their arm on all the keys at once. On one level, music is beautiful because of its manifold nature. But on another level, music itself is a fundamental unity. The system of harmony and disharmony, of keys and modes, exists outside of each individual song or performance of a song.

As I said, Plotinus does not offer us any specific instructions in meditation or contemplation, but in the passage I cite above, I think he hints at one. Here's how I reconstruct it:

Exercise: Plotinus's Contemplation

Each step is to be done over some period of time, perhaps five or ten minutes a day for weeks, before moving on to the next.

1. Begin by holding in your mind one of the images that Plotinus provides: a spring or a tree. Imagine the image vividly and contemplate how each of the individual things arises from a single source and is both separate from that source and not. A leaf is not a tree, but when we look at a tree, we see it as a unity of diverse leaves.
2. Extend this to your own examples. I used music above, but if you are fond of some other art, you can apply it to that or to any other practice or natural phenomenon. Again, the practice is to hold this idea in your head gently, returning to it when attention wanders but not forcing it to give up any secrets and not thinking about it too much. You are just a witness, a *theōros*, here to "see the sight."
3. Now, extend this to the experience of your own consciousness. Your consciousness is a stream, a branch, a song, or whatever other metaphors you have constructed. Trace your consciousness back now to its origin. Try to turn your observing mind, which is one of the streams, back to the source, to the spring. Ask yourself, If I am observing my mind, what is the *I* that is observing?

—

I have found this a productive exercise. As I said above, I'm not sure it's anything Plotinus would approve of, or anything like what he himself did in his contemplations, but I have found it useful.

The View from Above

I am interested in theurgic meditation, which is not necessarily synonymous with Platonism or Neoplatonism. In fact, many other schools of philosophy had their *meletai*, their exercises. The View from Above is a method of contemplation practiced by two very different schools of philosophy: the Stoics and the Hermetics.

The Stoic school, founded by Zeno of Citium, was a school of philosophy mostly remembered for its praxis, which is to say, the advice it offered for how to live a good life. Stoicism had a complex cosmology as well as an entire system of logic, but the reason we read the Stoics now, as a rule, is for their advice. They generally believed that human suffering came from a misapprehension of what was in our control and what was not. What was in our control was our own mind's reactions to things. What was not in our control was our wealth, status, health, relationships, or lives. We could certainly have influence over those things and should strive to; that was fine. But ultimately, we had to realize that the only thing we could do when unavoidable suffering struck was to master our own mind's reaction to it.

Easier said than done.

Because the Stoics were practical philosophers, they recognized that saying, "You have control over your own mind" isn't enough to help people. So they developed exercises to help people learn to direct their minds to more rational places. Not incidentally, the Stoic school of philosophy, among others, influenced the psychological practice of cognitive behavioral therapy, which helps many people with depression and anxiety and other psychological disorders.

Marcus Aurelius is one of the three most famous Stoics, though it helps that we really only have substantial surviving writing from four Stoic philosophers: Marcus Aurelius, Epictetus, Seneca, and Musonius Rufus. We have fragments of other, lesser-known authors, but these four provide complete works. Of these, Aurelius is perhaps the most famous. Again, it probably helps that he was emperor of Rome. He kept a personal diary, which he called

To Myself. It is usually now better known as *Meditations*. He records some of his mental exercises for maintaining control of his mind in times of hardship.

Along with many other useful exercises, he lays out the "view from above," an exercise that encourages us to perceive reality as a whole and our small place in it: "Think of existence, all together, and how little a share of it you have. Of the whole of eternity, how short and brief an interval is marked off for you; and of what is allotted by destiny, how much you are a part."[134] What he suggests here is seeing ourselves in the context of eternity.

The Stoics were interested in what I might call the psychological benefit of this practice, but there's also a larger, spiritual benefit described in the *Hermetica*:

> *Make yourself grow to immeasurable immensity, outleap all body, outstrip all time, become eternity and you will understand god…. Go higher than every height and lower than every depth. Collect in yourself all the sensations of what has been made, of fire and water, dry and wet; be everywhere at once, on land, in the sea, in heaven; be not yet born, be in the womb, be young, old, dead, beyond death. And when you have understood all these at once—times, places, things, qualities, quantities—then you can understand god.*[135]

The principle is quite similar: expand your awareness. Marcus Aurelius more or less restricts this to the dimension of time, but the *Hermetica* goes further: expand in space and time and then beyond time. The text also offers a specific benefit: then you will understand god. The word translated "understand" here is νοῆσαι, *noēsai*, which also means "perceive" or "observe," particularly as a mental act rather than just seeing. It's also worth pointing out that the original text uses the word θεός, *theos*, for god, which does not

....
134. Marcus Aurelius, *M. Antonius Imperator Ad Se Ipsum*, ed. Jan Hendrick Leopold, book 5, chapter 24, section 1, Perseus Digital Library, https://www.perseus.tufts.edu/hopper/text?doc=Perseus%3Atext%3A2008.01.0641%3Abook%3D5%3Achapter%3D24%3Asection%3D1. My translation.
135. Brian P. Copenhaver, ed., *Hermetica: The Greek Corpus Hermeticum and the Latin Asclepius in a New English Translation, with Notes and Introduction*, reprint ed. (Cambridge University Press, 1995), XI.20, 41.

necessarily mean a specific god, but can be used to refer to the Divine as a whole. One might also translate it as "then, you will be able to perceive the Divine."

Exercise: The View from Above

When putting this into practice, I recommend doing it in stages and not being discouraged if you cannot complete the whole contemplation in one sitting. In my personal experience, this is one of those contemplations that belies the idea that meditation is always relaxing. I find it a bit mentally strenuous to hold all that in my mind at once.

1. Start with space. See yourself in your room, sitting or standing or lying down, and then expand your view outward to the building, the city or town, the state or province or country, then to the whole earth. Imagine yourself watching from above as the earth turns.
2. Now, incorporate the entire solar system. Fly outward from the earth to the inner planets and the sun, then outward to the outer planets. You may find it helpful to watch some videos that actually animate this expansion of perspective; there's one great advantage we have over the ancients.
3. Now, expand to hold the galaxy, and then outward to the whole universe, mostly dark space with dots of galaxies floating in it, each as filled with stars as our own. You might see this whole thing as a tiny dot inside a tiny dot inside of a tiny dot in *one* of those tiny dots.
4. Now, add time to the mix. The universe is about 13.7 billion years old. It will last at least 22 billion years more. Our own sun will burn out in about 5 billion years. Stretch your mind out to the beginning, when space-time itself unfolded from a singularity, until the end of the universe when it cools and suffers heat death, all 35 billion years in a moment.[136]

---

136. Scientific accuracy doesn't matter here at all. If you prefer to imagine a more ancient view of the universe, where it's composed of crystal spheres, that'll work as well. We're not doing science here; we're just using our understanding of the universe to put ourselves into perspective.

5. As a final step, if you are able, now shift your perspective slightly. Instead of being that tiny flickering dot existing for only a tiny fraction of time in the tiniest part of the universe, imagine that you are, in fact, the universe you observe. You're every atom, from the beginning of time to the end of it.

   This final step is brief, but it's significant, and you may find it difficult. You are trying to imagine your mind expanding out to join the mind of the universe itself, even if for just a moment. Doing so can trigger that experience of unity with the Divine, henōsis. This goal is a step beyond the Stoic goal of *apatheia*, or control of the mind. But even if you are unable to achieve this shift in awareness, you will reap some benefits, perhaps, from the enlarged perspective of seeing yourself in the context of eternity.

Meditation on Virtue

One of the advantages of theurgic meditation is that it doesn't necessarily require elaborate ritual, special postures, or even particular states of mind. I've engaged in this particular contemplation while drinking my morning coffee, taking my morning shower, or brushing my teeth. This meditation on virtue is a spiritual exercise derived, again, from the Stoics, but it works well even if you don't necessarily espouse the Stoic view of the world. To understand how this works, we need to understand the theurgic understanding of virtue.

Virtues are qualities that reflect moral goodness. To many Greek philosophers, morality was less a question of what we should *do* and more a question of what we should *become*. If we developed morally good qualities, the question of what to do solved itself: We would do what was right in the situation. Advocates of this kind of virtue ethic listed the qualities they regarded as virtues, and Plato codified them into four, a codification later also adopted by Aristotle. These four are:

- **Courage:** Unfortunately, the word most often used for courage is ἀνδρεία, *andreia*, which translates to "manliness." But we can just say courage and not feel the ancient need to gender our virtues.

- **Wisdom:** This virtue speaks for itself: It's the ability to reason out solutions to problems, apply our values to situations, and learn and think cleverly. It's not intelligence so much as it's the rejection of willful ignorance.
- **Self-control:** The word σωφροσύνη (*sōphrosunē*) can also be translated as "temperance," but that word has taken on historical connotations in the United States as meaning absolute abstinence, particularly from alcohol, so I prefer "self-control." Self-control is the ability to identify what is enough and then to stop. For some things, enough may be none: There are many people who simply don't indulge in some habits because they know they might be carried away (which is, of course, an application of wisdom). Another good translation for this virtue is "moderation."
- **Justice:** Within the concept of ancient justice lies the idea of mercy. Justice isn't simply meting out punishments, but also deciding when not to punish, when to punish leniently, or when to offer an opportunity for growth. Justice is dealing fairly with those you meet, whether or not you have power over them.

You might notice that these are all intertwined. It's hard to exhibit courage without justice, self-control without wisdom, and so on. The ancients called these the *cardinal virtues*, because like the cardinal directions, they can help us map out our lives.

These aren't the only virtues, and a full discussion of virtue is outside the scope of this essay. For our purposes, it suffices to begin with these four as an inspiration and decide what virtues you yourself value as qualities that exhibit inherent moral goodness. For example, I like to add *compassion* to the list. Others may add *honesty*, though yet others may see honesty as already present in justice. Those who admire Benjamin Franklin can find his own list of virtues, if they like, or borrow virtues from their faith traditions. (Christianity adds faith, hope, and love to the cardinal virtues for a total of seven.)

So, how do you use these virtues in contemplation? Through rehearsal and recapitulation.

Exercise: Rehearsal and Recapitulation

The rehearsal occurs in the morning and can happen formally or informally. In rehearsal, you run through your coming day in your mind and ask yourself for each virtue, "What opportunities will I have to exhibit this virtue today?" Then, you imagine what it would look like if you do. For example, if you have a business meeting, you might speak your mind—for you, that might require courage. So, you quickly imagine yourself standing up at the meeting and contributing. Or perhaps you will deal with family, which might require justice or compassion. If you adopt a long list of virtues (such as Franklin's), this may take a while. But for me, it only takes a couple seconds for each of the virtues and one quick imagined image before I move on.

The recapitulation is the same, but this time, just before bed, you run through your day and ask yourself, "How have I exhibited this virtue today?" If you are susceptible to rumination or guilt, you want to guard against that. If you fell short, that's okay: You're a human who is growing and learning, and falling short of your virtues is quite human. Just recognize that you did not live up to your hopes for yourself, accept that, forgive yourself, and move on. In other words, exhibit the virtues of compassion and justice to yourself as well as to others. Similarly, the goal is not to pat yourself on the back and underline what a good person you are before you fall asleep. It's just to keep those two anchors of virtue in your day so that you can build a bridge between them day-to-day, like a spider spinning a web between fence posts.

Dwelling in the Nous

This final meditation is a meditation that isn't a meditation. It's a technique or state of mind that I call *dwelling in the nous*.

The Greek word νοῦς, *nous*, means "mind" or "perception."[137] In the Neoplatonic cosmology, there are multiple levels of reality, and the *nous* is one of them. This mind isn't the individual small mind of daily concerns and worries, but the underlying consciousness of the universe itself.

It's difficult to give precise instructions for this meditation. It arises with the realization that your mind already partakes of the essence of the universal

---
137. You'll also sometimes see νόος, *noos*, which is a dialectical variation.

nous. The other methods of meditation can lead you to that realization, but you can also learn to shift your mind to this perspective directly.

One way to approach this realization is the *via negativa*, or "negative way." This method occurs in Christian mysticism, Hindu meditation, and many other religious and spiritual paths. The method transcends doctrine. In fact, it transcends everything: That's the point.

Exercise: Via Negativa

You can begin the practice of the *via negativa* by considering something you often identify with: maybe your job, your religion, or your political beliefs. If you had a different job, a different religion, or different political beliefs, would you be the same person? You might not have the same personality, but people often do change these things, and when they do, they don't lose their coherent identity. They may act differently, but we don't usually say that they're different people entirely.

Now, move to something more personal, such as your family, loved ones, and so on. If you were to lose them, would you become a different person? You would change, again, in your personality and actions, but you wouldn't stop being who you are. They matter, certainly. They're part of who you are, and you wouldn't be the same, but you wouldn't cease to exist without them.

Then, you can take this a third step further. What if you lost your limbs? Got a transplant? Or grew frail in old age? These aren't pleasant things to contemplate, certainly, but they happen to people, and we don't usually say they're no longer themselves.

In fact, you have often undergone radical changes. You have been a child, a baby, and only potentiality. You've never been just one thing. There has never been a permanence to anything that we usually call a self, and yet you experience a continuity of identity.

Why?

What is that thing that is you, that does not change when you grow or age, get a new job, or meet a new friend? You might call it a soul, which in English is an imprecise and vague term. I'd say it's the underlying consciousness of your mind: not the thoughts it thinks or the beliefs it holds, but the framework upon which those things rest. That's ultimately what you are.

Learning to move the center of our awareness from the structures we build to the framework upon which we build them can give us an experience of henōsis.

Henōsis

Henōsis (ἕνωσις) means "combination into one" or "unification." It describes a state of what might be called "enlightenment," an experiential rather than purely intellectual awareness of some underlying reality of the universe. Unlike enlightenment in Buddhism, which is a fundamental awareness of the impermanence and *anattā* (no-self) of the universe, henōsis is a realization of fundamental unity.

In practice, the distinction seems one of definition more than experience. Both experiences are ineffable, and for much the same reason. To use language is to call on duality. A word means something because it doesn't mean other things. *Red* only takes on its meaning because it's not *green*. *Being* only means something because of *not-being*. Some philosophers, for elaborate reasons, equated the concept of Unity to that of Goodness, but even that equation—which is experientially valid—is misleading when cast into words. It implies that there's an evil that exists separate from the Goodness of Unity, and that is not the case. Though at the same time, it's not true to say good and evil are the same thing from the viewpoint of henōsis—not quite.

I suspect you begin to perceive the conundrum. To speak of henōsis at all is to fall short of it. Even to say it's an experience implies an experiencer separate from the experience, which is not the case. Those who experience henōsis still remain human, but with an experiential awareness that their identity is part of an underlying unity of reality. Of course, "part of" is an approximation of the experience. There is no "part" of the One.

Does the individual cease to exist in the experience of the One? That's a complex question. You cannot cease to exist, because that would imply that there are two states: being and nonbeing. Similarly, one cannot say that you *don't* cease to exist, because if there is both a you and the One, then there isn't a full experience of unity. This seems like a paradox, but the truth is simple:

Once you have the experience of henōsis, nothing changes about the way the universe is. Only your direct apprehension of reality changes. In other words, you understand the paradox in a way you cannot put into words.

Conclusion

The Neoplatonic spiritual practice is often described as having two paths: the contemplative path (exemplified by Plotinus), and the experiential or ritual path (described by Iamblichus). In truth, I think there is one path. The spiritual path of theurgy is a practical one: The practitioner adopts what works, adapts what doesn't, and pursues their own road toward henōsis. Whether that's a solid half hour contemplating Beauty every morning or five minutes taking the View from Above during your lunch break, investing some time in contemplative practice over time can lead to spiritual growth.

You do not need to invest hours a day in meditation, contrary to the claims of some spiritual leaders. You can, in fact, receive the benefits of meditation in as little as ten minutes a day. The good news is that you can also do it in smaller chunks. You can do five or ten minutes in the morning, then steal chunks of five minutes throughout the day. There is something to be said for an extended period of meditation as well, but one doesn't need to carve hours out of the day in order to meditate productively.

If you are going to pursue the theurgic path, I recommend you find some sort of contemplative practice, either from the variety presented here or elsewhere. It can be simple or complex, but just as it's a good idea to stretch your muscles and grab a few minutes of exercise a day, it's a good idea to focus a few minutes a day on your mind. And in the process, you will discover how to make use of your own mind as part of your practice in your own way.

Like the rivers in Plotinus's metaphor, all paths to the One wend their own peculiar and individual ways, but all lead back, ultimately, to the source, which is ineffable and unspeakable, but not unknowable.

IMMORTAL THEURGY
BY JEAN-LOUIS DE BIASI

Today, most of us spontaneously reduce the "theurgic path" either to "ceremonial magic," "high magic," or simply "rituals." The books written from the nineteenth century through today give a romantic idea of magicians invoking spirits in a magic circle. The rise of modern social media spreads this idea even further. By reading the ancient texts and biographies, we understand that initiatory ceremonies were associated with private teachings, demonstrations, experiments, and certain sorts of inner trainings.

Ceremonies and rituals exist in the theurgic path. Magical tools, symbols, and dedicated apparel can be used by the theurgist. However, all of that is used differently than how a magician would use it. I should remind you that even if theurgy can be seen as a simple magical practice, it remains essentially different. A theurgist working to ascend to the Divine can use similar formulas and rituals, but their motivation and goal is spiritual. There are some requirements needed before even thinking about performing a successful ritual. Besides the effectiveness of the practice, these elements are required to avoid ego inflation, absence of morals, and, eventually, delusion.

An authentic theurgic path should combine several components. But before beginning, the first requirement is to live according to the highest moral standards, which we can summarize in a short sentence: Do not harm. It should apply to everything in your life, from waste reduction to violent urges. The teachings given by the initiator help us understand and apply this simple first rule. It is not the only moral rule or principle a theurgist will learn and practice. However, this is an important foundation. It is essential to understand that nothing serious and successful can be achieved in this path without this precondition. Having said that, you understand now that theurgy is neither a religion nor a simple magical practice. This is something different and greater that traditionally starts with a preparation followed by an initiation. But achieving these preliminary steps doesn't mean we have completed the work. On the contrary, now the real work begins, and it must essentially be internal.

An Initiatory Tradition

Theurgy didn't appear from a vacuum. It has a long story worthy of admiration. When I was graduating with a degree in philosophy, I discovered that the main figures of classical philosophy travelled in Egypt and spent several years learning in the temples. It was there that Julian the Theurgist created theurgy, which is said to have been received through revelations during magical rituals. Reading the works of theurgists, Neoplatonists, and famous figures, such as Proclus and the emperor Julian, it is evident that all of them were initiated to these mysteries. All the famous figures of this tradition travelled to learn from masters of this chain, receiving direct oral teachings and eventually what is called "initiations." It was a central required step, revealing that a personal effort was necessary but couldn't achieve what was enacted during a true and real initiation.

Among most of the classical philosophers who travelled to Egypt to learn the great mysteries, the emperor Julian is a wonderful example of such a famous figure traveling to meet Maximum of Ephesus, who was taught by a disciple of Iamblichus. It was then that he received the teaching and this direct initiation. Before him, Apuleius followed a similar initiatory process, and later, Proclus did the same. Anywhere you look, an initiatory process, which couldn't be self-accomplished, was obvious. I followed the same example as a humble pilgrim, traveling on the most sacred lands of the Mediterranean world. Then, I was initiated into several traditions and eventually in the Hermetic and theurgic tradition of the Aurum Solis, becoming its lifetime

Grand Master. The theurgic path cannot really be understood in its entirety without starting with this essential step: being received through a mysterious ceremony and inner process called an initiation. The journey can begin, and you can go a long way on your own. You can even perform self-initiations, but at some point, someone else will be needed.

There is a lot to say about the way an authentic theurgic initiation works, but the essential focus today is to briefly highlight the three main goals.

1. The first goal is to help you awaken your inner abilities that are unused and undeveloped.
2. The second goal is to teach you a safe and effective method to rise to the Divine.
3. The third goal is to teach what you will find after your death and give you the practical keys to go there during your training and come back.

If you succeed in this theurgic initiatory process, you will be able to keep your memory intact and come back in your next life with more control. If not, you will be dragged down randomly, losing what you just learned. As you can see, being trained for this is paramount.

The Eightfold Theurgic Path

In the Aurum Solis, we have identified eight main categories we call *rays* that should be used and mastered by the theurgist to be successful in their quest. These eight rays of the Glorious Star are the expression of the whole theurgic path understood as a holistic system. These rays are (1) mindfulness, (2) breathwork and sacred sounds, (3) calisthenics, (4) devotion, (5) energy healing and the Mediterranean diet, (6) philosophy (7) astrology, and (8) theurgic rituals. These numbers are symbolic and not a progressive sequence the student must follow in order. The eighth ray, Hermetic number of the original Egyptian Ogdoad, corresponds to the theurgic practices. However, you should keep in mind that while this ray is dedicated to theurgic ceremonies and rituals, practicing all eight rays is essential to achieve your inner theurgic transformation. As a consequence, the numbering of the rays is a reference that can be symbolic but does not indicate a sequence you must follow, as all rays are interconnected and simultaneously combined and used in the practice to achieve balance and spiritual transformation.

Everything is combined to make your daily life enjoyable and successful along with your inner spiritual process. This unbroken lineage of Grand Masters and initiates of such theurgic tradition offers effective tools that can empower and improve your life on every level.[138] This traditional school is often called the "yoga of the West" today, and since the Aurum Solis traces its heritage to pre-Christian traditions, which include ancient Greece and Egypt, we lovingly also refer to it as "Mediterranean yoga" (*yoga* meaning "to join" or "to unite"), the Aurum Solis being the heart of this school.[139]

Let us go deeper into each of these categories, or rays, providing you with a clear insight and some practices you can use right away, keeping in mind that you can start with the category you prefer.

Mindfulness

Today, mindfulness has become an important part of the yoga world. At first, mindfulness seems to have nothing to do with theurgy. We cannot find any mention of this word in the theurgic tradition, and it could be difficult to see its importance for the practitioner. Nevertheless, it is crucial to highlight the various applications of such an important topic.

In a theurgic practice, there are things you can see and others you cannot. For obvious reasons, the former has been the focus of most beginners. This is a hot topic on social media. It seems that nice apparel, fascinating ritual rooms, large circles full of Latin and Hebrew words, and more are today what matter for many practitioners. Everything you can imagine will be added according to the traditional rule of accumulation. (This rule means that practitioners believe the more they add of symbols, tools, etc., the more efficient the work is.) If you are not sure that you have enough physical presence, add more items. If you are not sure about disconnecting your body and soul, add more incense and candles. If you practice in a small place, you have a good chance of becoming intoxicated, which will cause you to see lights or

---
138. We are talking here about the theurgic and initiatory tradition of the Aurum Solis, one of the rare theurgic Orders teaching the holistic system of theurgy.
139. For more information, visit www.MediterraneanYoga.org.

hear voices. I do not suggest practicing this way. I am sure you understand my point and can apply this "rule of accumulation" in behaviors you have witnessed.

On the opposite side, things you cannot see can turn out to be the most important aspect of your practice. The heart of mindfulness is dealing with this dimension. The theurgist must learn how to focus and keep concentration during a certain period, building and controlling a vivid visualization while being fully relaxed and detached from the work. All of that cannot be achieved simply by drawing symbols on the floor or declaiming archaic formulas that are just unintelligible gibberish. Everything should start with the realization of who we really are.

Practice: Seeking the Hidden Self

A simple exercise can help us to get closer to this hidden self. You can consider this the first step in this endeavor. It has been formulated by the French philosopher Descartes. Even in a different context, this is the kind of meditation you can immediately use. Take a moment and think of the five "classical" senses: touch, taste, smell, hearing, and sight. Each one gives you a perception of the world that surrounds you. Each one can fool you, being a source of illusion. Each one gives you a sensation of existence but is not the manifestation of who you really are. Now, imagine that you lost any sensation coming from touch. This is the most material sense. You are still there, ready to feel the world around you. Then you also lose your taste, then your smell. But you can still hear and see. Go forward and imagine that you also lose these two senses. Are you still there? Yes, you are thinking. But what are your thoughts? Are they based on memories you received through your senses? If yes, you must also abandon all the memories, keeping only what has not originated in the perceptions. As you can see, your mind at this point contemplates the emptiness of space and time. You are just a body, still alive, being present here and now, without any mental representation. This is an interesting experience, and I invite you to follow this process next time you are alone in a quiet place.

—

The point is mindfulness and is the inner attitude a theurgist should have while performing any ritual practice. As you can realize, we are far from the caricatural representation of a magus, grimoire in hands, standing in the magic circle and pronouncing the magic formulas of the magic papyri. However, we are at the heart of what makes the difference between a theurgist and a wizard. This is a golden key.

The next step is to know how to create this state of consciousness and how to keep it during our practice. As in the past, there are parts that are learned in a group. Deep relaxation, guided meditation, and creative visualization are psychic aspects the adept must learn and control. You do not have to reinvent the process. It has been tested and used for hundreds of years and is still used. In my book *Mysteries of the Aura*, I talk extensively about the training linked to the vision of the aura and everything related to it. Vision and perception of the invisible bodies and levels are paramount to practicing theurgy. Visualization is also one of the first things that must be learned. All of that is fundamental, but it is not even close to the heart of mindfulness. We must reach a state in which we can act while being here and now, detached but still acting. We must practice theurgy while being aware of the spiritual and material levels.

There are techniques for this. I have been lucky to learn them from the Eastern tradition Chan and from Gurdjieff inner circles a long time ago when I was living in France. The former originated in China and emphasizes meditation and direct experience of enlightenment, forming the basis of Zen Buddhism in Japan. The Gurdjieff teachings, known as the Fourth Way, focus on self-awareness, inner development, and harmonizing the mind, emotions, and body through practices like self-observation, sacred dances, and group work. These trainings were hard but unavoidable for someone who wants to progress.

It is difficult to imagine learning such things in a book, but I will give you a few insights. When I lead theurgic practices, I frequently remind participants to be aware of the sensation of their feet on the floor. I also ask them to focus on their breathing, the movement of their chest. A moment later, it is the sounds they can hear in the room and in themselves. These reminders must not be disconnected from the ritual work in process. The sounds of the bell used in practice are also a good way to remind everyone to come back to the sensation of their whole body. When students are more advanced, I invite them from time to time to do the same but being aware of two, three, or four senses simultaneously. For example, while they declare an invocation, to be aware of the soles of their feet on the floor, of the air on their skin, of the sound of their voice, and so on. Such a process clears the mind, keeping only the essentials that allow a real transformation and a successful practice. Mindfulness is simple but can take a lot of practice to assimilate. It constitutes one of the most important keys of theurgy.

Breathwork and Sacred Sounds

Breath is life and death. You came to life with your first breath, and you will leave life with your last breath. It is as simple as that. Breathing is a generally automatic movement of your lungs, diaphragm, and chest that keeps you alive. You get more from the air you breathe than just oxygen. It is also the carrier of subtle energy called *prana*, meaning "life energy." Pranayama is a breathing technique that has been codified by Eastern tradition (*ayama* meaning to "extend, draw out"). Similar specific teachings cannot be found per se in the Western tradition until modern times. Such a technique was probably taught, but undoubtedly in conjunction with ritual singing and healing techniques.

Today, the teachings of holistic theurgy entail learning breathing techniques that are frequently associated with mindfulness and healing. It's worth noting that breathing means nothing other than being here and now. For a beginner, the most important thing to remember is to disregard visualization, sounds, prayer, symbols, and so on. To begin, simply observe your breathing, chest movement, and the air leaving and entering your lungs through your nose. We are in the physical world, in the realm of sensations. *Observe* was the verb I used. However, the student should not even "observe," as this could indicate that consciousness is separated from the physical body breathing. Here, the student should "be" the physical body breathing. The practitioner must "be" the sensations themselves: the chest moving, the nostrils channeling the air, and more.

When this first step, which can take a long time, is completed, some controls are implemented. Exhalation length is increased, retentions are added, tongue and larynx positions are modified, and so on. The awareness of subtle energy is then associated with some visualizations. Mindfulness is maintained throughout the visualizations, avoiding any duality between the physical body and the mind. We must always be present. After months or even years of practice, some may achieve a level of inner enlightenment that is impossible to describe in words to those who have not experienced it. Nonetheless, anyone who uses these techniques in a traditional Eastern or Western school can gain huge benefits from them. It is critical to emphasize that I am discussing both physical and spiritual levels. Your health will improve, as will your mental concentration and the expansion of your consciousness. It is also essential to keep in mind that such results cannot be obtained by beginning with advanced techniques or without patience and persistence. They are critical values that should not be underestimated.

Breathing is the underlying aspect of invocation and ritual singing for anyone who has begun to practice rituals of any kind. Various ancient and magical languages are used in the Western tradition. Ritual texts frequently contain Sumerian, ancient Egyptian, Greek, Latin, Hebrew, and even Enochian. These languages' pronunciations are not the same. They are all connected to a group of people who created and sometimes used this language for a very long time. Their use in a religious or magical context built a real, invisible, semiautonomous world called an *egregore*. Anyone who uses this language and formula in the same context will be associated with this specific entity sooner or later. They are all unique, and some of them are more positive than others. There is a significant difference, for example, when using Enochian, Hebrew, or Greek.

It is interesting to note which languages were originally associated with theurgic tradition. Egyptian and Greek were obviously closer to the origin than Hebrew. It is not a matter of personal preference but a historical reality. Fifteen years ago in the Aurum Solis, we started to focus more on these languages, implementing research conducted with initiates from various countries and cultures. After analyzing the data, we discovered that the impact on spiritual work varied significantly. The egregores drawn by the invocations were not the same, and the spiritual light began to flow more freely, resulting in a stronger inner balance.

When I teach these sacred languages, I am frequently asked about pronunciation: How can I be certain that I am correctly pronouncing sacred words and texts? It's important to remember that people had different accents at different times. This remains true in all countries today. There is no standardized way to speak or pronounce English. Of course, proper pronunciation makes it easier to understand. There are ways to pronounce it more convincingly. As a result, you can practice and improve your pronunciation to achieve the desired effect. It is, however, more of a mental training than a linguistic one. This is how ritual declamations are learned and mastered. Even knowing the texts by heart is insufficient. There are breathing techniques for bringing the texts and names to life, and some languages, such as Egyptian, are more potent than others. Most of the techniques take some time to master. You can find an example of such a breathing technique in this section of the book. All of these elements cannot really be improvised or reinvented. It would be a complete waste of time. They have been used in some initiatory schools for many years. We know how to teach and how to get real results when techniques are used correctly.

There are words and sounds that are unique to all Western ritual texts. They don't have to be accompanied by lengthy invocations or prayers. Their power originates from the vibration that their sound produces and the association with the related egregore. These words are known as mantras in Eastern culture. Interestingly, they also exist in the West. A famous Western mantra I explained extensively in one of my books can be found in the Florence Baptistery. It surrounds a mosaic of the sun. It is "En Giro Torte Sol Ciclos Et Rotor Igne." The pronunciation of this mantra increases the power of the sun, which is universally applicable to anyone. To start, I encourage you to use your intuition to find the most appropriate tone for you. This mantra is often used with a prayer bead in turquoise for meditation and healing. The power of the sun increases all the positive energy you could need in your life. It is also used in some group rituals linked to the movements of the stars.

The ritual singing of the seven vowels is also extremely important in the theurgic tradition. Both the Egyptian temples and the Greek Magical Papyri attest to their existence. Each vowel is associated with a planet. They must be pronounced with a specific tone. There are ways to learn how to create a silent vibration and ways to progressively exteriorize the sound.

The next step is to learn specific techniques for working with sounds to raise your consciousness to the highest levels possible. This is referred to as throat singing and overtones. Both are distinct but share a common goal. The singer creates harmonics by using either the throat or the tongue in a different way. Consider the following scenario: You pluck a guitar string. Even if you can't hear it, the strings close to it are vibrating. This vibration contributes to the audible sound. When I sing an overtone, you can hear the vowel on a specific tone while also hearing other simultaneous harmonics. This work requires intense concentration and generates powerful vibrations throughout the body. Sound baths, typically involving singing bowls, are currently popular. These sessions use the same sound for everyone, wrongly assuming that everyone is the same and that frequency has the same effect on everyone. Overtones and throat singing are working in a similar way, but the instrument is your own body. As a result, the vibration produced is always adequate for who you are and what you require. These techniques are even more powerful when practiced in a group setting, and they open our inner selves to an amazing state of consciousness.

This brief introduction would be incomplete unless I mentioned the original musical instruments used in rituals. There are numerous things that could be said about the use of drums. They are used to induce trances in participants. The nature, shape, and paintings of these drums are not chosen by chance. Some are circular, while others are octagonal. Paintings of animals can also change the quality of the energy. They help to channel specific spirits and energies. The rhythms we use are significant because they correspond to the effects we want to achieve. Bells, pieces of metal, wood, or stone are also used to generate the vibrations necessary for specific sections of a ritual.

I want to mention two very useful and powerful musical instruments used in the practice. The first one is the bull-roarer, also known as a rhombus. It is a very old ritual instrument made of wood or stone, usually in the shape of a leaf, attached to a string. Sacred inscriptions and symbols can be painted or engraved on them. They are commonly used during outdoor practices, though this is not a definitive rule. They are moved in a circle, generating a strange sound that is said to call spirits and deities. I've been using these instruments for a long time. Their power always moves and amazes me.

Iynx is the name given to the second instrument. It is a wheel, like a gearwheel, made of metal, wood, or ceramic that is rotated by pulling two strings that run through two holes near the center. The sounds produced vary depending on how fast the wheel spins, its diameter, and its shape. They're used to summon spirits and deities. They are also used during meditation to help with out-of-body experiences and trance states. They must be used with caution for such practice because their shape can be harmful to the user if the string breaks. However, when handled and controlled properly, they are incredible instruments.

As you can see, this category, breathwork and sacred sounds, is extremely important. All these techniques are employed in the rituals. It's difficult to imagine a student succeeding on this path without extensive practice. It is yet another example of theurgy's cultural wealth. It is a living legacy that every initiate should treasure and be proud of.

Practice: Rhythmic Breathing

Once you've mastered this rhythmic breathing, you can use it whenever you'd like, especially during magical or meditative practices. The goal of this practice is to help you focus completely while clearing your mind of all thoughts. The practice of mindfulness will be a critical key to progress.

The rhythm of this type of breathing, which we can call "rectangular," consists of taking a breath in for four heartbeats, holding it for two, exhaling for four, then counting to two before beginning to inhale again. The critical point is the count of two before inhaling. Some students may find this pause difficult or stressful at first. If this is the case, I recommend that you lengthen your exhalation and continue with the cycle's inhalation. This allows you to slow down and relax during your practice. When you are more comfortable with this retention after the lungs empty, you can add it with a heartbeat count of two. This means inhaling on a count of four, holding the breath on a count of two, exhaling on a count of four, and coming to a two-heartbeat pause before inhaling again. The standard count will become second nature over time.

When you've mastered this simple technique, I recommend starting to extend the duration with a six-three-six-three cycle.

Calisthenics

The term calisthenics originates with the Greek words *kállos* (κάλλος), meaning "beauty," and *sthenos* (σθένος), meaning "strength." This practice uses the resistance of our body weight to develop muscular strength and control.

This form of training was practiced in places such as ancient Greece and ancient China. Alexander the Great's armies, the Spartans, and Han-dynasty physicians all used and promoted this type of exercise for training and health maintenance.

In modern times, yoga has adopted a comparable approach. Through the practice of asanas (postures), yoga also utilizes body weight to build strength, flexibility, and balance. Calisthenics typically emphasizes high-intensity, dynamic movements aimed at enhancing muscular power and endurance through exercises such as push-ups, pull-ups, and squats.

Conversely, yoga incorporates flowing sequences of postures, such as in Vinyasa or Hatha styles, that not only strengthen the body but also enhance flexibility, balance, and concentration, all while coordinating movement with conscious breathwork.

The Egyptian yoga that we practice today has a deep connection with calisthenics. Rooted in harmony and equilibrium, it relies entirely on bodyweight movements to develop physical strength while integrating mindfulness and breath awareness. This approach fosters a holistic discipline that nurtures both body and mind.

By blending the foundational principles of calisthenics with the fluidity and contemplative nature of yoga, practitioners benefit from a comprehensive practice that promotes overall health, resilience, and inner balance.

Minus a few exceptions, Western spiritual or esoteric traditions did not place much focus on the movements associated with the practices. This is a direct result of the development of the Judeo-Christian tradition, which emphasized the separation of body and soul from the start. Furthermore, the body was regarded as the source and cause of evil. The power of the flesh over the soul is deeply rooted in the original sin. This is a real disconnect between the two worlds as well as a strong incentive to concentrate solely on the spiritual path.

This mindset has had a profound impact on the spiritual world as a whole, including the vast majority of initiatory organizations. This is why it is critical to reintroduce and emphasize the importance of the physical body. Physical exercises that are linked to inner spiritual practices must be taught. Anyone seeking to embark on an initiatory path such as theurgy in a safe and balanced manner must regard the physical body as the true foundation of the inner work. The goal here is not to develop faith or to conduct preliminary theological research; being a believer is not enough on the theurgic path, nor is simply performing rituals.

Parts of the Judeo-Christian traditions reject the body using rituals, meditations, and visualizations. These traditions been extremely effective. In fact, visualizing your physical body decaying or its association with monstrous creatures helps the practitioner to be repulsed by it.[140] Similar processes can be found in shamanism, but the goal is different. However, the method and purpose of this work generally have a negative impact on the practitioner's psychology. We must remember that this path seeks both an ascent to the Divine and a positive transformation of our current lives. This path teaches that nothing stable and no real transformation can be achieved while rejecting the body.

In Hermeticism and theurgy, the body is regarded as a vehicle that must be cherished. It is both a source of pain and a source of great pleasure. This, paradoxically, is the best ally you can have because it almost never lies. Your mind can bend reality to your liking. Your mind has the skill to deceive you and lead you down the path of delusion. Meanwhile, your body is speaking the truth.

This is why you should educate yourself on the characteristics of this vehicle. Calisthenics are one of the best ways to lay a strong and trustworthy foundation upon which you can undertake whatever spiritual path you choose.

By extension of this physical work, it is recommended that you train your psychic abilities to see the subtle bodies. Several are related to the body. The development of this ability is part of a serious practice of the theurgic path. We can manage the energy that will eventually be used by our physical vehicle if we can see these invisible bodies. This, in conjunction with physical

---

140. "Let us bless pain. Love pain. Sanctify pain ... Glorify pain!" in Josemaría Escrivá, *The Way* (Four Courts Press, 1985), 62.

exercise and diet, is the most effective way to achieve a well-balanced body. If we are in good shape, we will be able to do our jobs more effectively. This is one of the reasons why the eightfold theurgic path includes calisthenics.

I teach Mediterranean yoga. Some may find it surprising to associate Egypt with yoga, which is now known as an Eastern tradition. In fact, the tradition provides us with very valuable indications of specific sequences of movements that can be compared to modern Eastern yoga. The lotus position, along with other well-known asanas, is one of the most ancient Eastern yogic representations. This position is commonly found in ancient Egypt. Chakras, or energy centers, are also depicted on the temple walls. Many statues depict positions that any yoga student is familiar with. Of course, some positions, sequences, visualizations, breathings, and sounds are unique. Vowel sequences were used as spells and a meditation guide, as evidenced by the Magical Papyri. Sequences were also used to align our physical body with the powers of the planets.

There are specific planet-related movements that have never been fully explained in published books. In my book *The Divine Arcana of the Aurum Solis*, I describe several movements associated with the planets, tarot arcana, astrological signs, and Greek and Hebrew alphabet letters. Each of these elements is described in several static positions. When they are linked, they depict an important sequence of movements, creating flows of energy that vitalize and tune you to the specific energies that correspond.

A planetary flow allows you to connect with a specific energy. Then, this light is channeled within your body, increasing your inner energy for both the physical and the subtle bodies' benefit.

It's exactly like turning a dynamo to generate electricity. There is enough energy at one point to light the lamp and keep it lit for an extended period of time. A similar effect can be obtained by performing a specific sequence of movements. With regular practice, you will feel a combination of physical and energetic sensations. Visualization and pronunciation are effective techniques. Involving the physical body, on the other hand, increases the inflow and quality of energy channeled.

While the presentation of this category could be expanded, it is also interesting to experiment with the principles presented here right away.

As an example, in my previous book *Mysteries of the Aura*, I described the famous sun salutation known as Surya Namaskar. I'd like to give you the opportunity to experiment with the power of the sun right now according to the teachings of Mediterranean yoga.

The practice of this Mediterranean sun salutation increases the presence of solar power in your aura, bringing success and health into your life.[141]

Practice: Sun Salutation

1. Stand with your feet parallel, aligned with your knees and hips. Arms are at your sides, relaxed.
2. On an inhale, extend your arms toward the ceiling, roll your head back, and join your hands.
3. On an exhale, place your palms together at your heart level, your fingers toward the sky.
4. On an inhale, join your arms in front of your chest, the inner part of your forearms touching together from the elbows to your wrists, and place your hands in a cup shape open to the sky.

Pause.

5. On an inhale, extend your arms to the sky above your head, forming a triangle with your thumbs and index fingers.
6. Exhale and fold forward. Bend your knees and relax your head. Frame your feet with your hands and step back with your right foot, with your right knee down on the floor.
7. Inhale, come back up to standing, extending your arms parallel and toward the sky with the palms of your hands facing each other above your head.
8. On an exhale, frame your feet with your hands, step back with your left foot, place your left knee down on the floor, and fully extend your arms on the ground in front of you.

---

141. This version of the sun salutation is what we use in Mediterranean yoga. If you'd like to see this performed in real time, visit this link: https://vimeo.com/852114595/a4f1c33b29.

9. Inhale, step forward with your right foot, with your left knee resting on the floor.
10. On an exhale, place your hands close to the top of the mat.
11. Inhale and move your left foot forward.
12. On an exhale, fold forward. Bend your knees as needed. Relax your head. Your feet are framed by your hands.
13. Inhale, stand, and extend your arms toward the sky, joining your hands and the tips of your fingers in the direction of the sky; look at your hands.
14. Exhale and cross your arms on your chest, with your left hand flat on the right of your chest, your right hand flat on the left of your chest. Your arms are crossed above the center of your chest.

Pause.

15. Release your arms on your sides, with the palms of the hands facing forward.

Devotion

Devotion is a crucial aspect of theurgy that is frequently misunderstood. This aspect of the theurgic path is distinct from religious observance. Faith is not viewed in the same way that a believer views it. It is an important part of a theurgist's spiritual work. The existence of deities is a hypothesis related to the philosophical and theological systems employed. Devotion is an attitude of reverence for the gods and goddesses. Deities have always been associated with theurgic practices in some way. Given that one of the primary goals of this path is to ascend to the Divine, it seems natural to regard deities as part of this highest level.

This tradition is essentially polytheist. This is not the place to get into a lengthy theoretical debate about whether ancient Egyptian, Greek, or Roman religions, to name a few, were polytheistic, shamanistic, animistic, monotheistic, theistic, or pantheistic. Obviously, all religions mention one or more deities. The same is true for religions based on the Bible and the Koran. These deities are thought to exist at the highest level or, in some cases, at an intermediate level. At one point the practitioner will have to deal with them.

Immortal Theurgy

A full degree is focused on a theurgic devotional practice in some traditions, such as the Mediterranean yoga and the Aurum Solis. This can be compared to deity yoga and Bhakti in the Eastern traditions.

Modern practitioners have concluded that anyone can speak to gods or goddesses at any time. The concept of a god who is present everywhere at all times, ready to listen to and obey someone's prayers, appears more monotheistic than polytheistic. If immortal deities exist, they must be superior to us in every way. As a result, we cannot pretend to interact with them with impunity or without extensive preparation. You can easily imagine the amount of preparation required to attend a job interview or speak with the president. So, how could meeting a god be any easier? Our frailty as humans gives us hope that some powerful deity is waiting for us. We must admit that such optimism is understandable but overly hopeful. Meanwhile, when we begin to use visualization, prayer, meditation, or ritual, our mind is always ready to assist us. With a good ritual, we can be confident that such divine communication has occurred. However, we must remember that our minds are easily deceived. This path is prone to delusion.

Here is the center of the most dangerous and fascinating paradox: Devotion is an essential component of theurgic practice, but it is also one of its most dangerous aspects. We must use it, but we must be concerned about the possible consequences. Clearly, the assistance and supervision of a master and a serious school are required. If this is not possible for any reason, the theurgist must adhere to a few simple guidelines:

- If you believe a god or goddess is speaking to you during a ritual or spiritual practice, proceed with caution. I'm not saying such manifestations are impossible. However, genuine communication of this kind is so rare that the message is almost certainly coming from your subconscious. If you think about it, it's both interesting and useful. If you are duped by it, this is extremely dangerous.
- A divinity must not be summoned. Attempting to proceed in this manner is either arrogant or insane. The realization of their essence and our own human nature should serve as a reminder that the only attitude to cultivate is humility. The latter must be the foundation of any devotional practice on the theurgic path.

- Approaching divinity with love and selflessness is essential. In a ritual, symbols and declamations can be used to aid our visualization and focus. Only a strong emotion, such as love, can open a channel between you and a divinity. There is no need for any kind of request in this case. If communication is established in this manner, the divine power will immediately know what your needs are.
- Devotional practices are characterized by their simplicity and beauty. Beauty is the highest level of the Divine in the Neoplatonist tradition. As a result, everything must exude harmony and balance. The accumulation of symbols, perfumes, clothing, and other items can result in chaotic and unbalanced inner development.

These are not the only considerations you should bear in mind as you begin this spiritual practice. They are, however, necessary and must accompany the practitioner throughout this journey. Only then can visualizations, movements, mantras, and all the other components be used safely. The mysteries that you can uncover are among the most sacred of this tradition.

A Kemetic Practice

Prayer beads have been used in many cultures for a long time. I even dedicated a full book (*The Magical Use of Prayer Beads*, 2016) to this wonderful spiritual tool. Even if they are not attested in ancient Egypt, they can be used to increase our concentration and meditation.

Kemetic prayer beads are made of twenty-four stone beads: three turquoise beads, seven carnelian beads, seven aventurine beads, and seven howlite beads.[142] They are associated with an Egyptian cartouche with three sacred Egyptian hieroglyphs: *ankh* (life), *wedja* (prosperity), and *seneb* (strength, health). For this bracelet, use the three hieroglyphs on a representation of a cartouche, such as on a charm. This text formula was often used by Egyptian kings. Using such prayer beads with the real turquoise, red, green, and white beads is beneficial. However, you can use the invocations below in the same

---

142. For a visual example of these prayer beads, please visit https://www.mediterraneanyoga.org/product-page/kemetic-prayer-beads.

way without them. In that case, the only thing you should do is visualize and count.

If you have the Kemetic prayer beads, place your fingers on the cartouche. (You can choose to use the Egyption or the English words.) Say:

> *I invoke at this moment the presence of Serapis, Horus, and Isis!*
> *O Immortal Deities, make me forever alive, intact, and healthy!*
> *May [ankh or life], [wedja or prosperity], and [seneb or strength or health] be manifested!*

On each red bead of the first series, declaim:

> **Serapis, give me health!**

On each green bead of the second series, declaim:

> **Hor-Pa-Khered, give me strength!**

On each white bead of the third series, declaim:

> **Aset, give me life forever!**

Observe a silent pause and declaim the following invocation:

> *The bright Eye of Horus comes, the bright Eye of Horus comes,*
> *   welcome in peace and resplendent like Re on the horizon.*
> *He repels the power of Seth before the one who makes it manifest.*
> *He was the one who took it, and he is burning against him.*
> *Its flame comes, having left the sky following Ra, in front of your*
> *   two sisters, Ra.*
> *The Eye of Horus is very much alive.*
> *The Eye of Horus is alive and well.*

Breathe and relax. Then, place the cartouche in contact with your forehead for a few seconds and say:

> *May [ankh or life], [wedja or prosperity], and [seneb or strength or health] be manifested!*
> *May Serapis, Horus, and Isis protect me now and forever!*

You can repeat several cycles if you feel the need and add the visualization of the divinities.

Energy Healing and the Mediterranean Diet

Subtle energy is inextricably linked to the theurgic path. We can have doubts about the effectiveness of our practices if we do not understand how subtle energy works on an invisible level. To work effectively, we must first learn to see and feel energy. We must complete exercises and training to succeed on this path. Even more than simply being aware of and controlling this energy, we can use it to help ourselves and others.

When I was initiated many years ago, it was assumed that anyone eager to embark on this path already understood the fundamentals of what is known as *animal magnetism*, also known as *mesmerism*. It is still necessary to have prior knowledge of energy work, astral vision, and out-of-body experiences. Working with these subtle energies allows access to the other world and its inhabitants. This energy work is essential for anyone who wants to start this healing journey.

As I explain in my book *Mysteries of the Aura*, Eastern and Western traditions present subtle bodies in different ways at different times.[143] Speaking about the physical body is easier because anyone with or without training can see what we discussed with their own eyes. This is not true of subtle bodies. The presentation of these spiritual bodies varies according to culture and tradition. When it comes to chakras, for example, some people say there are seven, while others say there are five or even ten. Differences between cultures can become even more pronounced, as in ancient Egyptian or Jewish tradition. The aura is a malleable manifestation of energy that incorporates components of the spiritual system in which you practice or were raised. There are fundamentally identical aspects, but the overall description can

---
143. Jean-Louis de Biasi and Patricia Bourin, *Mysteries of the Aura: How to See, Interpret & Work with Subtle Energies* (Llewellyn Publications, 2023).

differ, as can the impact on your life. To be effective, any work with a healing process must consider this cultural aspect. The same is true when working with theurgic systems and specific energies.

Before going anywhere, we should evaluate our education as children and later as adults. Then, it is critical that we do the same with the traditions and rituals that we have used. All these aspects are parts of what compose our subtle bodies, as well as the nature and structure of the energies that make up our aura. After such a thorough examination, we will be able to cleanse and organize the energies around us and then take a fresh start on the path.

Similarly, egregores play an important role in the equation. They are powerful energy sources, and any connection to them through initiations or practices must be considered. Because everything is energy, we must exercise extreme caution when making spiritual decisions. You are made of invisible energy, and everything around you is the same.

You are working with energy in any type of practice, whether it is prayer or ritual. Your hands, eyes, and sometimes your entire body are shaping energy waves, weaving a living web of light all around you. Only after you have fully mastered this energy work will you be able to begin the healing process. It has been the focus of the order *Eudiaque*, a French initiatory organization whose name comes from the Greek Eudia, "serenity." The Eudiaque Order, which is rooted in Egyptian tradition, employs animal magnetism in their rituals and healing practices. Today, we call this essential part of the theurgic path "Egyptian Sekhem." *Sekhem* is an ancient term that means "power" or "force." It refers to a sacred healing tradition that harnesses the universal life-force energy. Deeply rooted in the spiritual and mystical heritage of ancient Egypt, Sekhem serves as a gateway to deep personal transformation and holistic well-being.

Grand Master Henri Durville and other Grand Officers were medical doctors who wrote several books and papers about the spagyric tradition and what is now known as the Mediterranean diet.[144] The energy of nature, in fact, is fundamental. One of the most important aspects of assimilating this power is to follow a highly effective and scientifically proven diet. The Hermetic

---
144. I suggest the introductory book *L'initiation eudiaque*, Bibliotheque eudiaque, Theurgia Publications (French Edition).

theurgic tradition corresponds to the Mediterranean diet and, in some cases, vegetarianism. Furthermore, in the United States, the Mediterranean diet is the only diet recognized by the American Heart Association.

In a nutshell, this diet allows you to eat and drink whatever you want as long as it is organic and safe.[145] Aside from this wide variety of options, there are two main rules that everyone should follow. The first is to avoid excess, which is often the origin of pain, imbalance, and, eventually, disease. The second option is to adhere to the Mediterranean diet pyramid. It can be summarized as follows: Food intake ranges from small to large amounts. Less meat and sweets, more legumes and beans, olive oil, grains, and fruits and vegetables. Moderation should also be a rule. I am a graduate of the University of Athens with a degree in the Mediterranean diet.

I am confident that you now understand why it is critical to maintain a healthy physical body, as everything is interconnected in the strong web of energy that we are made of.

Practice: Magnetization and Energization

Specific hand movements can be used to perform energization or healing. The effectiveness of such techniques has been demonstrated over centuries of practice. Passes, imposition, application, stroking, and rubbing are the five main types of movements. They are dynamic flows that can be applied to a variety of situations. The best way to test this is to do it with a partner who will be seated while you stand in front.

Passes can be made with either one or both hands. Longitudinal and transversal passes are the two types of passes.

Longitudinal Passes

Longitudinal passes, when performed slowly and at a distance of 2–4 inches from your partner, charge the subtle bodies of your partner, resulting in a sense of calm and comfort. A very slow longitudinal pass takes at least thirty seconds. When performed more quickly, at a distance of 6–12 inches, they become stimulating. Their action is almost always perceptible in

---

145. The USDA organic certification is a good reference, but we focus on products that are without harmful chemicals.

the form of a mild current in the interior of the body that follows and even precedes the motion made by the magnetizer's hand. Long passes are practiced rapidly in a downward direction 12–16 inches from your partner. These actions are stimulating, clearing the mind and chest, warming the extremities, and clearing and balancing the aura.

In this experiment, I invite you to make longitudinal passes from the top of the head to the lower part of the trunk, or even from the head to the feet. You move your hands always in a downward direction and never the opposite.

A longitudinal pass from the head to the lower part of the trunk is practiced in two steps as follows:

First step: Begin at the top of the head and work your way down the length of the trunk. Make no use of muscular strength. Maintain a relaxed and stretched-out hand, with fingers slightly separated from one another. Your palms should be facing down, and your hands should be flat. Then, lower your arms as if you were going to draw ten perpendicular lines on the body's surface with your fingers. Assume you want to spread astral energy downward from the head to the chest. When your hands reach the bottom of their descent, close them as if to hold the energy for a second.

Second step: Draw your upper body back to separate yourself from your partner and raise your hands a little above the top of your head, passing them with fists closed in front of your chest. When your closed hands reach the top of your head, you open them slightly, as if to pour or spread the energy, and then slowly lower them again, as you did the first time.

It is best to keep such passes going for a few minutes, but no longer than five minutes. Your partner should be seated with their eyes closed and their back straight.

Transversal Passes

Transversal passes relax and clear the aura of aggregates that do not belong to your partner. As a result, these passes have a balancing effect, clearing the mind and removing any feelings of oppression. They always leave a feeling of peace and comfort, which is enhanced by the pleasant brightness of the aura.

Transversal passes, like longitudinal passes, are made in two steps.

First step: Cross your forearms around the middle of your chest. The palms of your hands are facing your partner, thumbs down, and fingers slightly apart. Your arms are spread out, and your palms remain directed toward the patient with your thumbs up. Your arms are spread wide apart and form a horizontal line. The palms of your hands face your partner, and the fingers are still slightly separated.

Second step: With your arms largely open in the final position, your forearms only need to be returned to the initial position. Then repeat these two movements.

Transversal passes are typically performed above the head, on the face, and on the chest. They can, however, be executed on the sides, spine, and legs.

Philosophy

It might seem strange to link philosophy and theurgic practice at first. Philosophy does not seem natural, but devotion, rituals, and the development of psychic abilities do. It takes a while to realize that throughout the majority of theurgy's history all the masters were essentially philosophers. But first, let's clarify what exactly we mean when we refer to philosophy in this context. The meaning of this Pythagorean term is "love of wisdom," which currently has no immediate connection to knowledge. The primary objective is to become a wise person—not a priest, a high priest, or a saint—someone who exemplifies significant life-building principles rather than acquiring more knowledge.

The philosophical past can be deceptive. Socrates is supposed to be the first to formally advance this way of thinking, and Plato established it as a tradition. It's interesting to note right away that the Neoplatonist school, which served as a key hub for the dissemination of theurgic philosophy, originated from this Platonic Academy. However, before becoming the "Academia Platonica," which lasted hundreds of years, it is good to remember that

Pythagoras, Plato, and almost all the main figures of this time spent years in Egypt. They underwent a difficult process before being approved by the Egyptian clergy. They learned both scientific and mystical secrets.

Pythagoras, who lived about a century before Plato, appears to have been the first person to embark on such a journey. When Pythagoras returned to his native land, he established a school with two main sections—one exoteric and one esoteric—reserved for those who had been initiated into the Pythagorean mysteries. Sadly, a few writings and the discovery of a secret underground Pythagorean Basilica in Rome are the only things that have survived from this school. However, he was undoubtedly the first to establish an esoteric and initiatory school in the form that we are familiar with today, including the use of symbols, rituals, secret signs, the distinction between initiates and noninitiates, a particular diet, the application of moral principles, a way of thinking, visualization techniques, and more. The secret lineage he founded lasted for hundreds of years. All the other famous figures, from Plato to Plethon, pretended to be initiated into the Pythagorean mysteries.

Plato founded his school and published his books based on the figure of Socrates after traveling in Egypt and other countries. His school is the true foundation of what we call philosophy today. Socrates is credited with developing the critical thinking method and the maieutics, which can be compared to the "art of giving birth"—in this case, "of ideas." We don't have direct evidence of this invention by Socrates, but Plato based his public teaching on such a technique. It is a method of discovering the answer to our questions within ourselves. The discussion between the philosopher and the student helps to discover eternal truths that have always existed. But, in addition to these public teachings, Plato, following Pythagoras's rules, was teaching what are known as "unwritten doctrines" and offering secret practices to a small number of students.

We must remember that philosophy has always been an inner practice, not just a mental exercise. This is the hidden part of philosophy that theurgists used. Before even considering rituals, it was necessary to master the mind and control and order the thoughts. Before we could join the ranks of students, we had to develop a moral attitude, purify, and change our lives. The first prerequisite was to study the philosophical works of the past masters and begin the inner purification process. A serious theurgic school in the twenty-first century should be structured similarly. It is the only way to provide a proper and safe path to more knowledge and, eventually, to enlightenment.

In the modern manifestation of this lineage, for example, students must read the works of Western philosophers who have become increasingly associated with the tradition: Iamblichus, Pythagoras, Plato, Emperor Julian, Plotinus, Proclus, Epictetus, Marcus Aurelius, Epicurus, Apuleius, Plethon, and other famous figures. Of course, some of them have developed different schools and differ on various subjects. However, large parts of their philosophy have become increasingly associated with the theurgic path. Some concentrate on how we should live our current lives, while others concentrate on the spiritual world. Obviously, it is not necessary to read everything before starting your theurgic journey.

We know that Judeo-Christians spent countless hours reading, meditating on, and studying the Bible. Hermetists and theurgists do the same with their sacred books, the *Corpus Hermeticum* and *Chaldean Oracles*, as well as the philosophers mentioned earlier. This is humanity's most brilliant manifestation. They are the greatest examples to emulate, and their voices are as relevant today as they were centuries back. They will not expect you to obey an invisible ruler who dictates every aspect of your personal life. They will assist you in discovering what is correct, avoiding delusion, and organizing a clear and stable mind. This is what our philosophy can provide and accomplish.

Astrology

Astrology is a well-known tradition. In the theurgic tradition of the Aurum Solis, we are using astrology coming from the Mediterranean tradition, focusing more specifically on the Egyptian and Hellenistic astrology. Obviously, some things are different from one to the other, and our use is linked to specific ritual practices. There is also a specific way to understand and use astrology in relation to the theurgic path. It is called *transformative astrology*.

Our system is simpler than the astrology you may know. We are following the ancient Hermetic vision: four elements plus one (the aether), seven planets, twelve signs, and the thirty-six decans.

The masters of this tradition were only using these planets and nothing more. Following their teachings, we use only the planets we can directly observe as they did in the past. We should keep in mind that the choice of the deities associated with each one was carefully chosen. They combine the powers at work, the symbolism of the gods, the seasons, and so forth. When astronomers discovered the other planets, they used names coming from mythology but without knowledge of these archetypes. Consequently, these identities, such as Pluto, Neptune, and so forth, are random and without any symbolic value.

Among these seven planets, two are more important: the Sun and the Moon. As a matter of fact, theurgy has been seen by many as a solar tradition. The Sun is at the center of the spiritual ladder used by the initiate to reach the ennead. On the physical level, the Sun gives life to everything on the planet. Without it, nothing can exist, and if it disappears, everything dies. The Sun is the first thing to consider when we build or read a natal chart. It is essential to know where this star was when we were born and its position on every following birthday. The power of the Sun is something real. If you go outside, you can see it. It could burn your skin or give you vitamins. It is evident that it cannot be compared with a planet like Jupiter or Mars. Their power can be real, but they are not as self-evident as the Sun.

The Moon is the second planet manifesting its effect in a very visible way. We can feel its power in our body and around us. We can see the energy of the Moon moving the ocean and affecting our dreams. Any ritual a theurgist performs should consider these two "planets." It is the same for the combination of their power, during a total eclipse, for example. I had the opportunity to do that a couple of times, once in France and once in the United States. For the second one, I travelled to the north of the country in Idaho to be right at the center of the path and chose the top of a mountain. I was expecting to be at the center of an amazing experience in the sky, but something happened also on the ground. A unique experience occurred on the ground, not in the sky. Attending a total eclipse is an amazing experience, but at the top of a mountain with a 360-degree view is even greater. I saw the shadow of the Moon moving fast in my direction as the temperature was dropping very fast and the Sun was disappearing. When the Moon was fully obstructing the Sun, suddenly all became still. Everything was cold and silent. I watched the moving corona that is usually hidden by the bright light. The movements of the loops and plumes were fascinating. It is what is also called the *ring of fire*. I was lucky, as this eclipse lasted more than three minutes. When I looked around me, I realized that I was at the center of a gigantic circle of light. Being at the top of the mountain and at the center of the eclipse path, I was able to see the sunrise all around me. A magic circle was created, and the combined powers of the Sun and the Moon were at their peak. It was a deep and intense experience on a human level, but also on a magical one.

Another aspect not often used by modern astrologers is the seasons, which were very important for ancient Egyptians. The time of year is essential to know yourself. There is a strong seasonal effect on the psychology and physical body of someone. Being born in summer, winter, spring, or fall makes us different. It is also the case for the time of your birth. The exact hour is used for the calculation of the ascendant and the position of the planets, but it is far from limited to that. Being born at 3 a.m., 5 a.m., 6 p.m., or midnight makes your body and your psyche different. But we must also consider all the powers that were in motion when we were born. This includes the country, the location, its elevation, the ley lines, the topography, and so forth, and even the building and the room itself. If you were born on a mountain in South America or in central Europe very far from the sea, you would be different from someone born on an island. This is not just a question of culture and genetics, but also the combination of the power of the stars and the land. Consequently, a student in theurgy should analyze not just the planets and the astrological signs, but everything that has been linked to their birth.

As it is explained in Mediterranean yoga, another essential aspect of astrology is the day of the week. According to the traditional teachings, each of the seven planets is associated with a day of the week. It is very important for you to know which planetary day you were born on. But don't be fooled by the civil calendar. The days of the week you know have no link with the powers of the planets. They have no value for an initiate. Sunday in the civil calendar cannot be the real planetary day of the Sun, as it has no connection with the cycles of the stars. I spoke extensively about this aspect and its history in my book *Rediscover the Magick of the Gods and Goddesses*. To be simple and understand the connection with the luni-solar calendar, you should know that the day of each New Moon is a day of Saturn, the following day being the day of the Sun, Sunday. The full sequence is Saturn (Saturday), Sun (Sunday), Moon (Monday), Mars (Tuesday), Mercury (Wednesday), Jupiter (Thursday), and Venus (Friday). As I explained in my previous book, this system was used in ancient Rome and Greece. It was almost the same in Egypt, even if the Full Moon was associated with Thoth. The first day of the first cycle of the lunar month, Saturnian day (Saturn/Cronos), is the day of the New Moon. The second day of the lunar month, day of the Sun (Helios), is the day after the New Moon. The third day is the day of the Moon (Selene). The fourth day is the day of Mars (Ares). The fifth day is the day of Mercury (Hermes). The sixth day is the day of Jupiter (Zeus). The seventh day is the day of Venus (Aphrodite).

This cycle of seven days continues until the next New Moon. If days remain after the end of the fourth cycle and the next New Moon, they are dedicated to the aether.

The following New Moon starts the new cycle by the Saturnian day, followed by four cycles, and so on for the rest of the year.

The next component to analyze is also linked to the planets. Each day can be divided into planetary hours, their durations being different during the night and the day. Consequently, you can be born on the day of Saturn but in the planetary hour of Mars, for example.

The last influence I want to highlight is called "velocia."[146] These periods of the day manifest the power of the elements: earth, water, fire, air, and aether. Knowing the predominant element gives you another important indication.

As you can realize now, there are a lot of things linked to material and celestial energies, which you can quite easily identify. Then, you can start to know yourself, your past, and your future.

So far, we have described the various elements used in connection with theurgic practices. However, it is the way to use astrology that is drastically different in theurgy. When someone is helping you to build and read your natal chart, you usually passively receive this information and interpretation.

---

146. The velocia are calculated from the time of sunrise. The first flow in the series is Akasha, followed by Vayu, Tejas, Apas, and Prithvi. Each lasts for twenty-four minutes. The sequence, therefore, repeats every two hours throughout the twenty-four-hour period.

If the astrologer has not been properly trained, the freedom you have could indirectly be reduced. Anything that is said is received by your subconscious as a prediction and not as an indication, which you can use to build your future.

A theurgist in the Aurum Solis tradition is not using astrology as passive knowledge but as a tool. The main theurgic work occurs each year on your birthday.[147] This is the moment when the planets are re-creating your birth and giving you the opportunity to perform a very important spiritual work. You can compare this operation to a birthday party. Imagine you have invited seven important guests for a dinner. You may have figured out that these seven attendees are the planets. However, you didn't decide where they would sit, and you let them choose freely. You don't know exactly how these people will behave. Sometimes, they can be nice, or, on the contrary, they can decide to argue about anything. They can fight, start to talk about politics, religion, and unpredictable subjects. Such a dinner is not always peaceful. Symbolically, this is what is happening not just on your birthday, but also every day of the year. It is essential for you to understand this process and take control of it. Some theurgic rituals can give you the tools you need to create the best outcome. But even without knowing all the complex ritualistic processes, there are things you can do immediately.

First, you should welcome these divine guests. You do not have to control the place they choose yet, but you can be happy, welcoming, and do your best to create an enjoyable moment. You are looking for harmony. You should build a relationship based on desire and love for the planet—more precisely for the divine power symbolized by the planet. You should know who they are, their story, their life, their personality, what they like, their names, and everything you can gather about them. You are not trying to impose your will on these deities. It is not a fight. You are welcoming them and trying to find the best combination possible between these important guests and you. The theurgist is using their knowledge and calculation to find the best dinner table organization possible. This table is the representation of the yearly chart. Every cycle, you will have an opportunity to try again, always looking

---

147. This is the reason why we are using the expression of "transformative astrology."

for the best outcome. You will extend this effort all through the year by manifesting your love toward these celestial powers. As a matter of fact, they can help you in your life and in your path. As you can realize now, astrology used in the theurgic path is an opportunity to learn more about the Divine while creating a more harmonious and balanced life around you.

Practice: Transformative Astrology

This practice is used the day of your birthday to balance astral energies and create the best outcome for the new yearly cycle of your life.

Introduction

Ideally, you should choose your birthday and the exact time of your birth. If you don't know it, start your practice in the minutes following sunrise.

Position of the Planets

If you know a little about astrology, find where the planets are in the zodiac for this special moment in relation to your location.

Organization of the Place

Choose a quiet room in which you can create a circle on the floor while standing or being seated in the center. The circle can be made of a cord or just materialized with white flour, chalk, or anything you choose and that can be easily cleaned after.

Distribute symbols of the zodiac inside and around the circle. You can use symbols drawn on flash cards or use the arcana from the Aurum Solis Tarot, which have been created for such a practice. The sign of the ascendant should be in the east, and all the other signs follow in their usual order. Then, place the seven planets on the circle where they are at this very moment.

Note that if you cannot use and organize a room as described, you can perform the whole practice in visualization. In this case, you just need to find a quiet place, close your eyes, relax, and follow the ritual indications in meditation.

Offerings and Symbols

You should choose different offerings for the deities of the planets. It could be food, beverages, flowers, perfumes, or a combination of all. Additionally, choose a metal linked to the planet and maybe also a stone.

Apparel

The traditional apparel recommended in this tradition is a white linen robe. If you do not have one, feel free to choose clothes that are comfortable and can adapt to the seriousness of the moment.

Practice: Ascent to the Light

I invite you to use this practice to embody what you just learned.

Ascent to the Light

When everything has been properly prepared, go to the center of the circle, sit, and take a few minutes of meditation. The best way to do this is to be aware of your breathing: observe the movement of your chest and the sensation of the air coming in and out of your nose.

Proceed with a simple and effective practice explained below called *Acessio Lucis* (Ascent to the Light).

Start by feeling the surface of your skin, the contact between your skin and your clothes. Switch to the awareness of the energy surrounding your physical body. Do the same after for your aura. When you are aware of or visualize your subtle body, transfer your consciousness into it and imagine that your size progressively increases. Your consciousness widens. Feel this sense of vastness as you continue to extend your subtle body. At one point, you stop and feel that you are a part of the cosmos. You are in peace, separated from the physical world, nevertheless aware of your physical body still in your room.

After a time of contemplation, release the visualization and continue your practice.

Activation of the Zodiac and Welcoming the Gods

Visualize the circle of the zodiac around you with the background of a starry sky. Symbols of astrological signs can appear in gold.

Keeping this vision in some part of your mind, recite the *Hymn to the Gods* by Proclus offered in the introduction of this book.

Face the direction of the first astrological sign on the east. Visualize the symbol in front of you. At this level, it's best to use the same color gold for all of the signs. This color is very efficient. However, using different colors will not improve their effectiveness.

Every time your visualization is established, inhale and pronounce the name chosen in the list provided below. Then, move to the next astrological sign and proceed in the same way. Notice that such order of the zodiac is counterclockwise. You can do this while keeping the same position, facing east and simply moving your mental focus around the circle. You can also rotate physically and face each sign when visualizing it. Feel free to choose what you feel is the most appropriate.

- Athena (Aries)
- Aphrodite (Taurus)
- Apollo (Gemini)
- Hermes (Cancer)
- Zeus (Leo)
- Demeter (Virgo)
- Hephaestus (Libra)
- Ares (Scorpio)
- Artemis (Sagittarius)
- Hestia (Capricorn)
- Hera (Aquarius)
- Poseidon (Pisces)

When you are back to facing east, take a moment of pause to focus on your breathing and your awareness of the zodiac all around you. Do not exceed a pause of three minutes.

Welcoming the Gods

Next, you should start your connection with the deities associated with the seven planets. It is very important to keep in mind what has been explained previously. The connection with the planet is based on respect and love. You are not trying to impose your will on a celestial power. Instead, you are building a real relationship with a deity that is unique. This is why you will use offerings and hymns for this purpose. The sequence you should use for each planet is the following: visualization, eight pronunciations of the sacred name, hymns, offerings, improvised declaration to the planet or eight pronunciations of the same sacred name, sealing of the divine connection.

Visualization: The representation you should visualize can be found in my book *The Divine Arcana of the Aurum Solis*. You can also use the representation of the divinity you like the most.

Sacred name: Pronounce the sacred name of the deity eight times. You should use your breath to create a regular sequence in this pronunciation.

Hymns: You can find in the appendices original translations of these hymns specially crafted for ritual use. They are used to easily activate the connection with the deities.

Offerings: Place the offerings you prepared on the floor in the direction of the planet. You can have a small plate or tray on which you place these offerings in front of the divinity you visualize.

Improvisation: Welcome the deity with words expressing your love and respect. If you are not comfortable with this kind of improvisation, just pronounce the sacred name of the deity eight more times.

Sealing: It is important to properly seal the relationship you just created with the deity. Focus on the representation of the divinity and visualize a light shining upon you. Take the time to feel this light surrounding you, filling your whole physical and subtle body. When this feeling is clear enough in your mind, place your left hand on the center of your chest and your right hand upon the left. Focus on the blessings of this divine presence within you. The best of this planetary power has been activated.

Balance the Powers

When the seven planets have been invoked one by one in such a way, be aware of their presence around you and of the connections that have been created. Visualize that harmony and balance between the deities themselves and with you have been created and sealed. Your new annual cycle, which will begin with your birthday, has been sealed, and you are ready to welcome the best divine support. Keep in mind that such events that will occur during the year are the consequences of past actions. This level of ritual practice can give you the best outcome possible by taking account of your past.

Pronounce the *Hymn to the Gods* by Proclus to end the practice before taking a few minutes to meditate and relax.

Theurgic Rituals

The Divine's presence has always been one of the greatest mysteries of the theurgic path. Several times in ancient texts and on the walls of Egyptian temples, magical and living statues are mentioned.[148] To approach these sacred rituals, extensive training and advanced initiations are required. However, the principles of this sacred process can be used to manifest the presence of a divinity in your life. This is what I'd like to present to you in this final section.

Practice: Consecration of a Divine Statue

Here is a powerful and very ancient practice you can use with large benefits.

Preparation

The altar can be placed in the west. The statue is placed close to the west side, facing east. You will be facing the statue.

The following ritual tools should be ready: a beeswax candle; salt; a large cup of water; perfume; anointing oil; offerings of food, alcohol, clothing, and possible jewelry for the statue; a white cloth to wipe the statue; and the statue itself.

---

148. Brian P. Copenhaver, ed., "To Asclepius," in *Hermetica: The Greek Corpus Hermeticum and the Latin Asclepius in a New English Translation, with Notes and Introduction*, reprint ed. (Cambridge University Press, 1995).

Immortal Theurgy

Opening
Everyone present gathers facing west. The officiant faces the assembly.

Ritual
Begin the ritual.

Officiant:
  May the ancient mysteries be once again accomplished!

Silent pause.
A bell is rung, and the officiant says:

  Salutation and again salutation to the High Guardians of the Glorious Star, who were, are, and are to come.

Assistant(s) or officiant:

  Salutation and again salutation in the splendor of the star which unites us.

Officiant:

  O you High Guardians, Hidden Adepti, Dwellers in Eternity.
  You have given signs and you have shown wonders, and you have revealed yourselves unto your children.

Assistant(s) or officiant:

  En Giro Torte Sol Ciclos Et Rotor Igne!

Officiant:

  Such are the words, such are the greetings!

Immortal Theurgy

A bell is rung, and the officiant says:

O Luminous Beings, see and hear us!
We work today in perfect harmony with your plans. We seek the fulfillment of our endeavor and ask the sowing shall be crowned in the harvest.
By the permanence of our plan, by this joy of research which is the wine of the will and which transforms the inexplicable, we invoke you!
By the living light and by the luminous life on this day and at this hour, I invoke you O Occult Beings!
Thus, light and life will rise to the radiance of a star, and this star will climb the summits forever illuminated.

A bell is rung, and the officiant says:

O Powerful and Immortal Deities, behold and hear my voice!
I am [surname and first name], your child, the guardian of the triple sacred flame of love, beauty, and truth.
I ask you to approve the work that I begin so that I can effectively and truly consecrate the statue of [name of the divinity].
May this sacred representation become the visible manifestation of the sacred powers of this god [or, this goddess].
May the blessing of the sacred and triple flame of goodness, beauty, and truth remain on this statue!
May love be the link and the seal of this operation!
So must it be!

A bell is rung.

Purification

The officiant extends their hands above the water.
The officiant keeps their hands in this position while saying the following:

> *Water has always been considered the purifying element that erases all stains. You, liquid and universal matrix whom I call, listen to me!*
>
> *Become again what you were at the beginning of time, when beings were born within you. Purify and sanctify this statue that I am going to wash so that it can welcome all the forces of the god [or, goddess] that he [or, she] represents.*

The officiant takes some salt and puts it in the water, saying:

> *You, salt, which is part of every living being, may your invisible structure be combined with this water to give life to everything that will be immersed in it.*

The officiant extends their hands above the water, visualizing this indissoluble union between these two elements at the origin of all life.

The officiant takes the statue and completely immerses it for a few moments. If this is not possible, the officiant simply pours water over the statue. If the material of the statue does not allow it, the officiant only sprinkles it with water. During this immersion, the officiant pronounces the following sentence:

> *By the power of water, be purified. May all the parts that you are made of be cleansed and vivified. As at the beginning of time, salt and water penetrate you and give you all the elements of life that you may need to begin to exist in the physical world. Be now as pure as when your form arose.*

The officiant takes the statue out of the water and wipes it with a clean, white cloth. As the officiant performs these gestures, they say:

> *The visible form of [name of the deity] has been purified and is now ready to receive the divine spirit it represents.*

Consecration

The officiant places the statue in the center of the altar and takes the perfume. The officiant raises the censer in the direction of the statue, saying:

May this fragrance penetrate the deepest parts of your being,
giving birth to the invisible body that surrounds you.

The officiant circles the statue clockwise three times with the censer. The first circle is at the level of the feet of the statue, the other at the middle level, and the other at the highest level of it, saying:

May this invisible wall that I create around you allow you to live
in peace in this sacred representation.

The officiant replaces the perfume on the altar, opens their arms, palms up, and declaims the hymn of the divinity of their choice.

Once the hymn has been declaimed, the officiant continues by saying:

O [name of the deity], hear my voice as I invoke you!
Listen to our call and our desire.
I invite you to descend into the body of this statue which represents you and which we have prepared as the worthy receptacle of your power.

A moment of silence.

The officiant lowers their arms, closes their eyes, and visualizes the deity in its celestial realm.

The officiant directs the palms of their hands toward the statue and visualizes a channel of light coming from the sky that goes down into it, connecting the sacred representation to the divinity that has just been invoked.

The officiant visualizes this energy concentrating on the statue and maintains the channel of light in the invisible while saying:

O you, [name of the deity], allow your power to descend at this
moment in this statue.
May it become the visible image of your invisible presence!

May the hymns that will be addressed to you in the visible world be heard from your invisible realm!
May you accept the offerings that will be made to you!
May this channel of light that links this representation to your true nature remain a reality.

The officiant lights a candle and raises it above the statue while saying:

May the pure divine light be honored!

A moment of silence is observed, then the officiant continues by saying:

We call upon you,
You, the secret flame who resides in the luminous and sacred silence!
You, the light and the great gods and the life of the worlds!
You, the powerful, the resplendent, whose Spirit fills everything!
You, the sanctified fire who is called upon in each sanctuary of the skies!

The candle is replaced on the altar.

Animation

The officiant takes the vial of anointing oil and puts a few drops of oil on their right thumb to draw a continuous line of oil from the top of the head to the foot of the statue along its spine.

The officiant proceeds in this way while saying:

O [name of the deity], may your power descend into this statue and give it life.

Then, the officiant anoints the mouth, saying:

Blessed be your lips through which holy words may be spoken.

The officiant anoints the heart, saying:

Blessed be your heart, which manifests your presence and your life.

The officiant anoints the feet, saying:

Blessed be your feet, by which you travel the worlds to come to us when we address our prayers to you.

The officiant then pours a little oil on the top of the head while saying:

By the powers of this oil, now become the visible manifestation of [name of the deity].
May through you all hymns, words, offerings be immediately addressed to [name of the deity].
Thus, I declare that you are the living and sacred manifestation of [name of the deity].

A silent pause, then the officiant takes the clothes for the statue, or the fabric of the chosen color, to cover it. The officiant dresses the statue with this fabric, leaving the face or the head uncovered and places the jewels or symbols that have been prepared.

Leaving the hands in contact with these clothes, the officiant declares:

May these clothes and jewels sanctify your presence.
May they manifest the love I have for you.

Offerings

The officiant then takes the offering of food and places it in front of the statue, saying:

Receive this food that I offer you.
May you accept this offering so that your visible appearance and your invisible bodies be vivified.

The officiant then takes the offering of alcohol (or other appropriate beverage) and places it in front of the statue, saying:

> *Receive this beverage that I offer you.*
> *May you accept this offering so that your visible appearance and your invisible bodies be vivified.*

The officiant raises their arms in a double salutation and declaims:

> *Thus, I, [surname and first name], consecrated this statue and invited [name of the deity] to reside there.*
> *In this visible and invisible statue, [name of the deity] resides now.*
> *May all who live there remain under this protection.*

The officiant lowers their arms and says:

> *May the blessings of the immortal divinities be ours, ever present in our hearts and homes.*
> *May we always honor them with dignity.*
> *May this place and all who live there always be protected and helped by the divine presence of [name of the deity].*
> *So must it be!*

A bell is rung, and the ritual is closed, usually with a meal shared with all the participants.

Before You Go

Theurgy is sometimes regarded as a type of ceremonial magic with a pinch of philosophy. A theurgist is typically depicted as an adept standing in a magical circle surrounded by candles and incense, conversing with the gods and goddesses. The theurgist, dressed in exotic or eccentric attire, may also be viewed as a kind of wizard, a relic of the past.

In reality, theurgy is a holistic system that encompasses all of the most important aspects of the Western tradition. From psychic ability development to physical body control, from a specific diet to knowledge of our subtle bodies, theurgy provides answers and guidance. Theurgy, which is neither a religion nor a set of superstitions, has been linked to the most famous Western philosophies. Learning and practicing the entire system of this tradition can positively transform your life and is the best preparation you can find for what comes next.

THEURGY: AN INTIMATE PATH TO THE GODS
CLIO AJANA

The theurgic path at its core stems from the desire for a strong connection with deity. While the specific term *theurgy* may be unknown to those outside of metaphysical or esoteric audiences, many feel the need to make a conscious effort to form an intense relationship with deity. In short, those who journey along the theurgic path are willing, hungry, and eager to gain understanding of what constitutes a deity connection. For some, it can occur through study of a specific metaphysical path, while others find the awareness comes from seemingly random or casual encounters, such as those often found in childhood. If such experiences later cause an individual to develop a connection based on more evolved experiences, the adult awareness of theurgy as an intimate path to the Gods can be both rewarding and challenging.

The Birth of My Desire

As a child, I began to hear what I thought was the voice of God calling my name. While the voice was at times softer in tone, like my mother's, and other times a bit heavier and husky, like my father's, the call always came in the middle of the night. The first two times, I raced from my tiny, green-canopied bed to knock hard on my parents' bedroom door, certain they had called me. Instead, they reassured me that they had not called my name. With a child's process of deduction, I presumed it was God. Who else would know me by name and wake me up in the middle of the night? Why would someone call a name if the desire to communicate was not present? The child, in simplicity, seeks to discover first who is calling and second why the individual is calling.

As adults, the human experience leads many onto a path to find the answers to these two questions. The nature of being human compels us to uncover the hidden when a discernable answer eludes quick discovery. From a child's simple curiosity, my desire grew into a craving for closeness and intimacy on a spiritual level. To uncover the why, there needed to be a conversation, yet to have that conversation, I needed to discern, discover, and identify the "who" that I could not explain.

Raised in a traditional Christian theological framework, I was grounded in Trinitarian doctrine, the concept of God as Father, Son (Jesus), and Holy Spirit (Catholic) or Holy Ghost (Protestant). No other possibilities existed in my world as a child. As a result, as a child of nine, I wondered why a doctrine that showcased the trinity as a coequal measurement presented Jesus (the son) as the most important in reality. In my family, filled with ministers and missionaries, the focus was on maintaining adherence to Christian orthodoxy, or the right belief system. Orthopraxy, doing the right thing per Christian teaching, would serve as a guide to living a fulfilling life. A devout Christian life meant believing that connecting with "God" or deity meant using actions to ensure salvation or a positive afterlife.

I saw the continued pattern of unanswered questions, perhaps due to my young age or just being female, evolve into a bitter resentment. In the end, my animosity fueled a resistance that symbolized the start of my theurgic journey. I had a simple desire to find, know, and understand God in the same way that I would have an ordinary friendship or relationship with another person. As a child, I did not know that what I sought was *henōsis*, a union or oneness in mystical terms; however, the path to this sense of oneness would take several decades of wrong turns, which provided fodder to continue the journey within.

After more than a decade of wandering and ignoring the call, I thought I found connection with G-d, upon my conversion to Judaism. I was attracted to the practice of *Tikkun Olam*, the responsibility within Judaism to repair the world in its present form through social justice. In mystical terms, the need to do good by healing the fractures present in what I would later understand in Hellenic Alexandrian Witchcraft as the world soul appealed to me. The spiritual appeal would be through actions defined by and understood by my fellow humans.

Looking back, I realize that my first conversion to another monotheistic religious tradition became my first contact with theurgy. It was limited to knowledge as stated through the lens of an individual relationship with the manner of the Christian God or G-d/Hashem ("The Name") as a Jew. In Christianity, my primary focus was orthodoxy with assumed belief. In Judaism, my inspirational focus was orthopraxy, taking on the mantle of correct action. This allowed me to presume that it is not blind faith but right action that would lead to divine closeness.

In truth, these steps performed an internal dance, common to all Seekers on the path toward intimate divine connection. While they work for some, for me, these monotheistic paths did not open the well of devotion and closeness with deity.

There are many reasons one might choose to leave a particular religious or spiritual path. While some reasons can involve trauma, anger, and hurt, I consider myself lucky that my partings never contained sorrow or pain. I mention this because some reading this work might presume that choosing a new path must be accompanied by anger, grief, fear, frustration, or other negative emotions. While it is important to empathize with those who are traumatized by past religious experiences, it is significant to recall that not all converts feel spiritual distress through this process.

As one seeks intimate connection with the Divine, there is a need to acquire increased faith. This process occurs while simultaneously shedding unneeded parts of the self by transforming them into what is useful on the theurgic path. This personal realization came as I was about to step off my previous path and experience a transformation.

Brush with the Theurgic Path

At dawn on my thirty-seventh birthday in Bryce Canyon National Park, my first connection with the Gods, as I came to know them, occurred. Red spires of hoodoos rose in the distance. The tall, jagged edges of rust, greenish-gold, and burnt orange appeared almost mystical through the thin veil of tall green trees. The air was still, crisp, and calm. The sun would not rise fully for another forty-five minutes. Outside a space where I was not meant to be, due to a mix-up in accommodations, I took the opportunity to meditate and to reconsider where my life was going. In silence, I saw my life; I did not like the image. My best friends were leaving town with promises to stay in touch that few manage to keep. My job paid the bills but held little excitement. The words in the *siddur*, the Jewish prayer book, were reduced to recitation based on principle rather than on faith. I recited the words as my heart ran close to empty. I *davened* (prayed) twice a day, and regularly during services in *shul*, only to find few answers.[149] If G-d was talking, I did not understand.

As the tendrils of predawn sunlight spilled across the rocks, my body relaxed in enveloping warmth, so warm that I removed my heavy sweater and one of my thick T-shirts. The air caressed me. While I heard no voices and I was physically alone in the predawn darkness, I knew that my lifelong desire was happening: My soul truly was conversing with the Divine. I felt a presence, neither completely masculine, nor feminine, just gentle and loving.

Like the fairy tale of "Goldilocks and the Three Bears," the God of my childhood represented a stern, disciplined life, focused on salvation through Jesus. This connection was too harsh. The Jewish G-d of my twenties and thirties exemplified the presence of a more loving but still distant deity. While Judaism fulfilled my needs for a vibrant social community and the elaborate religious rituals that I missed from childhood, it still did not feel strong enough.

I needed more of deity's embrace. Although I did not know it at the time, my awakening in Bryce Canyon National Park represented a middle path,

---

149. To *daven* (pray) in a traditional *shul* (Orthodox) or a synagogue follows specific rhythmic body patterns, sometimes appearing as bowing, which are repeated throughout the service. The practice is known as "davening." In shul, and later in synagogues, my level of religious devotion was at times acknowledged based on how much how I patterned my davening.

one that was neither too harsh, nor too understated. It would be the theurgic path I needed to thrive and share with others.

In those moments in Bryce Canyon National Park, I embraced the presence of a loving warmth and a sense of rightness with the world and my life. For a split second, I saw a complete image of my life spread before me in a mosaic pattern. For the first time, it was good. Time in this space did not flow in seconds, minutes, or even millennia. As a recipient, I understood the offer. For brief moments, I could not feel my legs. I did not fall, yet I could not feel the ground. The wind itself held me and provided a sense of true communion and a sense of unity. The image disappeared.

In that moment, I no longer experienced isolation or separation from the whole. My spiritual and everyday life merged. My soul became complete.

First Steps on the Path

Theurgy at its core is nostalgia—a way to navigate through pain the way "home" to a solid connection with the Divine. Home is the standard that we seek as humans yet cannot claim because we do not know the boundaries. The theurgic path is a journey of discovery. Each person walks the path and experiences encounters along the way

Four years after my experience at Bryce Canyon, I found myself at the opposite end of my family of origin's worship patterns. I was now a pantheist polytheist fostering a relationship with the goddess Hekate. In addition, I was newly following a witchcraft tradition that was also both pantheistic and polytheistic. I would later discover that this tradition utilized a theurgic path.

On some level internally, I realized that the process of henōsis, joining with the Gods, was finally in reach when I began study with Hellenic Alexandrian Witchcraft and Spiritual Tradition (hereafter known as "HA"). As a pantheist and polytheist tradition, HA encourages working with several deities simultaneously in magical workings. The tradition embraces a core reliance upon a strong connection with the Gods through religious practice, including prayer, divination, and conscious effort to connect with the Divine. This undertaking would encompass a number of years: In terms of theurgy, the journey truly is far more valuable than the destination.

In HA, theurgic experiences common for new Glorian (Initiate), Protogonos (First Degree), Mystagogos (Second Degree), and Pantos Psyche

(Third Degree) include a variety of exercises, which allow the individual to explore without knowing that the very use of a variety of texts provides a deeper connection with the Gods overall.

Some texts used to effect this internal change included Thomas Taylor's *The Hymns of Orpheus*, Stephen Flowers's *Hermetic Magic*, Sallustius's *On the Gods and the World*, Cicero's De Natura Deorum (*On the Nature of the Gods*), the Roman virtues, *The Chaldean Oracles (Zoroaster)*, the maxims on ethics of Democritus and Diogenes, Epicurus's *Principal Doctrines* (also known as his *Sovran Maxims*), Pythagoras's *The Golden Verses of Pythagoras*, and the wisdom of Iamblichus regarding the *Monad, Nous*, and psyche.[150]

Upon reflection, the training that reading and analyzing these philosophical texts provided was one of the best transitions to a theurgical path. I was learning as the philosophers themselves did by interacting with the Gods to acquire the wisdom and laws to form a deeper connection with the Divine. Learning arises from interacting with the philosophies.

The use of texts such as *The Chaldean Oracles (Zoroaster)*, *On the Gods and the World*, and *On the Nature of the Gods*, as well as practices found in the Greek Qabalah in particular, became a part of the earliest theurgical practices advocated in HA. Perhaps I did not realize it at the time, as my entry into HA occurred simultaneously with the completion of a graduate degree program that required a heavy reading load and a touch of philosophy.

While immersion in philosophical texts engaged the mind, the traditional daily rites of prayer, ritual, and meditation trained the body. Development of a morning routine of regular and full prayer using the *Dialexis Stauros, Dialexis Phos*, and *Dialexis Latreia* provided an energetic foundation that effectuated a deep focus and practice with the Gods overall. These exercises cleanse the spirit, and during the first several years of my theurgic connection, it was the consistent repetition of practice that provided an additional layer to the feeling of devotion to each of my deities. This perfects the

---

150. These philosophical texts, including those addressing Greek, Roman, and Egyptian philosophy, were required reading to allow the initiate to learn and understand the concepts that form the basis of Hellenic Alexandrian Witchcraft and Spiritual Tradition (capitalized as full title of the tradition here). In addition, initiates were encouraged to find more philosophical texts to increase connection with the Divine.

human body and soul. Regular use of these practices provides closeness to the Divine and nourishes an overall theurgic connection with the Gods.

Other symbols that I used on a regular basis to maintain this connection included the maintenance of a "Magickal Journal," which recorded my findings and my expansion into outside resources. I considered these materials resources to start finding the answers rather than the answers themselves. In HA, the encouragement of adding texts falls squarely into the scholarly realm rather than the popular culture realm. Engagement of the mind with the text and honing of the body with regular practice sculpted the path from novice to dedicant and from initiate to more advanced theurgical study.

The traditional pathworking in HA encourages the use of both a Magickal Journal and a Book of Shadows for two different purposes. I considered the first a subsection of the second, including my magical and solitary practice, while I used my larger Book of Shadows as a complete record of my dreamwork, spellwork, conversations with the Gods, and insights on my work with herbs.

The terms *Magickal Journal* and *Book of Shadows* can be interchangeable, as it is the overall purpose that matters, not the name given to the collected receptacle of wisdom.

What I did not know at that time was how the reading of these philosophical texts and the repetition of rites would effectuate a deep connection with the Gods in a divine manner.

Daily engagement with rites such as the *Dialexis Stauros*, *Dialexis Phos*, and *Dialexis Latreia* provided an energetic foundation that assisted in theurgic connection with the Gods.

The exploration of working magical acts with the Gods and in concert with deity is far different than the commonly seen thaumaturgy, which many define as what we consider miracles, incantations, and outward spellwork.

The choice to manipulate natural forces for a specific gain in spellwork is thaumaturgy and commonly seen and expressed in what many consider to be "magic." What I would learn in the HA tradition would be working with the Gods rather than my own individual, perhaps too-human, selfish desires. Overall, within the practice of theurgy, I found the answer to a more perfect union with the deity because my goal was communication with the deity.

As a budding theurgist, what I appreciated about the exercises at each level of pre-initiation and initiation was the specificity in form. As a living pantheist polytheist practice, the HA tradition encourages practices specific to the goal of achieving henōsis (oneness with the Gods).

When we take a pantheistic point of view where nature and divinity are in all things, then the base understanding of theurgy and henōsis, the "oneness," are no longer vague concepts but moments of pure awareness and awakening.

Constellation of the Worshipped

In the HA tradition, the Constellation of the Worshipped is a list indicating the deities with whom a devotee, dedicant, or *mageia* continues to forge a relationship.[151] Depending on the individual's observance, this can be a permanent list featuring the same deity or deities with no changes ever, or it can change based on the growth and evolution of spiritual ties with deity. The choice of when to create and change the list of deities varies with the individual.

As a dedicant and early initiate, my primary goal was to gain a deeper intimacy with the Gods in a more successful manner than that gained by exposure to previous religions. To that end, the use of prayer and meditation, the practice of writing entries in a Magickal Journal, and a continuation of exercises meant to strengthen my spiritual development in solitary practice were crucial.

I quickly realized that the formation of a solid relationship with at least one or two deities became easier when a spiritual foundation was integrated fully into one's life. For example, I found a key component is the use of

---

151. *Mageia* as a term has many connotations depending on context. For example, in reference to Goetia, the term *mageia* is considered low magic use, while theurgy is known as divine magic. Within HA, its general meaning is anyone who is a witch and who is practicing HA. As the entire tradition focuses on divine connection and divine magic (e.g., theurgy), the tradition does not see the use of the term *mageia* as negative, but neutral. In addition, the obligation of the mageia in continuing to learn and practice the HA tradition are the requirements of learning about the self, connecting with the Divine, and using the exercises given within the tradition to improve the individual.

divination within ritual circle, both to demonstrate a level of required proficiency for the individual and as a manner to connect more deeply with the Gods.

My earliest circles with Hekate, Hermes Mercurius Trismegistus, and Apollo focused on the need for knowledge acquisition in a spiritual sense and in a literal academic sense, as I was in graduate school in a new place where I needed guidance as to how to navigate an uncertain path.[152] This is not unlike the very path I was seeking to navigate with the Gods themselves.

Within a year of my first-degree initiation, I noticed the more I used divination within a ritual circle, the stronger my connection with various deities became. The goal of individual religious personal development through divination presents the reward of continued elevation within a given tradition; moreover, the use of divination assists in self-growth over the longer period. The following four exercises form just some of the core beginning steps in theurgic practice.

Exercise 1: Daily Practice—Deity of the Day

My personal theurgic practice includes working with deity partners to achieve spiritual goals using a specified timeline of devotion.

As a new polytheist, one of my earliest exercises consisted of fleshing out a relationship with individual deities through a deity-of-the-day calendar. A deity-of-the-day system helps to develop awareness as to where the individual is starting and where they would like to be. Honesty and openness about how close an individual is to a particular deity assists in forming a continuing religious ethic. After spending my first few years working with a deity each day, it became unwieldy, and I was able to narrow my focus to a deity-of-the-month calendar—in other words, doing essentially the same daily practice outlined below but changing the primary deity with whom I was communicating each month instead of each day.

My daily practice consisted of a short grounding and meditation session followed by a visit with one deity in ritual circle. This ritual contact includes the use of tools, such as a basic altar dedicated to chosen deities and

---
152. In HA, we see Hermes Mercurius Trismegistus as a syncretic deity combination of Hermes, Thoth, and Anubis, with aspects from each of these deities.

divination tools like tarot cards, runes, or a pendulum. Divination practice assists in further skill development, which enhances the depth of your connection to deity.

Within ritual circle space, conversations with the Gods about everyday problems eventually evolve into a way to understand the cosmos with regular practice. Relationships with the Gods become more active than passive. This foundation lends itself to practices that connect us to the Divine through intuitive knowing. This deeper wisdom eventually leads to the immaterial, which brings about henōsis.

I encourage everyone to try this. Create your own deity-of-the-day calendar and build a daily practice incorporating elements from your tradition. Choose some deities for your Constellation of the Worshipped with whom you are unfamiliar, as this is an excellent way to start building familiarity with and knowledge of them. For the chronologically inclined, keeping a calendar record for the deity of the day may be useful. Try incorporating divination into your meetings. The point is the connection. Consistent effort leads to meaningful results.

Exercise 2: Prayer Circle for the Deity of the Day

This prayer circle uses the deity-of-the-day format, but instead of a standard circle formation with one deity, it focuses on the presence of multiple deities and the impartation of knowledge. My initial group consisted primarily of Greek Olympian (Poseidon, Aphrodite, Artemis, Hermes, Athena), Chthonic (Hekate, Demeter, Persephone, Hades, Hermes as psychopomp), Egyptian (Sekhmet, Thoth, Seshat, Ptah), and Roman (Jupiter, Juno, Minerva, Vulcan) deities who worked with me as guardians and guides during my pre-initiatory, first- and second-degree periods.

Sit or stand at your altar. Ground and center in the usual way common to your tradition or spiritual practice. Banish or purify the space, again according to your tradition or path.

Following the HA tradition, I cast a circle and bless it using the four elements of water, earth, air, and fire. In HA, water and earth are paired for the blessing, while fire is paired with air for a similar purpose. If this is not a part of your tradition, then find a meaningful way to denote sacred space, a safe container in which to call your deities.

As you create sacred space, your focus is a prayer for sensitivity to the Gods, such as being able to hear and understand them, as well as maintain awareness during the healing process.

Call all of the deities you have been working with in your deity-of-the-day calendar.

Within the circle or sacred space, after calling all deities, spend time speaking with each. Take notes with a writing instrument. Build up from 5–6 minutes per deity to a regular practice of 20–30-minute conversations and activities with a deity after two or three months. This can include reading parts of one's Magickal Journal and conversing with the Gods. The most important part of theurgic practice is to see the Gods as true relationships. After the allotted time is through, thank the deities, release the circle or the sacred space you've created, and add any additional notes to your Magickal Journal.

Exercise 3: Magickal Journal Review with Deity During Ritual Circle

One thing I found that seemed small at first, but very helpful, was the suggestion by several of my deities, especially Hekate, that every two to six months I give an honest read of my journal and the steps that had been suggested by the Gods. While they did not say "today's the day," they noted patterns that I could work on and helped to figure out how to work with deities both individually and in group form to correct these patterns.

During the early days of one's path, the initial tendrils of communion with the Divine may not be necessarily 100 percent solid. As humans, the tendency to be cocky or too sure about the certainty of the connection occurs until something happens that reminds the individual that human frailty is also a part of the theurgic-divine connection.

One exercise that helps with this part of the journey is a periodic review of one's Magickal Journal, which some call a *Book of Shadows*. During my regular circle time with a particular deity or deities, I would take my book out and review my notes with that particular deity or deities. Some were very light on the review. Hekate is not—or at least not with me. I needed the firm structure and review. My connection with her now is due in great part to those regular sessions and reviews of my Magickal Journal notes. My review would include requests I made of her, requests she made of me, insights gathered during circle time, notes from any divination done during circle time, and notes from any spellwork done in ritual circle.

Example for In-Circle Deity Review (Hekate)
This example is based on my years of working with Hekate.

Items I would review in my Magickal Journal during ritual circle include:
- Requests made of Hekate.
- Requests she made of me.
- Insights from time spent with Hekate in ritual circle.
- Notes from any divination done for the self during ritual.
- Notes and results from any spellwork started during ritual.

Questions I would pose and add to my review in my journal:
- Ask Hekate about any changes in preferred food, drink, and other sacrificial offerings to her.
- Ask Hekate about the best time and method for contact with her.
- Ask myself how close I felt with her both during and after the working: very close, close, kind of close, not as close, need to feel closer, or not at all close.

This last question was often the most important, as it provided guidance not just on my theurgic path, but my overall spiritual path and growth in my tradition.

Like any solid relationship, the connection needs regular feeding and nourishing on both sides. Taking 15–20 minutes early on can save a great deal of anguish and uncertainty regarding the divine connection later. Overall, the review is a gift to the self as well as encouragement to dive more deeply into one's relationship with the self on an individual level as well as with the Divine.

Try doing a Magickal Journal review. Banish or purify and create sacred space as you normally would. Call your deity into circle. Look through the past several months of your Magickal Journal for the workings or communications you've had with them (or those since your last review) and apply the questions from the template above. If your deity has different requests of you, they will let you know and you can tailor the template to your needs. Try to be as open to receiving honest feedback as you can, and you can learn a lot from this review.

The biggest lesson is in the realization that the failures and mistakes are just as big a part of the theurgic path as the joyous aspect. At a certain point, the connection made—reinforced with each ritual, each sabbat observance, each gathering with community and like-minded souls—goes to renew and refresh the soul.

This renewal or refreshment of the soul is necessary for the Divine and the individual. The theurgic path requires that the individual check in with the Divine as well as themselves to make sure this is the direction where one either wants or needs to be. One irony is that the more you delve, the deeper you realize whether the path is for you or not.

Exercise 4: Remapping the Constellation

As mentioned earlier, in the HA tradition we will sometimes change or adjust our Constellation of the Worshipped according to different priorities or goals, or simply because sometimes our time with a given deity has come to an end and it's time to move on. The choice of when to change the Constellation varies with the individual.

Personally, I enjoy starting the new year, during the sabbat of Saturnalia, with an extended reflection on deity connection. Saturnalia within the HA tradition is a season roughly equivalent to December 17–23, with the full feast and celebration on the longest night and shortest day—the Winter Solstice. As it is the start of the active, or light, half of the year, ritual activities are focused on what might be considered secular New Year's wishes or resolutions. For me, it's a good time to dedicate myself to a group of deities for a yearlong focus. Many choose other dates of importance to them. Which date you choose doesn't matter as long as it is significant and you remember to revisit your commitments each year.

This was how my personal practice evolved after the first several years of just effectuating connection through a deity-of-the-day calendar, followed by a deity of the month. Don't feel you need to do this exercise if you aren't ready. However, if you feel you are at a stage where you could switch things up, choose a time of year, make your goals, and start connecting with a new Constellation annually.

Progress Becomes Evident

The methods outlined above for you to try will produce results. As a new initiate, this practice of meeting and working in depth with a particular deity for a set period, starting with a day, then a week, and then a month, allowed me to discern traits that I wished to emphasize or discard in my relations with the Gods themselves. During an early two-year period, for example, my deity-of-the-day records marked strengthening in my relationship with Hestia, goddess of the hearth, through baking, anything involving the kitchen and home, and making my workplace peaceful.

Another result of a strengthened theurgic bond is the presence of tender and intimate moments, such as when Hekate, one of the first deities who guided me onto my path, acted as nurse when I was ill with a respiratory infection. I was mobile enough to hear and respond to her voice as her aspect Hekate Soteira, the Divine Nurse. Upon urging me to get out of bed, she led me to the back of my kitchen cabinet where I kept a bottle of whiskey or bourbon, not for myself, but for her as an offering. She had me drink a small glass with a mixture of teas that I cannot recall to this day, topped with a bit of lemon. It tasted quite foul, but it worked both to bring up the crud and to sweat out whatever it was that I had. I felt gratitude for her presence in those moments. This was after about three years of near-constant daily devotion in which we engaged in many conversations, and I would often read my creative and academic works to her, developing our bond. After the health incident, I noticed an increased closeness and connection to her, which remains until this day.

In later initiatory stages, the use of the four exercises above provided benefits when starting, amending, or concluding a deity relationship with grace. The long-term result from the above example was a deeper engagement with Hekate. While she remains a part of my permanent deity grouping, there are times when our ritual conversations result in the need for other deities and deity projects to take precedence. And with the annual revision of my Constellation of the Worshipped, that is both understandable and possible.

While individual practice will vary, I spent between 30 and 90 minutes each morning in a state of meditation, conversation, or ritual practice with one of my deities. Barring unavoidable circumstances, I was advised to always perform these rites in a well-prepared space set aside for maximum focus and minimum distractions. In our hectic society, not everything can be done in the car or in a rush. These morning sessions became my solace when life became overwhelming. Clear exceptions would be for those who, due to circumstances, have no privacy except for time spent in their car, their workplace, or outdoors.

As HA is a pantheist and polytheist path, I would gain lists of tasks from one or all my deities. These lists worked as a method to streamline my external life with my spiritual life and theurgic aspirations. I learned to accept changes as a part of my journey to connect with the Gods with resentment as well as joy.

In many ways, true connection comes through practice, repeated memorization, and continued exposure to, awareness of, and understanding of a desired connection.

Continuing the Theurgic Path

The juxtaposition of certain divination systems, such as astrology, numerology, and tarot, added to planetary hours, deity correspondences, and invocation through hymns, provides a method for a deepening of practice and a greater integration of the process of henōsis. Through repetition, I find the use of divination elicits a type of intimacy that furthers closeness with the Gods in a consistent manner. Divination utilization furthers work on a given theurgic path, thus expanding an appreciation for divine communion.

The Johari Window is a four-paned communication tool a bit like a rectangular Venn diagram that shows parts that are known or unknown to the self overlapping with areas known or unknown to others.[153] Not surprisingly, the largest area of mysteries consists of items not known to the self or

---

153. Joseph Luft and Harrington Ingham, *The Johari Window, a Graphic Model of Interpersonal Awareness* (Proceedings of the Western Training Laboratory in Group Development. University of California, Los Angeles, 1955), https://www.hee.nhs.uk/sites/default/files/documents/Johari%20window.pdf.

to others. In a way, the practice of theurgy is a type of heuristic practice, as it does indeed enable the individual to learn something for themselves, with the assistance of and communion with deity.

Combining these four areas (deity-of-the-day ritual practice, divination, planetary hours, and deity correspondence) helped me to increase my individual self-awareness while reducing areas that remained unknown due to lack of closeness and communication with the Gods.

This openness and willingness to speak with the Gods frequently and to listen carefully generates a type of synergetic increase, which can be best understood as steps toward a type of perfection and connection with the Gods.

A combination of ritual, divination, and conversation creates a more active connection with the Divine on the theurgic path. As individuals, if the goal is to seek oneness with the Gods, then effective practices to help the individual reach this state of unity are both varied and necessary. We talked about conversation above; now, let's turn to a couple of methods that can help you further fine-tune your ritual work with deities.

Exercise 5: Crafting with Planetary Hours

There are many ways to craft a ritual, and the use of planetary hours is a common Western Magical Tradition tool that provides an excellent guide to pinpoint the timing of communication with the Gods, as well as any thaumaturgic spellwork. You can use the planetary hours to help with the effects or outcomes desired in the spellwork being performed. Remember, there are two parts: What is the desired result, and what is the required outcome? While less important during urgent situations, I recommend entering a circle on a day or at a time most suited for the deity in question. When in doubt, ask the deity as to the best day to use. For example, Friday is a common day for love deities and excellent for conversations with Aphrodite, Venus, and Hathor; however, if the focus is on communication, Wednesday might work well as a backup when one cannot wait for two days. Once the day has been chosen, you can choose the appropriate planetary hour to begin conversation or do magic with the deity. For example, if you wanted to work on relationship issues but couldn't wait until Friday, you could choose the planetary hour of Venus on the day of your choice instead. If you wanted to work on

Theurgy: An Intimate Path to the Gods

abundance, perhaps you would choose the planetary hour of Jupiter, while if your focus is clear communication, you would choose the planetary hour of Mercury or do spellwork on a Wednesday.

If this is of interest to you, pursue it further by incorporating planetary hours into your next ritual or spell. A good practice is to plan your ritual working around helpful days and times. There is an online planetary hours site that calculates planetary hours for most any city or town on the planet, which is far easier than calculating by hand: https://planetaryhours.net/. To learn more, *Planetary Magick: Invoking and Directing the Power of the Planets* by Melita Denning and Osborne Phillips is an excellent primer for the novice or advanced practitioner.

To engage even more deeply in planetary motions, an excellent reference site at the time of this writing is the United States Naval Observatory Astronomical Applications Department Data Services; one subsection hosts a variety of links for dates from 1700 to 2100 for a variety of planets, bright stars, our sun and moon, and other bodies.[154]

Exercise 6: Use of Numerological Calculations

Numerological calculations accomplish a similar function as planetary hours. Before entering a circle, it is helpful to calculate the number for the universal year, month, day, and essence for a particular date. For a personal ritual to speak with deity, it helps to complete one's individual calculation. For example, let's calculate the numerology for the Pomonalia Sabbat (Rite of Hecatia) that occurred on October 31, 2024. The full calculation for the universal year is 2 + 0 + 2 + 4 = 8. To get the universal month, you add the month number to the year; the universal month for October was a 9 for the year 2024 (because 1 + 0 + 2 + 0 + 2 + 4 = 9). The universal day is calculated next by adding the day (3 + 1) to the universal month (9), which comes to 13, and that reduces to a 4 (1 + 3 = 4). Finally, the essence is calculated from adding together the universal year, month, and day and then reducing it to a single digit: 8 + 9 + 4 = 21,

---

154. The primary index for the Astronomical Applications Department Data Services is https://aa.usno.navy.mil/data/index. The page "Dates of Primary Phases of the Moon" contains data spanning from 1700 to 2100 and allows querents to see timing for past ritual acts and spellwork, as well as calculate current or future rituals: https://aa.usno.navy.mil/data/MoonPhases.

and 2 + 1 = 3. This essence is the overall vibration of the day. As an example, this indicates a good date for working, organizing, and building a strong foundation (4), with the overall glow of celebration and creativity (3).

While there are many books that are available on numerology, for those just starting out, find reprints from the 1970s. My personal favorite is Kevin Quinn Avery's *The Numbers of Life: The Hidden Power in Numerology*. It covers the Pythagorean and Chaldean systems. The book also has a section called "The Second Study," which includes several in-depth techniques and introduces a Qabalistic system that he calls "A New Quaballah" for those with interest. You may wish to find the numerological system that makes the most sense to you and work exclusively with it.

Applying numerology will help alert you when a chosen day is completely unsuitable for your ritual goal, and you can reschedule it. Or it can highlight the energies of the day so you can best use them to your advantage in ritual and with deity communication.

Theurgy Is Worth the Effort

Effective practices to help the individual reach henōsis, a state of unity with the Gods, are both varied and necessary. The utilization of a deity-of-the-day construct, the adoption of a regular conversation with individual deity or deities in ritual space, and a strong connection with the Divine requires a path of active learning about the Gods and a practice that integrates the Gods in every aspect and at every level of an individual life.

For those beginning their theurgic paths, do not lose hope. My theurgic journey began within monotheism and blossomed with my initiation into and practice of the HA tradition, where I began to recognize and exercise theurgy on a larger scale with regular practice. What keeps me going is a full commitment to the experience of the connection with deity.

The journey is one of understanding, hope, and discovery. Shrouded in mystery for some, the search for connection with the Divine represents theurgy in its purest form. The role that Pagan, Heathen, and polytheist traditions play in any given practice and discovery of a theurgic path varies; however, the result is the same: a uniquely carved path to achieve oneness with the Divine overall and the Gods as we understand them. Theurgy is the answer to my search for a more perfect connection with the Divine.

The theurgic path demands a brutal honesty of the self and with the deities with whom one is working. It is not always convenient, either in time or focus, as the crux of the issue may not appear to be clear, understandable, or of immediate benefit. As a devotee or practitioner of theurgy, at times only faith as the individual understands it will assist in untangling the situation. A core relationship formed by the bond of honesty, a consistent practice, and the overall feeding of the divine connection makes the effort formed on the theurgic path worth it.

A QABALISTIC APPROACH TO THEURGY
TONY MIERZWICKI

Theurgy can certainly be dated back to the Greco-Roman period, with its roots stretching back to even earlier times. It was thought of as a highly technical path practiced by philosophers using the magickal and spiritual techniques available to them, yet its fundamentals are readily understandable. Its basic principles are still being taught within magickal orders such as the Hermetic Order of the Golden Dawn, the A∴ A∴, and the Ordo Aurum Solis ("Order of the Gold of the Sun").

This chapter presents a plan of attack for those wanting to incorporate theurgy into a path where it is not taught. The Qabalah comes to mind, because an important aim of theurgy is ascension through the planetary spheres, and the Qabalah has ascension baked into it. The Qabalah can be seen as a cosmic "filing cabinet," which has numerous correspondences for the planetary deities and archetypal energies ruling the days of the week, making it a great example and starting point.[155]

---

155. Israel Regardie, *A Garden of Pomegranates: An Outline of the Qabalah*, rev. and enlarged, 2nd ed. (Llewellyn Publications, 1985), 37.

Attunement to these archetypal energies refers to forging a link between aspects of ourselves and the corresponding aspects of the Divine. Thus, for example, a link can be forged between our intellect and divine intellect or our capacity to love with divine love. Bringing the Divine into everyday life can be used to enhance all aspects of ourselves in a systematic fashion.

As a bonus, attunement to these energies will enhance many magickal practices not connected with theurgy, and this benefit will be discussed later. Another important matter to be discussed is the need to exercise discernment when communications from deities are received. Finally, those already practicing contemporary theurgy may well benefit from a different perspective.

A flexible approach to theurgy may yield results for those who do not respond to more traditional methods.[156]

Before the fun practical aspects of attunement can be discussed, it is necessary to cover some background information. John Opsopaus's essay in this anthology, "Practicing Theurgy in the Platonic Tradition," provides a wonderful overview of the history of theurgy.[157] Theurgists would master a range of techniques, which led to the soul purifying itself from the pollution of matter and ascending to its source to effect union with the Divine (*henōsis*).[158]

Ascension Processes in the Ancient World

The importance of attunement to the planetary deities and archetypal energies ruling the days of the week becomes apparent once it is understood that each of the planets is a stepping stone for the soul in its ascent to its heavenly home.

The Chaldean Oracles were believed by theurgists to be of divine origin. The surviving fragments of the Chaldean Oracles have "references to

---

156. Brandy Williams touched on the need for flexibility in *For the Love of the Gods: The History and Modern Practice of Theurgy*.
157. E. R. Dodds, *The Greeks and the Irrational* (University of California Press, 1951), 293–9; Garth Fowden, *The Egyptian Hermes: A Historical Approach to the Late Pagan Mind* (Princeton University Press, 1993), 283–85.
158. Dodds, *The Greeks and the Irrational*, 130–31.

initiations, purifications, and consecrations."[159] These suggest a temporary experience of immortality by way of ascending to the realm of the Divine. The process involved a breathing technique of inhaling the sun's rays, and with the help of angels, the soul would separate from the body.[160] The most obvious references are Fragments 9a, 110, 115, 116, 122, 124, 130, 131, 158, 164.[161]

Within the *Greek Magical Papyri*, we find the "Mithras Liturgy" [*PGM* IV:475–829] dating back to the early fourth century, which gives instructions for a soul to ascend past the planets and various forces by using a number of hymns, names of power, breathing techniques, and sounds. The end result is that the soul gains immortality.[162] Very similar techniques of ascent are used in the *Nag Hammadi* text *Marsanes*, which uses hymn recitation, angel names, and vowel chants.[163]

Ascents also occur in Jewish writings, such as that of Rabbi Nehunya in the fourth-to-sixth century text *Hekhalot Rabbati* (*Greater Palaces*).[164] The goal of this ascent to the chambers of the palace of the seventh heaven is not made clear; however, in another Jewish text, the *Merkabah Rabbah* asserts that it will "lengthen days to eternal life," meaning that it will confer immortality.[165]

The primary aim of Hermeticism is to attain knowledge of the Divine. This idea is common in Jewish and Christian usage but rare in classical and Hellenistic paganism. In Hermeticism, however, knowledge of deity wasn't

....
159. Naomi Janowitz, *Magic in the Roman World: Pagans, Jews and Christians* (Routledge, 2001), 80.
160. Janowitz, *Magic in the Roman World*, 80.
161. Ruth Majercik, trans., *The Chaldean Oracles: Text, Translation, and Commentary* (Brill, 1989), 53, 91, 93, 95, 97, 99, 109, 111.
162. Janowitz, *Magic in the Roman World*, 80–81.
163. Birger A. Pearson, trans., *Marsanes*, in *The Nag Hammadi Library: The Definitive Translation of the Gnostic Scriptures Complete in One Volume*, ed. James M. Robinson, rev. ed. (HarperCollins, 1990), 460–71; Janowitz, *Magic in the Roman World*, 114.
164. Morton Smith, trans., *Hekhalot Rabbati: The Greater Treatise Concerning the Palaces of Heaven*, corrected Gershom Scholem, transcribed and ed. Don Karr (updated 2024), https://constable.blog/wp-content/uploads/HEKHALOT_RABBATI.pdf.
165. *Merkabah Rabbah*, quoted in Janowitz, *Magic in the Roman World*, 81–82; Rebecca Macy Lesses, *Ritual Practices to Gain Power: Angels, Incantations, and Revelation in Early Jewish Mysticism* (Trinity Press International, 1998), 336–44.

the end goal, but rather it was important to strive for this to enable the soul to be released from the material world and acquire immortality.[166]

The first text in the *Corpus Hermeticum*, the *Poimandres*, also features an ascent. Poimandres (*poimên*, "shepherd" and *anêr*, "man"), the primary deity in the text, is equated with Hermes Trismegistus. The ascent culminates in deification (becoming a deity). Interestingly, the *Poimandres* contains numerous Jewish components, including allusions to Genesis 1–2 and Isaiah 6:3 extracted from the liturgical Kedusha, which was attributed to the Cherubim when they bore the throne of the Lord but was later used in deification rituals.[167]

Deification is actually a constant thread throughout the *Corpus Hermeticum*, although the details vary from tractate to tractate:

- The eleventh tractate states that in order to achieve deification, all time and all knowledge has to be found within, which is analogous to saying that humans are a microcosm of the macrocosm.[168]
- The fourth tractate states that humans cannot be engaged in the mortal realm as well as the divine realm and must hate their bodies in order to love their mind, which is connected to the Divine. Making this choice leads to divinization.[169] "Hate" is a very strong word carrying a lot of baggage. The body is a vehicle for the spirit and must be looked after for optimal results; however, there is a huge difference between vanity and living a healthy lifestyle.
- The thirteenth tractate uses the term "born again" a number of times, recommending that the reader "leave the senses of the body idle, and the birth of divinity will begin," resulting in a divinized mind.[170] This strongly suggests a need for meditative states.
- The tenth tractate states that deification occurs in souls that are separated from the body, indicating that deification cannot occur

---

166. Fowden, *The Egyptian Hermes*, 112–13.
167. Janowitz, *Magic in the Roman World*, 82–83; Brian P. Copenhaver, *Hermetica: The Greek Corpus Hermeticum and the Latin Asclepius in a New English Translation, with Notes and Introduction*, reprint ed. (Cambridge University Press, 1995), 1–7.
168. Copenhaver, *Hermetica*, 11.20.
169. Copenhaver, *Hermetica*, 4.6, 7.
170. Copenhaver, *Hermetica*, 13.1, 3, 7, 10.

while still in the body.[171] The Greek Magical Papyri seems to suggest that such rituals in the physical body achieve brief experiences of immortality or deification. A number of spells claim to offer transformation into a god or immortality. However, at the end of the spell, the magician goes back to their normal life. This, to me, suggests a temporary experience of godhood or immortality. Permanent deification, however, appears to only be possible after death.

- Nothing is as capable of uniting humanity with the Divine as the mind. Death remains the ultimate barrier.[172] Humans can be seen as mortal deities and the Divine as immortal humanity.[173]

The Hermetic text *Kore Kosmou* claims that Egyptian priests were presented by the Divine with three arts: magick and philosophy to nourish the soul, and medicine to care for the body. The text is similar to a Gnostic salvation teaching. Descending through the seven planetary spheres, the first human was ensnared by matter. Self-knowledge was revealed to be the key to leave the body and ascend through the seven planetary zones to the Ogdoad: the eighth zone, the realm of the Divine. Incarnation can then take place below the deities of the fixed stars. There is no need for a savior figure, as often happens in Gnosticism, as salvation is achieved by individuals, and matter was not considered evil.[174]

Among the Neoplatonists, Iamblichus of Apamea was the best-known exponent of theurgy. His system synthesized Chaldean, Egyptian, and philosophical (i.e., Greek) teachings. His rituals would combine acts that defied human understanding with unspeakable symbols, which would only be understood by the deities. The goal was to separate the soul so as to result in spiritual meeting with the Divine.[175] Iamblichus went to great pains to show

---

171. Copenhaver, *Hermetica*, 10.7.
172. Copenhaver, *Hermetica*, 10.23.
173. Copenhaver, *Hermetica*, 10.25; Janowitz, *Magic in the Roman World*, 83.
174. Erik Hornung, *The Secret Lore of Egypt: Its Impact on the West*, trans. David Lorton (Cornell University Press, 2001), 52; Dan Merkur, *Gnosis: An Esoteric Tradition of Mystical Visions and Unions* (State University of New York Press, 1993), 117–53.
175. Fowden, *The Egyptian Hermes*, 132–34.

that the theurgical practices were based on the teachings of Egyptian priests, based on the wisdom of Hermes Trismegistus.[176]

As is evident, ascension through the planetary spheres was widely practiced in the ancient world, although details varied from school to school. We will now look at how ascension can be practiced using Qabalistic techniques.

Qabalistic Tree of Life and Planetary Correspondences

While the Qabalistic Tree of Life postdates the practice of ancient theurgy by many centuries, it is a very useful tool for arranging the correspondences to be used, hence the above reference to it being a cosmic "filing cabinet."[177] It is a map of what we have within (consciousness and perception) and without (the world around us).[178]

There are numerous diagrams of the Qabalistic Tree of Life with planetary correspondences available online. Those who prefer to have a physical copy would do well to consult the one in *Godwin's Cabalistic Encyclopedia*.[179]

Rawn Clark has produced a wonderful analysis of a text titled *The 32 Paths of Wisdom*, which allegedly dates to the late thirteenth century CE. The number 32 represents the sum of the 22 pathways linking the 10 Sephiroth on the Tree of Life. Also useful are Aleister Crowley's *Liber 777*, James Eshelman's *The Mystical & Magical System of the A∴A∴* and *Pearls of Wisdom*, Nema's *Maat Magick*, and David Shoemaker's *Living Thelema* and *The Way of the Will*. The text associated with each of the Sephiroth from Yesod to Binah are the portions that are relevant in each of these works.

This section is for the benefit of those who are interested in working with archetypal Sephirothic energies either as an alternative to, or supplement for, the planetary deities.

---

176. Fowden, *The Egyptian Hermes*, 185.
177. Regardie, *A Garden of Pomegranates*, 37.
178. James A. Eshelman, *The Mystical & Magical System of the A∴A∴: The Spiritual System of Aleister Crowley & George Cecil Jones Step-by-Step* (The College of Thelema, 2000), 5.
179. David Godwin, *Godwin's Cabalistic Encyclopedia: Complete Guidance to Both Practical and Esoteric Applications* (Llewellyn Publications, 1997), xiv–xvi.

Each Sephirah on the Tree of Life represents an aspect of the Divine. However, the Qlippothic, or "shadow," side represents negativity. These two sides of each Sephirah need to be brought into a state of balance.[180]

A path of ascension can also be seen as a journey to discover the Divine within rather than an ascension without through spiritual realms. To quote David Shoemaker:

> *The Way of Return is the Qabalistic term describing the process of reuniting the incarnate human personality with its divine Source. Just as the universe (and each human being) was created in a "top down" process descending from Kether, so must each human seek to return to God in an upward path from Malkuth. This is an elegant and uniquely Qabalistic restatement of the mystical path common to all esoteric traditions. That is, by retracing the process through which we came into being, we may discover the divine nature within us, and transcend the limitations of physical existence.*[181]

Qabalistic writings are heavily peppered with technical terms that appear daunting at first, and so perseverance is necessary.

Malkuth

Malkuth ("Kingdom"), Sephirah number 10, corresponds to the Sphere of the Four Elements and signifies sensory reality.[182] This is referred to as the "Resplendent Consciousness" and causes an influence to flow from the "Prince of the Countenance," which is a reference to Metatron, the archangel of Kether.[183] This implies a flow from Kether through every part of the

---

180. David Shoemaker, *The Way of the Will: Thelema in Action* (Weiser Books 2024), 7.
181. David Shoemaker, *Living Thelema: A Practical Guide to Attainment in Aleister Crowley's System of Magick* (Weiser Books, 2022), chap. 1.
182. Eshelman, *Mystical & Magical System*, 5–6, 69.
183. James A. Eshelman, *Pearls of Wisdom: Gems from the Journal Black Pearl* (The College of Thelema, 2013), 240–41.

Tree of Life till it comes to an end in Malkuth.[184] The entire Tree of Life is interconnected.

The work of Malkuth is effectively the beginning of the path of initiation and preparation for further advancement. There is a beginning of awareness of subtle forces permeating life. It results in empowerment and balance through self-analysis, which in turn leads to self-knowledge, thus making the next Sephirah accessible.[185] Malkuth also represents practicality, health, and experiences with the senses.[186] Malkuth corresponds to the physical world and represents the tenth and densest level.[187] Malkuth is the bedrock on which all spiritual development is based and represents all aspects of mundane everyday life.

The shadow side of Malkuth can possibly be seen as the seven deadly sins of Christian theology: pride, greed, lust, envy, gluttony, wrath, and sloth.

Malkuth is symbolized by the earth.

Yesod

The work of Yesod ("Foundation"), Sephirah number 9, is to employ the astral personal self, or "(predominantly subconscious) psyche," to exercise power over the elements, applying the Malkuth experience of knowing the self while working toward self-transformation.[188] It imposes power on the personality, which renews the psyche.[189] Yesod represents automatic (or lunar) consciousness and serves to obtain control of one's own foundation.[190] Yesod is called "Pure Consciousness" (clean or unmixed), as it purifies all the Sephiroths' essences, which implies working down from Kether.[191]

Yesod is more fluid than Malkuth and includes the Astral Planes where all forms of dreaming and imaging take place; it is also a zone of instincts.[192]

---

184. Eshelman, *Pearls of Wisdom*, 240–41.
185. Rawn Clark, "The 32 Paths of Wisdom," Hermetic Library, accessed April 24, 2022, https://hermetic.com/jwmt/v1n3/32paths.
186. Shoemaker, *Way of the Will*, 8.
187. Nema, *Maat Magick: A Guide to Self-Initiation* (Weiser Books, 1995), 9.
188. Clark, "The 32 Paths of Wisdom."
189. Clark, "The 32 Paths of Wisdom."
190. Eshelman, *Mystical & Magical System*, 5–6, 85.
191. Eshelman, *Pearls of Wisdom*, 239–40.
192. Nema, *Maat Magick*, 17.

Yesod incorporates energy and fecundity. The shadow side of Yesod can be sexual obsession or abstinence, aggression or energy depletion, excessive projection or suppression of the unconscious part of the mind.[193]

Yesod is symbolized by the Moon. In *Liber 777*, Crowley stated that the influence of this celestial body at the moment of birth ("The Genethliac Values of the Planets") is "The Senses. Bodily consciousness."[194] The psyche is an expression of the senses and bodily consciousness. (*Genethliac* refers to the influence of the planet, or in this case, the Moon, at the precise moment of birth. Genethliac astrology uses the exact time, date, and location of birth to calculate a birth chart, which determines personality traits, strengths, weaknesses, and the possible future.)

Hod

The work of Hod (Splendor), Sephirah number 8, is to employ rational intellect to continue the self-transformation of the personality.[195] This is called the "Perfect Consciousness," as it is the "Plan of the Primordial," which comes about from the intellect of Hod.[196]

There is also the acquisition of knowledge about every facet of existence, in both inner and outer worlds, as well as a vision of the Universe in its infinite complexity. Just as the personality was understood in Malkuth, the complexity of the Universe becomes understood in Hod.[197] In Hod, there is a rapid flow of ideas, analysis, and organization.

The shadow side of Hod is the intellectual stagnation of being caught up in rigid thought structures and habits and resorting to cold logic.[198]

Hod is symbolized by Mercury. In *Liber 777*, Crowley stated that the influence of this celestial body at the moment of birth ("The Genethliac Values of the Planets") is "The Mind. Cerebral tissues and nerves."[199] The rational intellect is an expression of the mind, cerebral tissues, and nerves.

---

193. Shoemaker, *Way of the Will*, 8–9.
194. Aleister Crowley, *Liber 777 Revised* (Celephaïs Press, 2004), 41.
195. Eshelman, *Mystical & Magical System*, 5–6, 93.
196. Eshelman, *Pearls of Wisdom*, 238–39.
197. Clark, "The 32 Paths of Wisdom."
198. Shoemaker, *Way of the Will*, 9–10.
199. Crowley, *Liber 777*, 41.

Netzach

The work of Netzach (Victory), Sephirah number 7, is to explore desire and instinctual emotion.[200] This is referred to as the "Hidden Consciousness," which illuminates the mind's abilities.[201] The illumination may be from the shining mirror of Venus, to which it is aspected.[202]

There is a realization that the personality is bound by rationality and logic at one extreme and emotion and instinct at the other, represented by Hod and Netzach respectively. Experiences lead to an initial reaction on the "pre-rational, emotional gut level," which is interpreted by the rational mind, so "the work of Netzach therefore, is to look within the rational reaction and penetrate to the initial gut-level instinct… the direct perception of this force is what enables the completion of the transformation of the personal self."[203]

Netzach is the domain of emotional archetypes, and under the rational response to these lies the direct experience of them. Netzach corresponds to invocation of godforms (magickal possession), sex magick, and the creation of art.[204]

Netzach is associated with outpourings of love and emotion toward the self and others, as well as the easy achievement of ecstatic states. The shadow side of Netzach is emotional instability or religious fanaticism, without any rational thought to rein it in.[205]

Netzach is symbolized by Venus. In *Liber 777*, Crowley stated that the influence of this celestial body at the moment of birth ("The Genethliac Values of the Planets") is "The Lower Love."[206] While love is commonly attributed to Netzach, it falls short of the higher love, which will be experienced at Gedulah (Chesed).

---

200. Eshelman, *Mystical & Magical System*, 5–6, 103.
201. Eshelman, *Pearls of Wisdom*, 237–38.
202. Eshelman, *Pearls of Wisdom*, 237–38.
203. Clark, "The 32 Paths of Wisdom."
204. Nema, *Maat Magick*, 33.
205. Shoemaker, *Way of the Will*, 10.
206. Crowley, *Liber 777*, 41.

Tiphareth

The work of Tiphareth (Beauty), Sephirah number 6, is to explore the "Ego-center" and attain to the "center" or "self," which is in reality the reflected image of Kether.[207] (Kether will be discussed later.) Tiphareth corresponds to *ruach* ("breath" or "spirit") which is the self-conscious ego, which perceives the world as divided and differentiated. Hermetic Qabalists refer to it as "Mediating Consciousness," as it aptly describes the function of Tiphareth.[208]

There is an "Individual perspective" acquired at Tiphareth, which results in objective detachment when observing the personality and status in the material world.[209] This enables looking at the self and how it is interconnected with other individuals.

Tiphareth represents the Ego-center and sits at the center of the Tree of Life—the other Sephiroth can be arranged around it to form a hexagram. Here is the achievement of the Knowledge and Conversation of the Holy Guardian Angel (HGA), which is a being sent by the Divine as a guide and protector. The HGA is also referred to by others as an "exalted aspect" of the higher consciousness, called the *Higher Self*.[210] The nature of the HGA is resolved through experience. At this stage, the student has well and truly become an adept. It should be noted that some esoteric schools teach that before Tiphareth can be reached, the Veil of Paroketh must be passed through. This can be thought of as a barrier of sorts, adding a degree of difficulty in accessing this Sephirah.

While there are a number of techniques for accessing the HGA, the best known is found within the pages of *The Sacred Magic of Abramelin the Mage*. Another is to take a strictly binding magickal oath to repeat invocations of the HGA until union occurs.[211]

Tiphareth is a place of self-awareness channeled from the Divine, with a balanced understanding of the ego. There is an appreciation of beauty and harmony, and this influences interactions with others. The shadow side of

---

207. Eshelman, *Mystical & Magical System*, 5–6, 119–20.
208. Eshelman, *Pearls of Wisdom*, 235–36.
209. Clark, "The 32 Paths of Wisdom."
210. Eshelman, *Mystical & Magical System*, 122–26.
211. Nema, *Maat Magick*, 45.

Tiphareth is spiritual megalomania and an obsessive interest in spirituality, resulting in neglecting matters in the mundane world.[212]

Tiphareth is symbolized by the Sun. In *Liber 777*, Crowley stated that the influence of this celestial body at the moment of birth ("The Genethliac Values of the Planets") is "The Human Will. Vital Force. Spiritual Conscious Self."[213] Access to the HGA leads to knowledge of True Will, whereupon the individual path sanctioned by the Divine becomes known, and progress is rapid.

Geburah

The work of Geburah (Strength), Sephirah number 5, is volition.[214] This is "Radical Consciousness" (meaning "extreme, sweeping, revolutionary").[215] Individual Will begins at this point. It is the essence or substance that equates to the Unity.[216]

At Geburah, the individual power that can be harnessed for additional transformation of the Self is discovered.[217] The adepthood conferred in Tiphareth matures to fulfilment in Geburah, and great magickal power is achieved. Negative personality patterns result from weakness, and there is a danger of reactive overcompensation. The process is analogous to driving a high-powered sports car for the first time—caution and respect need to be exercised. Geburah is also the force that pushes all things apart that are not similar.[218]

While Geburah is aspected to augmented strength, it also has a subtler component of acquiring the endurance to overcome tiredness and negativity.[219]

Geburah provides energy to make it easier to steer through life in accordance with True Will. The shadow side of Geburah is aggression, tyranny, and cruelty, as well as dominion of others.[220]

---

212. Shoemaker, *Way of the Will*, 10.
213. Crowley, *Liber 777*, 41.
214. Eshelman, *Mystical & Magical System*, 5–6, 139.
215. Eshelman, *Pearls of Wisdom*, 233–34.
216. Eshelman, *Pearls of Wisdom*, 233–34.
217. Clark, "The 32 Paths of Wisdom."
218. Clark, "The 32 Paths of Wisdom."
219. Nema, *Maat Magick*, 51.
220. Shoemaker, *Way of the Will*, 10–11.

Geburah is symbolized by Mars. In *Liber 777*, Crowley stated that the influence of this celestial body at the moment of birth ("The Genethliac Values of the Planets") is "The Bodily Will. Muscular system."[221] Many adepts take up various forms of exercise, including strength sports, and it is at this point that they begin to excel in them.

Gedulah/Chesed

The work of Gedulah (Greatness)/Chesed (Mercy), Sephirah number 4, is with memory and freedom from delusion and the illusion of duality. It has been claimed by some that there is a release from "personal karma" at this point.[222] This is called the "Overflowing Consciousness" ("receiving"), and from it emanate all powers of the ruach ("breath" or "spirit").[223]

Some esoteric schools teach that just as the Veil of Paroketh marks the division between the triad of Gedulah/Chesed, Geburah, and Tiphareth from the Sephiroth below, so the Veil of the Abyss marks the division between the triad of Kether, Chokmah, and Binah from the Sephiroth below.

Gedulah/Chesed represents mastery over previous "enslavement" to lesser states such as intellect and emotion. This Sephirah is positioned at the boundary of the Abyss between the mundane Temporal realm and the Supernal realm of eternity. It is the launch point for journeying across the Abyss.[224]

Gedulah/Chesed and Geburah represent the opposite states of similarity and difference. Geburah is the repulsive force that pushes dissimilar things away from each other, while Gedulah/Chesed is "loving kindness," the attractive force that pulls things together.[225] Gedulah/Chesed gives rise to the "prophesies that seers behold in visions," which initiates can employ in their transformation of the Individual Self.[226]

Tiphareth represents union with the HGA and discovery of True Will, and Geburah represents the acquisition of the strength and endurance to walk the path dictated by the True Will. Gedulah/Chesed blends these into a

---

221. Crowley, *Liber 777*, 41.
222. Eshelman, *Mystical & Magical System*, 5–6, 153–54.
223. Eshelman, *Pearls of Wisdom*, 231–33.
224. Clark, "The 32 Paths of Wisdom."
225. Clark, "The 32 Paths of Wisdom."
226. Clark, "The 32 Paths of Wisdom."

harmonious union. There is a quest for individual perfection, which includes humility and forgiveness, as well as improving the world. There is an understanding that all the trappings of the mundane world are chains of Ego limiting our progress.[227]

Gedulah/Chesed gives the experience of prudent rulership coming from a place of spiritual attunement and a sense of obligation toward those around us. The shadow side of Gedulah/Chesed is similar to that of Geburah, except that the opportunity to practice aggression and cruelty is taken advantage of, as subordinates had not set rules of acceptable behavior.[228]

Gedulah/Chesed is symbolized by Jupiter. In *Liber 777*, Crowley stated that the influence of celestial bodies at the moment of birth ("The Genethliac Values of the Planets") is "The Higher Love. Wesenschaund of Krause."[229] The first of these is a reference to the higher level hinted at in the experience of Netzach. The second is a reference to the doctrines of German philosopher Karl Christian Friedrich Krause (1781–1832), which were called "panentheism" and were a fusion of pantheism and theism. This belief claims that God is *Wesenschaund* (German for "essence") and is composed of the whole universe. He emphasized the interconnectedness of individuals with the whole. The higher love experienced here is contrasted with the more mundane love of Netzach.

Crossing the Abyss, or "The Dark Night of the Soul"

The experience of Crossing the Abyss is often likened to "The Dark Night of the Soul" ("Noche oscura del alma"), a poem penned by St. John of the Cross (1542–1591), one of the best-known Christian mystics, a church doctor, and a cofounder of the Discalced Carmelites, a contemplative monastic order.

The protocol for mystical ascent was outlined by St John. It was a silent self-communion where the soul would separate from earthly attachments and the general chaos of the mundane world. The soul would have a personal experience of despair and hopelessness, having no sense of the presence of

---

227. Nema, *Maat Magick*, 59–68.
228. Shoemaker, *Way of the Will*, 10–11.
229. Crowley, Aleister. *Liber 777*, 41.

God and heaven, not unlike the Crucifixion of Christ. Eventually, this gives way to an exalted union of the soul with God.[230]

The concept of the Dark Night of the Soul has transcended its Catholic/Christian origins and has been embraced by numerous spiritual modalities. It ultimately deals with facing fears, encountering illusions of the ego, and experiencing a symbolic death, followed by a rebirth in Binah. The ego keeps us separated from the rest of humanity.

The experience of Gedulah/Chesed is of becoming as perfect as possible, following the path of True Will. Gedulah/Chesed is also the final limit of dualistic existence. The experience of the Abyss is akin to the onion analogy where the layers are peeled off, revealing a core of nothing, and so a lifetime of belief about our nature is shown to be false. Experiencing this nothingness leads to fear and denial and triggers the fight or flight response. The Abyss is a place of silence and is not bound by time.[231]

It should be noted that the Supernal triad of Binah, Chokmah, and Kether has little impact on psychological functioning, and so there is far less available information in a practical sense.[232]

Binah

After crossing the Abyss, the adept arrives at Binah (Understanding), which is connected with intuition, and is Sephirah number 3.[233] Binah is the "Sanctifying Consciousness" or "Foundation of Primordial Wisdom," and so Binah is to Chokmah as Yesod is to Tiphareth.[234]

Binah and Gedulah/Chesed lie on opposite sides of the Abyss. Binah is the realm of potentials, which begin their process of manifestation in Gedulah/Chesed, completing it as they descend the Tree of Life. When crossing

---

230. "St. John of the Cross: Spanish Mystic," Britannica, updated December 10, 2024, https://www.britannica.com/biography/Saint-John-of-the-Cross; St. John of the Cross, "Dark Night of the Soul." Carmelite Monks, accessed October 2022, http://carmelitemonks.org/Vocation/DarkNight-StJohnoftheCross.pdf.
231. Nema, *Maat Magick*, 69–74.
232. Shoemaker, *Way of the Will*, 11.
233. Eshelman, *Mystical & Magical System*, 5–6.
234. Eshelman, *Pearls of Wisdom*, 229–30.

A Qabalistic Approach to Theurgy

the Abyss, Binah initially appears dark but with perseverance is found to have a radiance on close inspection. Binah is a portal to infinity.[235]

In Binah, there is full awareness of the way individual lives are mixed with the universal life as a result of relinquishing ego attachments. There is also a receiving of the Word.[236] The Word, or *Logos*, is the interconnection between humanity, the world, and the Divine. The Word is normally spoken by a Magus as part of crafting a magickal system, with some examples being Aleister Crowley's "Abrahadabra" ("The Great Work Accomplished"), Anton LaVey's "Indulgence," Michael Aquino's "Xeper" ("I Have Come Into Being"), and Nema's "Ipsos" ("By the Same Mouth").

In Binah, the "onion layers" are reintegrated using knowledge that everything is actually illusion. This process will take at least weeks to complete and possibly even years. Those who have achieved liberation from illusion should then assist others in their quest to accomplish the same.[237]

Binah is symbolized by Saturn. In *Liber 777*, Crowley stated that the influence of celestial bodies at the moment of birth ("The Genethliac Values of the Planets") is "The Ego (*ahamkara*). Skeleton."[238] According to Yogapedia, the Sanskrit word *ahamkara* refers to the ego in Hindu philosophy. It is said that Lord Krishna instructed Arjuna (a figure in the *Mahabharata*) that ahamkara had to be removed, meaning that the ego had to be overcome before spiritual enlightenment could be achieved. Occasionally the ego is described as "the instrument of the spirit," which can manifest in negative emotions such as jealousy and pride.[239] To cross the Abyss is to die to the ego, so *ahamkara* removal is the analogous process in the Vedic texts.

Planetary attunement would normally end at this point. Chokmah and Kether are looked at for the sake of completion for those who want to understand where ascension building on workings on each day of the week can potentially lead to. This will be discussed below.

---

235. Clark, "The 32 Paths of Wisdom."
236. Shoemaker, *Way of the Will*, 15.
237. Nema, *Maat Magick*, 75–78.
238. Crowley, *Liber 777*, 41.
239. "Ahamkara," Yogapedia, updated December 21, 2023, https://www.yogapedia.com/definition/5235/ahamkara.

Chokmah

The work of Chokmah (Wisdom), Sephirah number 2, is the attainment of wisdom.[240] Chokmah is known as the "Radiant Consciousness" ("illuminating") or the "Second Glory," which is secondary to the "Primal Glory" of Kether.[241]

Binah represents Understanding, which relates to an object or a situation. Over time, Understanding matures into Wisdom, represented by Chokmah, which is a "continuous state" not requiring a focal point.[242]

In Chokmah, the Word, which is "the primal impulse of all the life of humanity" can be uttered.[243]

To speak the Word, which is the distillation of spiritual experience, is actually the duty of Chokmah. Crossing the Abyss revealed the illusory nature of the individual self, which can be used as a "mask" in the mundane world. Speaking the Word actually fulfills obligations toward the universe.[244]

Chokmah is symbolized by the Fixed Stars. In *Liber 777*, Crowley stated that the influence of celestial bodies at the moment of birth ("The Genethliac Values of the Planets"), which in his book is actually listed as "Herschel" but is obviously referring to the correspondence for Chokmah, is "The True Will. Spiritual Energy."[245] So, while the True Will is first known at Tiphareth, this knowledge gradually intensifies and only truly blossoms at Chokmah.

Kether

The apex of the Tree of Life is Kether (Crown), Sephirah number 1.[246] Kether is known as the "Wonderful Consciousness" or the "Primal Glory," and no living individual can attain to it.[247] In some traditions it is taught that Kether can only be attained after death, suggesting that ascension can be seen as a preparation for death.

---

240. Eshelman, *The Mystical & Magical System*, 6.
241. Eshelman, *Pearls of Wisdom*, 228–29.
242. Clark, "The 32 Paths of Wisdom."
243. Shoemaker, *Way of the Will*, 15.
244. Nema, *Maat Magick*, 81–84.
245. Crowley, *Liber 777*, 41.
246. Eshelman, *Mystical & Magical System*, 6.
247. Eshelman, *Pearls of Wisdom*, 226–27.

Kether represents Unity as absolute wholeness without division. The experience of Kether is to be consonant with all of existence, with everything happening simultaneously.[248]

Kether is the experience of the Source from which everything emanates and to which everything returns—the potential for everything that can manifest.[249]

Once the Word has been spoken, the True Will is completed. Living in Kether is to exist without Will but steeped in love and harmony, forming an open channel for influence to flow unimpeded from Kether to Malkuth. There is a sense of knowing that everything, both good and evil, is in accordance with divine decree.[250]

Kether is symbolized by the Prime Mover, which is responsible for the precession of the equinoxes. In *Liber 777*, Crowley stated that the influence of celestial bodies at the moment of birth ("The Genethliac Values of the Planets"), which in his book is actually listed as "Neptune" but is obviously referring to the correspondence for Kether, is "The True Self (*Zeitgeist*). Spiritual environment."[251]

Zeitgeist is a German philosophical term meaning "the spirit of the age," referring to the collective consciousness of an era distinguishing it from all other eras. At Kether, the True Self blends seamlessly with the Zeitgeist, as following one's True Will represents submission to the Divine.

Kether is completely integrated Unity without parts. There is no beginning, middle, or end, no duality. To attain to Kether is to be one with all creation, with action and reaction occurring at the same time and life turning into a state of just existing in perfect harmony with the Divine.[252]

It should be noted that the traditional model of ascension involves journeying through concentric planetary spheres. However, working with the Tree of Life enables exploring the dynamics between particular Sephiroth, especially Hod and Netzach, Geburah and Gedulah (Chesed), as well

....
248. Clark, "The 32 Paths of Wisdom."
249. Shoemaker, *Way of the Will*, 15.
250. Nema, *Maat Magick*, 85.
251. Crowley, *Liber 777*, 41.
252. Clark, "The 32 Paths of Wisdom."

as potentially Binah and Chokmah. For the purposes of attunement to the Sephirothic energies, the journey actually ends with Binah.

Sephirothic Energy Attunement Ritual
The ritual below outlines a number of ideas on how to effectively attune to Sephirothic energies.

Planetary and Sephirothic Correspondences
Many traditions already have correspondences for planetary deities, and these should be used unless the initiate strongly intuits that something is amiss. Those initiates working within a tradition that does not use planetary deities and would prefer to work with archetypal energies would do well to consult Aleister Crowley's *Liber 777*. The rows to be consulted in his text are Sephirah number 9 (Yesod/Moon) to Sephirah number 3 (Binah/Saturn.)

There are useful correspondences there including colors (there are four different color scales to choose from, but the Queen Scale is the one most commonly used) and perfumes, with plants and precious stones as a bonus.

There are also correspondences there for the Egyptian, Hindu, Scandinavian, Greek, and Roman deities for those not currently working with these pantheons but interested in them.[253]

Discernment is a very useful tool to cultivate. If a particular correspondence or attribution does not feel right, it should be changed after careful contemplation. As an example, the Greek deity correspondences in *Liber 777* vary from those in the *Greek Magical Papyri*, and so I chose to use the latter in my book *Graeco-Egyptian Magick*. While the deities chosen are those used at the time for the days of the week, I imagine that substituting Apollo for Helios as the solar deity and either Artemis or Hekate for Selene as the lunar deity would work quite well. We all need to find the correspondences that best resonate with us.[254]

---

253. Crowley, *Liber 777*, 2–17.
254. Tony Mierzwicki, *Graeco-Egyptian Magick: Everyday Empowerment* (Megalithica Books, 2006).

There is a more difficult option from the Ordo Aurum Solis, who use the same deities as were used in the Greek Magical Papyri but tie them into the lunar cycle rather than the days of the week:

Day 1 (New Moon): Saturn/Kronos

Day 2: Sun/Helios

Day 3: Moon/Selene

Day 4: Mars/Ares

Day 5: Mercury/Hermes

Day 6: Jupiter/Zeus

Day 7: Venus/Aphrodite

This cycle is repeated three more times. Any days left over between the end of the fourth cycle and the New Moon are dedicated to the aether. For more information on this, refer to Jean-Louis de Biasi's *Rediscover the Magick of the Gods and Goddesses*.

I mention this technique for the sake of completeness. It is challenging, as it involves changing over to using the lunar calendar.

Creation of a Sacred Space, Banishing, and Energizing

Normally for a ritual, a sacred space is required. This can be accomplished in one of two ways.

First, those lucky enough to have access to a temple have this already done for them. Through repetitive use, a temple has negative energies banished from it, and a vortex of energy is built up that can be tapped into.

Second, a sacred space can be created at a desired or convenient location. Some traditions will delineate the sacred space by tracing out, or casting, a circle. Other traditions will not bother with a circle or any other shape. Simply using smoke from incense, resin, or herbs, or asperging using a consecrated liquid, while visualizing negativity being removed from the space works well. For example, rosemary is a purifying herb that is easy to attain. An example of a consecrated liquid is water with salt.

Some traditions will energize the sacred space by calling in energy from the four cardinal directions, referred to as *calling the quarters* in Wicca, or perhaps working with a seven-direction system, referred to as *calling the sevenths* in my *Graeco-Egyptian Magick*.[255] For those working in the Golden Dawn Tradition, there is the Lesser Banishing Ritual of the Pentagram (LBRP), with an accessible version being produced by Donald Michael Kraig.[256] For those working in the Thelemic Tradition, there is the Star Ruby. Those working in a temple can dispense with this step.

Depending on the tradition being worked, this process can be of varying degrees of complexity. Simply using incense or resin while visualizing negativity being removed from the area works quite well.

Calling Planetary Deities or Sephirothic Energies

Many traditions already have techniques for invoking planetary deities, and these should be used. Their color and perfume correspondences will intensify the obtained results.

I personally like using spells from the Greek Magical Papyri, Orphic Hymns, and Homeric Hymns. Some students like to produce their own hymns. Meditating after calling in the planetary deities ensures that the maximum amount of information is absorbed.

To illustrate the suggested procedure, a Qabalistic approach will be used. The Sephirothic energies permeate the universe and are to be found within us. It is a matter of attuning to these energies by using the correspondences associated with them. At a minimum, we have a color, a number, and a fragrance. From this we know how many candles of a particular color we need and what fragrance should be used. Crowley's *Liber 777* is a wonderful starting point, with the only difficult color being for Malkuth.

The suggested procedure is a series of meditations on the Sephirothic energies using correspondences from Crowley's *Liber 777*:

---

255. Mierzwicki, *Graeco-Egyptian Magick*, 79.
256. Donald Michael Kraig. "Lesser Banishing Ritual of the Pentagram," Llewellyn, July 7, 2005, https://www.llewellyn.com/encyclopedia/article/5139.

- Place correspondences taken from Crowley's *Liber 777* on an altar to better attune to the Sephirothic energy being worked with.
- Create a sacred space for meditation using the LBRP.
- Relax, balance, and calm using the fourfold breath, otherwise known as *box breathing*. Inhale for 4 seconds. Hold for 4 seconds. Exhale for 4 seconds. Hold for 4 seconds. Repeat until centered.
- The eyes should be closed. Silently intone the name of the Sephirah repeatedly and focus on the lessons contained therein. Continue until no further knowledge manifests, whereupon the eyes can be opened.
- Repeat the LBRP.
- Monitor dreams for further information and journal all experiences.

Once a certain degree of proficiency is achieved with a Sephirah, keep repeating the process on the correct day of the week. At the same time, move on to the next Sephirah, focusing on it until proficiency is attained.

Sadly, some of the incenses listed below are threatened or endangered, so it would make sense to use a substitute. For example, experiment with incenses that have an association with the sun as a substitute for frankincense. When substituting, use what feels right to you. Additionally, the recommended incenses for Binah, Chokmah, and Kether are civet, musk, and ambergris respectively.[257] All three are of animal origin and usually involve cruelty. I would suggest either synthetic versions or plant-based equivalent fragrances.

Malkuth

This is a preliminary set of practices to be done prior to beginning the daily attunements designed to bring order into the frequent chaos of everyday life in the physical world.

Malkuth is the mundane-world bedrock on which the path of initiation is built. It focuses on the physical world and the physical body with which it is experienced.

---

257. Crowley, *Liber 777*, 13.

Maslow's Hierarchy of Needs provides a wonderful guide, with physiological (survival) needs being at the beginning, and these consist of breathing, food, water, shelter, clothing, sleep, and reproduction.[258] This means having fresh air to breathe, wholesome and nutritious unprocessed or minimally processed food to eat, clean water to drink, a place to call home, warm clothing to wear, and restful sleep. Shelter needs vary; so long as people are happy and have leisure time to work on themselves spiritually, the shelter chosen does not matter. Needless to say, nothing is free in life, and so a source of income is required to meet these physiological needs. The remaining needs will be covered once the ascension process up the Tree of Life begins.

Part of the work of Malkuth is to establish a temple space, procure an altar, and fashion magickal tools.[259] For this series of meditations, the only tool required is a dagger, crystal, or wand to perform the LBRP.

It was previously suggested that the shadow side of Malkuth can be seen as the seven deadly sins of Christian theology: pride, greed, lust, envy, gluttony, wrath, and sloth. Devout Christians will strive to replace the seven deadly sins with their opposites. Either extreme is counterproductive, and a balance point between the two is optimal.

Humility is the opposite of pride; however, pride in moderation is very positive. Pride in achievements and appearance is healthy so long as it is not excessive.

Charity is the opposite of greed; however, it needs to be applied with discretion, as excessive charity leads to dependence on handouts, leading to stagnation.

Chastity is the opposite of lust, but can lead to frustration, insecurity, and anxiousness. If lust is obsessive, then it becomes as destructive as any other addiction. Physical intimacy in moderation is very positive for many people. (Some people will wait till Yesod to deal with the chastity-lust duality. However, it actually makes sense to start in Malkuth and finish in Yesod, because there is a physical component as well as an astral one, where erotic dreams are experienced.)

---

258. Saul Mcleod, "Maslow's Hierarchy Of Needs," Simply Psychology, updated March 14, 2025, https://www.simplypsychology.org/maslow.html.
259. Nema, *Maat Magick*, 9–11.

Gratitude is the opposite of envy and is incredibly important. However, a little bit of envy can be a motivating factor when used constructively.

Temperance is the opposite of gluttony and is very positive as long as it does not lead to fasting for excessively long periods of time and developing an eating disorder.

Patience is the opposite of wrath. However, wrath can be channeled constructively, for instance to improve sporting performance.

Diligence is the opposite of sloth. However, a little bit of sloth is valid self-care.

Once the altar is procured, meditations on the mundane world can be helped by burning Dittany of Crete incense. As candles that are colored citrine, olive, russet, and black will be difficult to come by, perhaps ten candles with an earthy appearance can be used instead.[260]

Once your intuition tells you that proficiency has been achieved with Malkuth, move on to Yesod. It would not hurt to periodically revisit Malkuth to ensure grounding. A firm foundation is vital.

Yesod

Place nine purple candles on the altar and burn jasmine, ginseng, or an odiferous root incense. While initially the day of the ritual is unimportant, once it has been reasonably mastered, it should be performed on Mondays.[261]

Yesod represents the beginning of astral workings as well as working with the predominantly subconscious psyche. Erotic dreams can be symptomatic of sexual obsession, which can be just as unhealthy as abstinence. Channeling energy is important to avoid depletion, while being wary of it leading to aggression or energy depletion. The unconscious part of the mind should be worked on without excessive projection or suppression. Yesod is where Astral Projection takes place, and an Astral Temple could be established, perhaps mirroring the physical one established in Malkuth.[262]

Once a certain degree of proficiency is achieved with Yesod, keep repeating the process every Monday. At the same time, move on to Hod.

---

260. Crowley, *Liber 777*, 6, 13.
261. Crowley, *Liber 777*, 6, 13.
262. Nema, *Maat Magick*, 17–22.

A Qabalistic Approach to Theurgy

Hod

Place eight orange candles on the altar and burn storax incense. While initially the day of the ritual is unimportant, once it has been reasonably mastered, it should be performed on Wednesdays.[263]

Hod represents the rational intellect and the acquisition of knowledge about the inner and outer worlds. The study of the Qabala and Gematria is recommended, as is the study of sigils and symbols. A layperson's understanding of science will make the practice of magick more effective.[264]

It's important to be flexible and not allow rigid thought structures, habits, and cold logic to take root. As new information is absorbed, previously held views may need to be modified.

Once a certain degree of proficiency is achieved with Hod, keep repeating the process every Wednesday, as well as repeating the process with Yesod on Monday. At the same time, move on to Netzach.

Netzach

Place seven emerald candles on the altar and burn benzoin, rose, or red sandalwood incense.[265] While initially the day of the ritual is unimportant, once it has been reasonably mastered, it should be performed on Fridays.

The personality exists between intellect and emotion, represented by Hod and Netzach, respectively.

Netzach represents directly experiencing desire and instinctual emotion, which underly any rational response to them. Netzach serves to obtain control of attractions and repulsions. Experiments in the invocation of godforms (magickal possession), sex magick, and the creation of art should be begun. Note that in magickal possession, the deity chosen shares the body but does not take it over.[266]

Netzach is associated with deep emotions, a love for ourselves and other people, and ecstatic states, while avoiding obsession or volatile emotions.[267]

---

263. Crowley, *Liber 777*, 6, 13.
264. Nema, *Maat Magick*, 23–30.
265. Crowley, *Liber 777*, 6, 13.
266. Nema, *Maat Magick*, 34.
267. Shoemaker, *Way of the Will*, 10.

Once a certain degree of proficiency is achieved with Netzach, keep repeating the process every Friday, as well as repeating the process with Hod on Wednesday and Yesod on Monday. At the same time, move on to Tiphareth.

Tiphareth

Place six yellow (gold) candles on the altar and burn olibanum (frankincense). While initially the day of the ritual is unimportant, once it has been reasonably mastered, it should be performed on Sundays.[268]

Tiphareth represents exploration of the Ego-center and attainment of the "center," "self" or HGA as well as seeing how it is interconnected with other individuals through an appreciation of beauty and harmony.

Techniques for accessing the HGA include the prolonged ritual in *The Sacred Magic of Abramelin the Mage* or taking a strictly binding magickal oath to repeat invocations of the HGA until union occurs. Whatever method is chosen, the process generally takes quite some time. Knowledge of the name of the HGA greatly enhances access to it. (The name of the HGA should be kept secret.)

Through access to the HGA, there is knowledge of True Will, the individual path sanctioned by the Divine, and progress is rapid. There is a need to guard against spiritual megalomania and an obsessive interest in spirituality, which could result in neglecting matters in the mundane world.

Once a certain degree of proficiency is achieved with Tiphareth, keep repeating the process every Sunday, as well as repeating the process with Netzach on Friday, Hod on Wednesday, and Yesod on Monday. At the same time, move on to Geburah.

Geburah

Place five scarlet-red candles on the altar and burn tobacco. While initially the day of the ritual is unimportant, once it has been reasonably mastered, it should be performed on Tuesdays.[269]

---

268. Crowley, *Liber 777*, 6, 13.
269. Crowley, *Liber 777*, 6, 13.

Geburah represents harnessing individual power for additional transformation of the Self. Apart from augmented strength, it has a subtler component of acquiring the endurance to overcome tiredness and negativity. While many take up various forms of exercise, including strength sports and martial arts, yoga and meditation also have their place. To truly excel, it's critical to factor in sleep and relaxation. It is important to guard against aggression, tyranny, and cruelty, as well as dominion of others.

Once a certain degree of proficiency is achieved with Geburah, keep repeating the process every Tuesday, as well as repeating the process with Tiphareth on Sunday, Netzach on Friday, Hod on Wednesday, and Yesod on Monday. At the same time, move on to Gedulah/Chesed.

Gedulah/Chesed

Place four blue candles on the altar and burn cedar incense.[270] While initially the day of the ritual is unimportant, once it has been reasonably mastered, it should be performed on Thursdays.

Geburah and Gedulah/Chesed represent two poles of sequence, with Geburah pushing dissimilar things apart, and Gedulah/Chesed drawing all things together.

Gedulah/Chesed represents memory, freedom from delusion, and the illusion of duality, as well as mastery over intellect and emotion.

Tiphareth represents the HGA and True Will, and Geburah represents the strength and endurance to walk the path of True Will. Gedulah/Chesed blends these into a harmonious union. At this point, the Self can cross the Abyss between the mundane Temporal realm and the Supernal realm of eternity. Numerous visions are to be had.

At Gedulah/Chesed there is a quest for individual perfection, which includes humility and forgiveness, as well as improving the world. There is an understanding that all the trappings of the mundane world are chains of Ego limiting our progress.

For some, there is the experience of balanced, responsible rulership. It is important to not allow aggression and cruelty to be practiced by the subjects being ruled. Rules of acceptable behavior must be set.

---

270. Crowley, *Liber 777*, 6, 13.

Once a certain degree of proficiency is achieved with Gedulah/Chesed, keep repeating the process every Thursday, as well as repeating the process with Geburah on Tuesday, Tiphareth on Sunday, Netzach on Friday, Hod on Wednesday, and Yesod on Monday. At the same time, move on to Binah. Ascending to Binah has considerable challenges, as full access involves crossing the Abyss, and until then, it is only glimpsed from afar.

Crossing the Abyss, or "The Dark Night of the Soul"

Gedulah/Chesed represents near perfection by following the True Will and cognizance of the final limit of dualistic existence. Negative emotions such as pride, jealousy, and hate have to be overcome. To cross the Abyss is to peel off the "onion layers" that represent illusions of the ego or beliefs about ourselves built up over a lifetime. This reveals a core of nothing, leading to fear and denial, and it triggers the fight-or-flight response. There is a symbolic death, followed by a rebirth in Binah. The Abyss is a place of silence, and time is meaningless.

Binah

Place three black candles on the altar and burn myrrh or civet incense. (It should be noted that civet comes from civets and involves cruelty, so please seek out a plant-based or synthetic substitute.) This ritual should be performed on Saturdays.[271] By this stage, every other day of the week is being used for attunement to the other Sephiroth.

In Binah, there is a full consciousness of the interconnectedness of all lives, as the illusion of separation provided by the ego has dissolved. The stripped "onion layers" are reintegrated using knowledge that everything is actually illusion. This is a slow, gradual process that will take at least weeks and possibly even years to move from glimpsing Binah to full immersion.

There is also a receiving of the Word. The Word, or *Logos*, is the interconnection between humanity, the world, and the Divine. Unless your destiny is to channel an entire system of magick, this will be a Word with meaning to you alone.

---

271. Crowley, *Liber 777*, 6, 13.

Those who have achieved liberation from illusion should then assist others in their quest to accomplish the same. This should be done in a very practical manner, namely by assisting in the provision of food, shelter, healing, and protection to those who need it.[272] Those who are wealthy are in a position to supply a lot of financial assistance, while those who are poor should roll up their sleeves.

As pointed out previously, planetary attunement would normally end at this point, with meditations on the corresponding Sephiroth being incorporated into daily workings. Each passing week will strengthen the degree of attunement.

Binah, however, is a portal to infinity, with Chokmah and Kether softly beckoning. They will be briefly looked at for the sake of completion.

Chokmah

Place two gray candles on the altar and burn musk incense. (It should be noted that musk comes from musk deer and other animals and involves cruelty, so please seek out a plant-based or synthetic substitute.) While there is no assigned day, perhaps Saturday would be best, as it corresponds to the Sephirah closest to Chokmah.[273]

Binah represents Understanding, which over time matures into Wisdom, represented by Chokmah, which is a "continuous state" not requiring a focal point.[274] The Word, which was received in Binah, should be uttered in Chokmah, which completes True Will and fulfills obligations toward the universe.

Knowledge of the illusory nature of the individual self can be used to craft a "mask" in order to function in the mundane world. I imagine that it would be so much easier to live as a hermit while in Chokmah and not interact with the rest of humanity!

Daily attunements should be continued, with meditations on the corresponding Sephiroth being incorporated into daily workings. Saturday will be a busy day with meditations on Binah as well as Chokmah. Each passing week will strengthen the degree of attunement.

---

272. Nema, *Maat Magick*, 77–78.
273. Crowley, *Liber 777*, 6, 13.
274. Clark, "The 32 Paths of Wisdom."

Once it is felt that there is a reasonable degree of immersion into Chokmah, it is time to experience Kether.

Kether

Place one white candle on the altar and burn ambergris incense. (It should be noted that ambergris comes from sperm whales and involves killing the whale unless low-grade material washes up on a beach, so please seek out a plant-based or synthetic substitute.) While there is no assigned day, perhaps Saturday would be best, as it corresponds to the Sephirah closest to Chokmah and Kether.[275]

The journey ends at Kether, which represents an integrated totality, an indivisible Unity. There is an experience of being consonant with all of existence, with everything happening simultaneously, and also being part of the Source from which everything emanates and to which everything returns.

In Kether, there is a sense of knowing that everything, both good and evil, is in accordance with the Will of the Divine.

Living in Kether is to exist without Will but steeped in love and harmony. It seems to me that this is an angelic existence, with its continuous connection with the Divine, and manifesting love and harmony.

Daily planetary attunements should be continued, with meditations on the corresponding Sephiroth being incorporated into daily workings. Saturday will be a busy day, with meditations on Binah as well as Chokmah and Kether. Each passing week will strengthen the degree of attunement.

Dismissal of Planetary Deities or Sephirothic Energies

Normally, deities should be thanked for coming to a ritual and farewelled. However, those working with Sephirothic energies can omit this step.

The process of setting up the sacred space should be reversed by de-energizing the sacred space and performing another banishing.

---

275. Crowley, *Liber 777*, 6, 13.

Communicating with Deities

In my book *Hellenismos*, I expressed my belief that rituals can foster personal contact with deities, creating a two-way communication flow, and that this can manifest as messages in dreams or intuitive feelings. Keeping a daily journal is essential for tracking prayers, offerings, and experiences, starting with traditional offerings and experimenting with nontraditional ones.

The essence of polytheism is recognizing the Divine in all aspects of life. Deities respond quickly to sincere seekers, but one must open their heart and mind to the beauty of the world. This concept is known as *unverified personal gnosis* (UPG), which refers to personal experiences that may not be backed by historical texts.[276]

It's important to note that reconstructionists lack a complete understanding of ancient practices, leading to gaps in knowledge. Communications from spirit realms can be unreliable, as highlighted by Donald Michael Kraig, who cautions against blind acceptance of channeled messages without discernment, as none of the hundreds of books containing this material have radically improved life or provided new information.[277]

However, every religion began with personal spiritual experiences, often classified as UPGs. This, of course, excludes the tongue-in-cheek contemporary religions designed to elicit humor, such as the Church of the SubGenius and Pastafarianism. While new archaeological findings may validate some UPGs, discernment remains crucial. Practitioners should assess whether channeled information aligns with the deity's nature and ensure it promotes personal growth rather than ego-driven claims. UPGs can enrich personal practices, affirming the reality of deities.

This brings us back to those communications that cannot be verified. Is the channeled information roughly in keeping with the nature of the deity? Does the information feel like an expression of your imagination rather than something "alien"? Are you being prompted to endanger yourself or others? Are you projecting your own ego to make an exalted claim, such as being the spouse of a deity and hence their exclusive mouthpiece for the entire planet?

---

276. Tony Mierzwicki, *Hellenismos: Practicing Greek Polytheism Today* (Llewellyn Publications, 2018), 63–64.
277. Donald Michael Kraig, *Modern Magick: Twelve Lessons in the High Magickal Arts* (Llewellyn Publications, 2010).

These messages should be for your individual use and growth—they should enhance your life and hopefully the lives of those around you. UPGs add vitality to personal practice as practitioners realize that the deities are real.

Approaches to Planetary or Sephirothic Initiation

There are two approaches to planetary or Sephirothic initiation.

First, the planetary deities or Sephiroth can be worked with in sequence, starting with the Moon/Yesod and ending with Saturn/Binah. Once each of the energies has been mastered, they can be worked with on the appropriate day of the week. This is the approach I suggested above.

Second, those who have already worked with at least some of the planetary deities or Sephiroth should work with all seven right from the very beginning, on the appropriate day of the week. With each passing week, more and more benefit will be derived from each of the deities or Sephiroth. Attunement will come fairly quickly for the Moon/Yesod, Mercury/Hod, and Venus/Netzach. The process will slow down for the remaining ones, but with persistence, attunement to all seven deities or Sephiroth will eventually be achieved.

In the introduction to this article, it was stated that attuning to the planetary deities or Sephiroth will actually enhance many magickal practices not connected with theurgy. It is obvious that planetary attunement will offer a better connection to the seven deities ruling the seven days of the week. This will have the effect of making any system of magick that taps into these energies more potent. This includes, but is not limited to, manifestation, healing, working with herbs, folk magick, and preparation of sigils and talismans. In short, much spellwork will be made more potent.

Finally, those wanting to ascend through the planetary spheres or Sephiroth in order to experience union with divinity will have a solid foundation to build on by having attuned on a weekly basis.

APPENDIX A:
PROCLUS'S "ON THE HIERATIC ART OF THE HELLENES"
ORIGINAL TRANSLATION AND FOOTNOTE COMMENTARY BY JOHN OPSOPAUS, PhD

Just as the amorous (*erôtikoi*) progress along the way from beautiful things in sensation and arrive at the one principle of all beautiful and intelligible things,[278] so the priests organized the priestly (hieratic) science from sympathies among all phenomena, both toward each other and toward the unseen powers, apprehending all in all, and they were amazed to see the last things in the first and the first in the last, to see earthly things in the heavens as a cause in a heavenly manner, and heavenly things in the earth in an earthly manner. How are heliotropes moved by the sun, but selenotropes by the moon, turning around according to their ability with the celestial lights of the cosmos? For all things pray according to their own order and hymn the leaders of entire series (*seirai*), whether spiritually (*noerically*), discursively, naturally,

---

278. The allusion is to Plato's *Symposium*, in which the lover ascends the scale of being from the beauty of the beloved to Beauty Itself. See "Meditation on Beauty" in Patrick Dunn's chapter. The "Ascent by Love" is one of three Neoplatonic ascents to the One described in MacLennan, *The Wisdom of Hypatia*, chapters 10–12.

or sensibly.[279] When the heliotrope is opened by the sun, it is moved by it, and if indeed someone were able to hear it striking the air with its turning, they also would perceive through this sound that it brings the sort of hymn to the King that a plant is able to sing.

In fact, in the earth it is possible to see suns and moons in an earthly manner, but in the heavens to see in a heavenly manner all the plants, stones, and animals, living in a spiritual (*noeric*) manner. Contemplating these very things, the ancient sages, by applying them to one or another of the heavenly beings, invited divine powers into the mortal region and attracted them by means of similarity; for similarity connects beings to one another. Moreover, if someone has warmed a wick and holds it under a lamp not far from the flame, they see it catch fire, although not touching the flame, and what is below is kindled from above. Analogously then, understand the prior warming as the things here with a sympathy for those there, and the approach and favorable positioning as the use of materials in the hieratic art both according to a proper critical time (*kairos*) and in an appropriate manner, and the transmission of fire as the presence of the divine light to what is able to participate in it, and the kindling as the divinization (*theiou*) of mortals and as the illumination (*perilampsis*) of the enmattered (*enulon*), which indeed are moved toward what remains above according to their share in the divine seed (*sperma theion*), just like the light of the kindled wick.

The lotus also exhibits this sympathy, being closed prior to the sun's rays, but somehow opening during the day when Helios first appears, and spreading out as much as the light ascends, and drawing together again when it sets. So how then do people opening or closing their mouth and lips to hymn the sun differ from the lotus folding and unfolding its petals? For those parts of the lotus are in place of the mouth, and its hymn is natural. But why is it necessary to speak about plants, in which there exists some trace of generative life? But also one

---

279. That is, there are four levels or degrees of prayer: at the levels of the intuiting *nous*, discursive reason, living nature, and material reality.

Appendix A: Proclus's "On the Hieratic Art of the Hellenes"

may see stones inspired[280] by the emanation of the celestial lights, as we observe that the "sunstone" (*hêlitis*[281]) with its golden rays mimics the sun's rays, and the stone called "the eye of Bêl"[282] has a form resembling the pupils of eyes and emits a glittering light from the middle of the pupil in it (some say we must call this stone "the eye of Helios"), and selenite ("moon stone") in its figure and motion changes with the moon, and the "sun-moon-stone" (*hêlioselênos*[283]) is a sort of image (*agalma*) of the conjunction of the heavenly lights, which it resembles in their conjunctions and separations across the heavens. Thus all things are full of gods, things in the earth of heavenly gods, but things in heaven of the gods above heaven, and each proliferating series (*seira*) proceeds even to the last of things. For those things in the one-before-all (*hen pro tôn pantôn*) were revealed in everything, among which also were alliances (*sustaseis*) of various souls arrayed below various gods. Moreover there happens to be a multitude of solar animals, such as lions and roosters, and they also participate in the god according to their own order. And it is amazing that the lesser in power and size among them frighten the stronger in both respects, for the lion, they say, shrinks back before the rooster. It is not possible to grasp the cause of this from sense perception, but from spiritual (noeric) perception and the diversity of causes.[284] At very least, the presence of the solar symbols (*sumbola*) is more active in the rooster; clearly it shares in the solar revolutions and sings a hymn to the luminary as it rises and turns over the remaining cardinal points;

---

280. ἐμπνέοντας: breathing, living, inspired, perhaps enspirited or ensouled. Ficino paraphrases *imitationem et participationem*; Brian Copenhaver, "Hermes Trismegistus, Proclus, and the Question of a Philosophy of Magic in the Renaissance," in *Hermeticism and the Renaissance: Intellectual History and the Occult in Early Modern Europe*, ed. Ingrid Merkel and Allen G. Debus (Folger Books, 1988), 107, l. 37.
281. This stone has not been identified.
282. Pliny describes *Beli oculus* as "a stone of a whitish hue, surrounding a black pupil in the middle, which shines amid a lustre like that of gold" [book 37, chapter 55.1, *The Natural History of Pliny*, vol. 6, trans. John Bostock and H. T. Riley (Henry G. Bohn, 1857), 443, 452], perhaps tiger's eye or cat's eye chalcedony.
283. This stone has not been identified.
284. The reason may be that although lions are in the seira of Helios, because in astrology Leo is ruled by the Sun and is its domicile, roosters, as aerial creatures, are superior to lions, which are terrestrial; Copenhaver, "Hermes Trismegistus," 85–86.

also on account of this, some solar angels are perceived to have such shapes, for although formless they give themselves forms when appearing to us, who are bound in form. Now, some of the solar daimons appear lion-faced, and when a rooster appears, it is said, they become invisible, shrinking before the signs (*sunthêmata*) of the stronger ones, as many people, when they see the images (*eikones*) of divine men, are restrained by them from doing something defiled.

Simply stated, some things are stirred up by the revolutions of the celestial lights, such as the plants discussed, but others imitate the form of the rays, such as the palm, and others the empyrean substance, such as the laurel, and others something else. Therefore, you may observe the characteristics sown together in the sun distributed among participating angels, daimons, souls, animals, plants, and stones. For which reason the masters of the hieratic art have discovered from the things lying in front of their eyes the service paid to the higher powers, mixing some, but taking away others as is appropriate; the mixing is because they observed that each unmixed thing holds some specific character of the god, but does not truly suffice for his invocation (*proklêsis*); because of this, by mixture of many things they unite the aforesaid emanations (*aporroiai*) and they make the unity that arises from the many to be like the whole before the many. And they frequently prepare composite sacred images (*agalmata*) and incenses, mixing into one the dispersed signs (*sunthêmata*) and making by their art an essentially divine comprehension in accord with the unity of very many powers, the separation of which makes each feeble, but the mixture returns to the Idea of the paradigm. Sometimes it happens that one plant or one stone suffices for this work: for manifestation[285] the spurge-flax[286] suffices, but for protection the laurel, buckthorn, squill,[287] coral, diamond, and jasper, for divination a mole's[288] heart, and for purification sulfur and sea water.

---

285. αὐτοφάνειαν.
286. *Daphne Gnidium, Daphne oleoides*, or *Thymelaea hirsute*. Henry George Liddell, Robert Scott, comps., *A Greek-English Lexicon*, vol. 1, rev. Henry Stuart Jones, with Roderick McKenzie (Clarendon, 1968), under "κνέωρος."
287. Squill, *Urginea maritima* (Liddell, Scott, Jones, and McKenzie), under "σκίλλα."
288. A blind mole rat, *Spalax typhlus* (Liddell, Scott, Jones, and McKenzie), under "ἀσπάλαξ," but now named *Spalax microphthalmus*.

Appendix A: Proclus's "On the Hieratic Art of the Hellenes"

Certainly while they draw to themselves through sympathy, they banish through antipathy, purifying perhaps with sulfur and pitch, and lustrating with seawater, for sulfur purifies through the sharpness of its smell, but seawater through participation in the empyrean power.

In these initiations (*teletai*) and also the other services (*therapeiai*) concerning the gods they select proper animals and other things. Starting from these and suchlike, they came to know the daimonic powers, as their beings are closely connected to the energy (*energeia*) in nature and bodies, and through these things they bring themselves into association (*sunousia*) with them, and from them forthwith they retraced the very creations of the gods, on one hand learning some things from them, but for others they were moved by [the gods] themselves toward accurate knowledge of proper symbols (*sumbola*). In this way finally, leaving nature and natural energies below, they received revelations from the primary and divine powers.

Bibliography

Copenhaver, Brian. "Hermes Trismegistus, Proclus, and the Question of a Philosophy of Magic in the Renaissance," in *Hermeticism and the Renaissance: Intellectual History and the Occult in Early Modern Europe*, edited by Ingrid Merkel and Allen G. Debus. Folger Books, 1988.

Liddell, Henry George, Robert Scott, Henry Stuart Jones, and Roderick McKenzie. *A Greek-English Lexicon*. Clarendon Press, 1968.

MacLennan, Bruce J. *The Wisdom of Hypatia: Ancient Spiritual Practices for a More Meaningful Life*. Llewellyn Publications, 2013.

Pachoumi, Eleni. *Proclus' On the Hieratic Art According to the Greeks: Critical Edition with Translation and Commentary*. Brill, 2024.

Pliny. *The Natural History of Pliny*. Vol. 6. Translated by John Bostock and H. T. Riley. Taylor and Francis, 1857.

Proclus. *De sacrificio et magia*, in *Catalogue des Manuscrits Alchimiques Grecs*. Vol. 6. Edited by J. Bidez, F. Cumont, A. Delatte, O. Lagercrantz, and J. Ruska. Lamertin, 1928.

APPENDIX B:
PROCLUS'S HYMN IV: COMMON HYMN FOR THE GODS
ORIGINAL TRANSLATION AND FOOTNOTES BY JOHN OPSOPAUS, PhD

Hear, gods! who hold the helms of holy wisdom, who
lit anagogic fire, and to th' immortals draw
the souls of mortals,[289] which departed dismal vaults[290]
and purified themselves by secret rites and hymns.
Hear, great saviors, grant to me the holy light
from very sacred[291] books, dispersing mist so that
I might know well the deathless god and mortal man,[292]
that daimons doing deadly things not always hold
me under Lêthê's streams apart from blessed ones,
and that my soul, which fell in icy waves of birth,

---

289. The word used by Proclus, μέροψ, refers to an articulate being (i.e., a human), but might also refer to our "divided life" (Van den Berg, *Proclus' Hymns*, 210).
290. κευθμῶνα: a vault or hole, especially in Tartaros (Van den Berg, *Proclus' Hymns*, 231).
291. ζαθέων: very sacred or divine; etymologically: filled with gods (Van den Berg, *Proclus' Hymns*, 234), hence perhaps even ensouled by a god.
292. This is a slight paraphrase of the *Iliad* 5.127–28, where Athena disperses the mist from Diomedes's eyes so he can discriminate gods from humans.

my soul, which does not wish to wander much too long,
some chilly Penalty[293] not bind with chains of life.
But gods, ye leaders of enlightening wisdom, hear!
for those who hasten to the lofty path, bring ye
to light the orgies[294] and the rites of holy myths.

Bibliography

van den Berg, R. M. *Proclus' Hymns: Essays, Translations, Commentary*. Brill, 2001.

---

293. Ποινή (Poinê): penalty, price paid, recompense, redemption, personified as goddess of vengeance.
294. ὄργια (*orgia*): secret rites or worship.

APPENDIX C:
THE HERMETIC THEURGIC CREED
JEAN-LOUIS DE BIASI

This text was created from chapter five of the *Book of Laws* written by Gemistos Plethon. It is used in the Aurum Solis. As explained in the introduction, it can help to understand the beliefs shared by most of the theurgists.

1. I believe that the goddesses and the gods really exist.
2. I believe that, by their providence, the goddesses and the gods sustain and guide human destiny for the good. They accomplish this directly, by themselves, or through the divinities of the lower planes, but always in accordance with the divine laws.
3. I believe that the goddesses and the gods are never the origin of any evil, neither for us, nor for any being. On the contrary, they are, by their essence, the origin of every good.
4. I believe that the goddesses and gods act to bring about the best possible result, according to the laws of an immutable fate, which is inflexible and emanates from the Supreme Divine Principle.
5. I believe that the Universe is eternal. It did not begin at some point in the past, and it will never end. It is composed of many parts that are organized together and harmonized into a unique whole. It was created to be the most perfect it can be, and there is nothing

to add that would make it more perfect. It always remains steadily the same—in its original state—and it continues to be eternally immutable.

6. I believe that my soul shares the same essence as the divinities; it is immortal and eternal. The immortal divinities direct the soul, sometimes in one body, sometimes in another, according to the laws of universal harmony and from the perspective of what is needed for that being to ascend to the Divine. This union between the mortal and the immortal contributes to the unity of everything.
7. I believe that, in order to be in harmony with our divine nature, we must consider beauty and goodness to be the most essential aspects of what exists and the highest aspirations of our lives.
8. I believe that, in determining the laws that govern our existence, the immortal divinities have put our happiness into the immortal part of our being, which is also the most important part of us.

Bibliography

Plethon, Gemistos. *Plethon's Book of Laws*. Brill, 2001.

BIBLIOGRAPHIES BY CHAPTER

John Opsopaus, PhD

Addey, Crystal. *Divination and Theurgy in Neoplatonism: Oracles of the Gods.* Ashgate, 2014.

Akçay, K. Nilüfer. *Porphyry's On the Cave of the Nymphs in its Intellectual Context.* Studies in Platonism, Neoplatonism, and the Platonic Tradition. Vol. 23. Brill, 2019.

Athanassakis, Apostolos N., and Benjamin M. Wolkow, trans. *The Orphic Hymns.* Johns Hopkins, 2013.

Betz, Hans Dieter, ed. *The Greek Magical Papyri in Translation, Including the Demotic Spells.* Volume 1: The Texts. 2nd ed. University of Chicago Press, 1992.

Clarke, Emma C. John M. Dillon, and Jackson P. Hershbell, trans. *Iamblichus: On the Mysteries.* Edited by Johan C. Thom. Writings of the Greco-Roman World, no. 4. Society of Biblical Literature, 2003.

Ficino, Marsilio. *Three Books on Life: A Critical Edition and Translation with Introduction and Notes.* Edited and translated by Carol V. Kaske and John R. Clark. Renaissance Society of America, 1989.

Graf, Fritz. "Prayer in Magical and Religious Ritual." In *Magika Hiera: Ancient Greek Magic and Religion*, edited by Christopher A. Faraone and Dirk Obbink. Oxford University Press, 1991.

Hannah, Barbara. *Encounters with the Soul: Active Imagination as Developed by C. G. Jung.* Sigo Press, 1981.

Johnson, Robert A. *Inner Work: Using Dreams and Active Imagination for Personal Growth.* Harper & Row, 1986.

Jung, C. G. *The Black Books 1913–1932: Notebooks of Transformation.* 7 vols. Philemon Series. Edited by Sonu Shamdasani. Translated by Martin Liebscher, John Peck, and Sonu Shamdasani. W. W. Norton, 2020.

Jung, C. G. *Jung on Active Imagination.* Edited and with an introduction by Joan Chodorow. Princeton University Press, 1997.

Jung, C. G. *Memories, Dreams, Reflections.* Rev. ed. Recorded and edited by Aniela Jaffé. Translated by Richard Winston and Clara Winston. Random House, 1963.

Jung, C. G. *The Red Book: Liber Novus.* Philemon Series. Edited and with an introduction by Sonu Shamdasani. Translated by Mark Kyburz, John Peck, and Sonu Shamdasani. W. W. Norton, 2009.

Jung, C. G. *The Red Book: Liber Novus. A Reader's Edition.* Philemon Series. Edited and with an introduction by Sonu Shamdasani. Translated by Mark Kyburz, John Peck, and Sonu Shamdasani. W. W. Norton, 2012.

Lewy, Hans. *Chaldaean Oracles and Theurgy: Mysticism, Magic and Plantonism in the Later Roman Empire.* Nouvelle édition per Michel Tardieu. Études Augustiniennes, 1978.

MacLennan, Bruce J. *The Wisdom of Hypatia.* Llewellyn Publications, 2013.

Majercik, Ruth, trans. *The Chaldean Oracles: Text, Translation, and Commentary.* Brill, 1989.

Opsopaus, John. *Cebes' Path to Enlightenment: A Translation of the Tablet of Cebes with an Extensive Commentary on its Meaning, with Color Illustrations.* Pythagorean Pentagram Press, 2023.

Opsopaus, John. *Pythagorean Theology and the Esoteric Elements.* Pythagorean Pentagram Press, 2023.

Opsopaus, John. *The Secret Texts of Hellenic Polytheism: A Practical Guide to the Restored Pagan Religion of George Gemistos Plethon.* Llewellyn Publications, 2022.

Plethon, Georgios Gemistos. *Plethon's Laws and Other Works (Translated)*. Translated by John Opsopaus. Pythagorean Pentagram Pr., 2023.

Plutarch. "The Obsolescence of Oracles." In *Moralia: Volume V: Isis and Osiris. The E at Delphi. The Oracles at Delphi No Longer Given in Verse. The Obsolescence of Oracles*. Translated by Frank Cole Babbitt. Loeb Classical Library 306. Harvard University Press, 1936.

Porphyry. *On the Cave of the Nymphs*. Translated by Robert D. Lamberton. Station Hill Press, 1983.

Porphyry. *On the Cave of the Nymphs*. Translated by Thomas Taylor. Phanes Press, 1991.

Proclus. *Procli Diadochi in Platonis Cratylum commentaria*. Edited by Giorgio Pasquali. In aedibus B. G. Teubneri, 1908.

Proclus. *Procli Diadochi in Platonis Timaeum commentaria*. Edited by Ernestus Diehl. 3 vols. In aedibus B. G. Teubneri, 1903–1906.

Shaw, Gregory. *Hellenic Tantra: The Theurgic Platonism of Iamblichus*. Angelico Press, 2024.

Shaw, Gregory. *Theurgy and the Soul: The Neoplatonism of Iamblichus*. Pennsylvania State University Press, 1995.

Siniossoglou, Niketas. *Radical Platonism in Byzantium: Illumination and Utopia in Gemistos Plethon*. Cambridge University Press, 2011.

van den Berg, R. M. *Proclus' Hymns: Essays, Translations, Commentary*. Brill, 2001.

Hercules Invictus

Herodotus. *The Histories*. Everyman's Library. Translated by George Rawlinson. Introduced by Hugh Bowden. J. M. Dent/Tuttle, 1992.

Brandy Williams

Benavidez, Cordelia. *Victor Anderson: An American Shaman*. Immanion Press, 2017.

Betz, Hans Dieter, ed. *The Greek Magical Papyri in Translation, Including the Demotic Spells*. Vol. 1, The Texts. 2nd ed. University of Chicago Press, 1992.

Butler, Alison. *Victorian Occultism and the Making of Modern Magic: Invoking Tradition*. Palgrave Macmillan, 2011.

Cicero, Chic, and Sandra Tabatha Cicero. *The Essential Golden Dawn: An Introduction to High Magic*. Llewellyn Publications, 2003. Kindle.

Cicero, Chic, and Sandra Tabatha Cicero. *Golden Dawn Magic: A Complete Guide to the High Magical Arts*. Llewellyn Publications, 2019. Kindle.

Clarke, Emma C. John M. Dillon, and Jackson P. Hershbell, trans. *Iamblichus: On the Mysteries*. Edited by Johan C. Thom. Writings of the Greco-Roman World, no. 4. Society of Biblical Literature, 2003.

Crowley, Aleister. *Liber AL vel Legis*. O. T. O. U.S.A. Library. Accessed May 2, 2025. lib.oto-usa.org/libri/liber0220.html.

Crowley, Aleister. "Liber Astarte vel Berylli." *The Equinox* 1, no. 7 (1912): 39–58.

Crowley, Aleister. "Liber CXCIV, O.T.O., An Intimation with Reference to the Constitution of the Order." Accessed June 8, 2025. lib.oto-usa.org/libri/liber0194.html.

Crowley, Aleister. "Liber DCCXI, Energized Enthusiasm, A Note on Theurgy," *The Equinox* 1, no. 9 (1913), 17–46.

Crowley, Aleister. "Liber O Vel Manus et Sagittae." *The Equinox* 1, no. 2 (1909) 13–30.

Crowley, Aleister. "Liber XV: O. T. O. Ecclesiae Gnosticae Catholicae Canon Missae." O. T. O. U.S.A. Library. Accessed May 2, 2025. lib.oto-usa.org/libri/liber0015.html.

d'Este, Sorita, and David Rankine. *Wicca: Magickal Beginnings*. Avalonia, 2008.

Dominguez, Ivo, Jr. *Spirit Speak: Knowing and Understanding Spirit Guides, Ancestors, Ghosts, Angels, and the Divine*. New Page Books, 2008.

Dunn, Patrick. *The Orphic Hymns: A New Translation for the Occult Practitioner*. Llewellyn Publications, 2018.

DuQuette, Lon Milo. *Best of the Equinox: Sex Magick*. Vol. 3. Weiser Books, 2013.

Faerywolf, Storm. *Betwixt & Between: Exploring the Faery Tradition of Witchcraft*. Llewellyn Publications, 2017.

Faerywolf, Storm. *Forbidden Mysteries of Faery Witchcraft*. Llewellyn Publications, 2018.

Farrar, Janet, and Gavin Bone. *The Inner Mysteries: Progressive Witchcraft and the Connection with the Divine*. 2nd ed. Acorn Guild Press, 2012.

Farrar, Janet, and Gavin Bone. *Lifting the Veil: A Witches' Guide to Trance-Prophesy, Drawing Down the Moon, and Ecstatic Ritual*. Acorn Guild Press, 2016. Ebook.

Farrar, Janet, and Stewart Farrar. *Eight Sabbats for Witches*. Phoenix Publishing, 1981.

Farrar, Janet, and Stewart Farrar. *A Witches' Bible, The Complete Witches' Handbook, Part 2, Principles, Rituals and Beliefs of Modern Witchcraft*. Phoenix Publishing, 1984.

Farrar, Stewart. *What Witches Do: A Modern Coven Revealed*. Phoenix Publishing, 1983.

Filan, Kenaz, and Raven Kaldera. *Drawing Down the Spirits: The Traditions and Techniques of Spirit Possession*. Destiny Books, 2009.

Frew, Don. "Gardnerian Wica as Theurgic Ascent." Theurgicon. August 28, 2010. theurgicon.com/gardnerian.pdf.

Goodwin, Charles Wycliffe, ed. and trans. *Fragment of a Graeco-Egyptian Work Upon Magic From a Papyrus in the British Museum*. Deighton; Macmillan, 1852.

Heselton, Phillip. *Gerald Gardner and the Cauldron of Inspiration: An Investigation into the Sources of Gardnerian Witchcraft*. Capall Bann Publishing, 2003.

Howard, Michael. *Modern Wicca: A History from Gerald Gardner to the Present*. Llewellyn Publications, 2009.

Kaczynski, Richard. *Perdurabo: The Life of Aleister Crowley*. New Falcon Publications, 2002.

Lady Sheba. *The Book of Shadows*. Llewellyn Publications, 1971.

Lees, Frederic. "Isis Worship in Paris: Conversations with the Hierophant Rameses and the High Priestess Anari." *The Humanitarian* 16, no. 2 (1900), 82–87. https://www.golden-dawn.com/eu/displaycontent.aspx?pageid=143-isis-worship-in-paris. (Site discontinued.)

Majercik, Ruth, trans. *The Chaldean Oracles: Text, Translation, and Commentary*. Brill, 1989.

Mankey, Jason. "The Charge of the Goddess: A History." *Raise the Horns* (blog). Patheos. Updated April 7, 2015. https://www.patheos.com/blogs/panmankey/2015/04/the-charge-of-the-goddess-a-history/.

Mankey, Jason. *Transformative Witchcraft: The Greater Mysteries*. Llewellyn Publications, 2019.

Mierzwicki, Tony. *Graeco-Egyptian Magick: Everyday Empowerment*. Megalithica Books, 2006.

Opsopaus, John. "Practicing Theurgy in the Platonic Tradition." In *Theurgy: Seven Approaches to Divine Connection*. Edited by Jean-Louis de Biasi. Llewellyn Publications, 2025.

Opsopaus, John. "A Summary of Pythagorean Theology, Part V: Theurgy." Biblioteca Arcana. Updated January 26, 2010. wisdomofhypatia.com/OM/BA/ETP/V.html.

Owen, Alex. *The Place of Enchantment: British Occultism and the Culture of the Modern*. University of Chicago Press, 2004.

Paxson, Diana L. *The Essential Guide to Possession, Depossession & Divine Relationships*. Weiser Books, 2015.

Regardie, Israel. *The Golden Dawn: The Original Account of the Teachings, Rites and Ceremonies of the Hermetic Order*. 7th ed. Revised and corrected by John Michael Greer. Llewellyn Publications, 2016.

Regardie, Israel. *The Tree of Life: An Illustrated Study in Magic*. Edited and annotated by Chic Cicero and Sandra Tabatha Cicero. Llewellyn Publications, 2003.

Reidy, Richard. *Eternal Egypt: Ancient Rituals for the Modern World*. iUniverse, 2010.

Reidy, Richard. *Everlasting Egypt: Kemetic Rituals for the Gods*. iUniverse, 2018.

Reuss, Theodor, and Aleister Crowley. *O.T.O. Rituals and Sex Magick*. Edited by A. R. Naylor. I-H-O Books, 1999.

Shaw, Gregory. "Containing Ecstasy: The Strategies of Iamblichean Theory," *Dionysius* 21 (2003): 53–88.

Shaw, Gregory. "The Role of Aesthesis in Theurgy." In *Iamblichus and the Foundations of Late Platonism*, edited by Eugene Afonasin, John Dillon, and John F. Finamore. Brill, 2012.

Williams, Brandy. *For the Love of the Gods: The History and Modern Practice of Theurgy, Our Pagan Inheritance*. 2nd ed. Mnemosyne Press, 2022. Ebook.

Williams, Brandy. "Gnostic Priestess Prayer." Brandy Williams, May 24, 2014. brandywilliamsauthor.com/gnostic-priestess-prayer/.

Williams, Brandy. *The Woman Magician: Revisioning Western Metaphyiscs from a Woman's Perspective and Experience*. 2nd ed. Mnemosyne Press, 2022. Ebook.

Patrick Dunn

Aurelius, Marcus. *M. Antonius Imperator Ad Se Ipsum*. Edited by Jan Hendrick Leopold. Perseus Digital Library. https://www.perseus.tufts.edu/hopper/text?doc=Perseus%3Atext%3A2008.01.0641%3Abook%3D5%3Achapter%3D24%3Asection%3D1.

Copenhaver, Brian P., ed. *Hermetica: The Greek Corpus Hermeticum and the Latin Asclepius in a New English Translation, with Notes and Introduction*. Reprint ed. Cambridge University Press, 1995.

Plato. "Symposium." Translated by Benjamin Jowett. Accessed January 7, 2023. https://www.gutenberg.org/files/1600/1600-h/1600-h.htm.

Plotinus. *Plotinos Complete Works*. Vol. 2. Translated by Kenneth Sylvan Guthrie. Accessed January 7, 2023. https://www.gutenberg.org/files/42931/42931-h/42931-h.htm#iii_8.

Jean-Louis de Biasi

Copenhaver, Brian P., ed. "To Asclepius." In *Hermetica: The Greek Corpus Hermeticum and the Latin Asclepius in a New English Translation, with Notes and Introduction*. Reprint ed. Cambridge University Press, 1995.

de Biasi, Jean-Louis, and Patricia Bourin. *Mysteries of the Aura: How to See, Interpret & Work with Subtle Energies*. Llewellyn Publications, 2023.

Escrivá, Josemaría. *The Way*. Four Courts Press, 1985.

van den Berg, R. M. *Proclus' Hymns: Essays, Translations, Commentary*. Brill, 2001.

Clio Ajana

Afonasin, Eugene, John M. Dillon, and John F. Finamore, eds. *Iamblichus and the Foundations of Late Platonism*. Brill, 2012.

Avery, Kevin Quinn. *The Numbers of Life*. Freeway Press, 1974.

Cicero. *De Natura Deorum Academica*. Translated by Harris Rackham. Edited by E. H. Warmington. Vol. 19 of *Cicero in Twenty-Eight Volumes*. The Loeb Classical Library, Harvard University Press, 1967.

Denning, Melita, and Osborne Phillips. *Planetary Magick: Invoking and Directing the Powers of the Planets*. The Magical Philosophy, book 4. Llewellyn Publications, 2011.

Diogenes the Cynic. *Sayings and Anecdotes: With Other Popular Moralists*. Translated by Robin Hard. Oxford University Press, 2012.

Epicurus. "Principal Doctrines." Translated by Peter Saint-Andre. Monadnock Valley Press. Updated May 11, 2013. https://monadnock.net/epicurus/principal-doctrines.html.

Flowers, Stephen Edred, ed. *Hermetic Magic: The Postmodern Magical Papyrus of Abaris*. Samuel Weiser, 1995.

Guthrie, Kenneth Sylvan, compiler and trans. *The Pythagorean Sourcebook and Library: An Anthology of Ancient Writings Which Relate to Pythagoras and Pythagorean Philosophy*. Edited by Thomas Taylor, Arthur Fairbanks Jr., and David R. Fideler. Phanes Press, 1987.

Luft, Joseph, and Harrington Ingham. *The Johari Window, a Graphic Model of Interpersonal Awareness*. (Proceedings of the Western Training Laboratory in Group Development. University of California, Los Angeles, 1955), https://www.hee.nhs.uk/sites/default/files/documents/Johari%20window.pdf.

Majercik, Ruth, trans. *The Chaldean Oracles: Text, Translation, and Commentary*. Brill, 1989.

Sallustius. *Concerning the Gods and the Universe*. Edited and translated by Arthur Darby Nock. Cambridge University Press, 1926.

Shaw, Gregory. *Theurgy and the Soul: The Neoplatonism of Iamblichus*. 2nd ed. Angelico Press/Sophia Perennis, 2014.

Taylor, Thomas. "The Hymns of Orpheus." In *Thomas Taylor the Platonist: Selected Writings*. Edited by Kathleen Raine and George Mills Harper. Bollingen Series 88. Princeton University Press, 1969.

Waterfield, Robin, trans. *The First Philosophers: The Presocratics and Sophists*. Oxford University Press, 2000.

Wolfsdorf, David Conan, ed. *Early Greek Ethics*. Oxford University Press, 2020.

Tony Mierzwicki

Betz, Hans Dieter, ed. *The Greek Magical Papyri in Translation, Including the Demotic Spells*. Vol. 1, The Texts. 2nd ed. University of Chicago Press, 1992.

Boylan, Patrick. *Thoth: The Hermes of Egypt*. Ares Publishers, 1987.

Budge, E. A. Wallis. *The Gods of the Egyptians: Or Studies in Egyptian Mythology*. Vol. 1. Dover Publications, 1969.

Copenhaver, Brian P. *Hermetica: The Greek Corpus Hermeticum and the Latin Asclepius in a New English Translation, with Notes and Introduction*. Reprint ed. Cambridge University Press, 1995.

Crowley, Aleister. *Liber 777 Revised*. Celephaïs Press, 2004.

de Biasi, Jean-Louis. *Rediscover the Magick of the Gods and Goddesses: Revealing the Mysteries of Theurgy*. Llewellyn Publications, 2014.

de Biasi, Jean-Louis, and Patricia Bourin. *The Ultimate Pagan Almanac 2022: Northern Hemisphere*. Theurgia, 2021.

Dodds, E. R. *The Greeks and the Irrational*. University of California Press, 1951.

Eshelman, James A. *The Mystical & Magical System of the A∴A∴: The Spiritual System of Aleister Crowley & George Cecil Jones Step-by-Step*. The College of Thelema, 2000.

Eshelman, James A. *Pearls of Wisdom: Gems from the Journal Black Pearl*. The College of Thelema, 2013.

Fowden, Garth. *The Egyptian Hermes: A Historical Approach to the Late Pagan Mind*. Princeton University Press, 1993.

Freke, Timothy, and Peter Gandy. *The Hermetica: The Lost Wisdom of the Pharaohs*. Judy Piatkus, Ltd., 1998.

Godwin, David. *Godwin's Cabalistic Encyclopedia: Complete Guidance to Both Practical and Esoteric Applications*. Llewellyn Publications, 1997.

Hornung, Erik. *The Secret Lore of Egypt: Its Impact on the West*. Translated by David Lorton. Cornell University Press, 2001.

Janowitz, Naomi. *Magic in the Roman World: Pagans, Jews and Christians*. Routledge, 2001.

Kraig, Donald Michael. *Modern Magick: Twelve Lessons in the High Magickal Arts*. Llewellyn Publications, 2010.

Lesses, Rebecca Macy. *Ritual Practices to Gain Power: Angels, Incantations, and Revelation in Early Jewish Mysticism*. Trinity Press International, 1998.

Luck, Georg, trans. *Arcana Mundi: Magic and the Occult in the Greek and Roman Worlds*. The John Hopkins University Press, 1985.

Majercik, Ruth, trans. *The Chaldean Oracles: Text, Translation, and Commentary*. Brill, 1989.

Mead, G. R. S. *Thrice Greatest Hermes: Studies in Hellenistic Theosophy and Gnosis*. Kessinger Publishing Company, 2010.

Merkur, Dan. *Gnosis: An Esoteric Tradition of Mystical Visions and Unions*. State University of New York Press, 1993.

Mierzwicki, Tony. *Graeco-Egyptian Magick: Everyday Empowerment*. Megalithica Books, 2006.

Mierzwicki, Tony. *Hellenismos: Practicing Greek Polytheism Today*. Llewellyn Publications, 2018.

Nema. *Maat Magick: A Guide to Self-Initiation*. Weiser Books, 1995.

Pearson, Birger A., trans. *Marsanes, in The Nag Hammadi Library: The Definitive Translation of the Gnostic Scriptures Complete in One Volume*. Edited by James M. Robinson. Rev. ed. HarperCollins, 1990.

Regardie, Israel. *A Garden of Pomegranates: An Outline of the Qabalah*. Revised and enlarged. 2nd ed. Llewellyn Publications, 1985.

Robinson, James M., ed. *The Nag Hammadi Library*. Rev. ed. HarperCollins, 1990.

Shoemaker, David. *Living Thelema: A Practical Guide to Attainment in Aleister Crowley's System of Magick*. Weiser Books, 2022.

Shoemaker, David. *The Way of the Will: Thelema in Action*. Weiser Books, 2024.

Smith, Morton, trans. *Hekhalot Rabbati: The Greater Treatise Concerning the Palaces of Heaven*. Corrected Gershom Scholem. Transcribed and edited by Don Karr. Updated 2024. https://constable.blog/wp-content/uploads/HEKHALOT_RABBATI.pdf.

Stanley, Thomas, trans. *The Chaldaean Oracles: As Set Down by Julianus*. Heptangle Books, 1989.

Williams, Brandy. *For the Love of the Gods: The History and Modern Practice of Theurgy*. Llewellyn Publications, 2016.

Online Sources

"Ahamkara." Yogapedia. Updated December 21, 2023. https://www.yogapedia.com/definition/5235/ahamkara.

Clark, Rawn. "The 32 Paths of Wisdom." Hermetic Library. Accessed April 24, 2022. https://hermetic.com/jwmt/v1n3/32paths.

Kraig, Donald Michael. "Lesser Banishing Ritual of the Pentagram." Llewellyn, July 7, 2005. https://www.llewellyn.com/encyclopedia/article/5139.

Mcleod, Saul. "Maslow's Hierarchy Of Needs." Simply Psychology. Updated March 14, 2025. https://www.simplypsychology.org/maslow.html.

St. John of the Cross. "Dark Night of the Soul." Carmelite Monks. Accessed October 2022. http://carmelitemonks.org/Vocation/DarkNight-StJohnoftheCross.pdf.

"St. John of the Cross: Spanish Mystic." Britannica. Updated December 10, 2024. https://www.britannica.com/biography/Saint-John-of-the-Cross.

ABOUT THE AUTHORS
(IN ALPHABETICAL ORDER)

Clio Ajana

Clio Ajana is an Archieria of the Hellenic Alexandrian Witchcraft and Spiritual Tradition, a theurgic initiatory tradition in Minnesota. She also practices as a Balkan Heathen and a Greco-Buddhist. Her primary tradition embraces Greek, Roman, and Egyptian gods with an emphasis on welcoming all LGBTQIA2S+ since 1998. Her devotional areas include prison ministry, death midwifery, divination (numerology, astrology, and tarot), and exploration of Pagan voice as a minority within a minority. A monthly columnist for *The Wild Hunt*, her other contributions include the anthologies *Shades of Ritual: Minority Voices in Practice* and *Bringing Race to the Table: Exploring Racism in the Pagan Community*. A professional and religious educator, Ajana's writing often addresses the intersection of current events with aging, divination, death, menopause, and spirituality. She lives in Minnesota, where, in true theurgic fashion, she considers everything in her life to be touched and guided by the Gods. Facebook: Clio Ajana. Website: www.clioajana.com.

Jean-Louis de Biasi

Jean-Louis de Biasi is an author, lecturer, and philosopher. A published author in multiple languages, including English, he teaches philosophy, spirituality, ancient traditions, and various forms of yoga. A Freemason since 1990, he is currently a member of the United Grand Lodge of England (UGLE). Before joining Canadian and American Masonry, he was instrumental in reactivating and organizing Egyptian Freemasonry within the Grand Orient of France (GODF).

Specializing in ancient traditions and rituals from around the world, he has received all degrees of Egyptian, Scottish, and other high-degree Freemasonry. Additionally, he holds the 32 degrees of the American Scottish Rite (earned in Washington, D.C.) and the Royal Arch in Canada.

Jean-Louis is currently developing a heritage museum in the southwest of France that includes Masonic and Mithraic sections; you can explore at www.castillonnes.org. He can be found on Facebook.

Patrick Dunn

Patrick Dunn is the author of several books on magic and esoteric topics, including *The Practical Art of Divine Magic* and *The Orphic Hymns: A New Translation for the Occult Practitioner*. A poet, teacher, and writer, he lives near Chicago.

Hercules Invictus

Hercules Invictus is a Lemnian Greek, a proud descendant of Argonauts and Amazons. He is openly Olympian in his spirituality and worldview, dedicated to living the mythic life, and has been exploring the fringes of our reality throughout his entire earthly sojourn. For over five decades, he has been sharing his Olympian odyssey with others.

Having relocated the heart of his Temenos to Northeastern New Jersey and the greater New York metropolitan area, he has been establishing his unique niche locally and contributing to his community's overall quality of life in any way he can.

Hercules currently produces and hosts several podcasts, launched a YouTube channel, has written numerous articles, has published two e-books, and has contributed to over twenty published anthologies. He frequently conducts Olympian workshops and serves as a guest speaker on multiple platforms.

You can subscribe to Hercules Invictus on YouTube.

Tony Mierzwicki

Tony Mierzwicki is the author of *Hellenismos: Practicing Greek Polytheism Today* and *Graeco-Egyptian Magick: Everyday Empowerment*. He has contributed to various anthologies and has been featured extensively in print, online, and in broadcast media. Tony writes a regular blog for Patheos, *Holistic Spirituality*, which features musings on contemporary issues and book reviews. He also interviews many of the authors whose books he reviews on his podcast. Tony developed a fascination with ancient religions in the early 1980s, which led him to immerse himself in ceremonial magick in 1990. He has been running regular workshops and rituals re-creating ancient magickal and religious practices in the United States and on the east coast of Australia since 2001.

John Opsopaus, PhD

John Opsopaus, PhD, has been practicing Hellenismos (the worship of the Greek gods) since the 1980s. He has more than forty publications in various magical and Neopagan magazines and frequently presents workshops on Hellenic magic, Neopaganism, Pythagorean theurgy, and spiritual practices. He is the author of *The Oracles of Apollo: Practical Ancient Greek Divination for Today* (Llewellyn, 2017) and *The Secret Texts of Hellenic Polytheism: A Practical Guide to the Restored Pagan Religion of George Gemistos Plethon* (Llewellyn, 2022). He also designed the Pythagorean Tarot and wrote the comprehensive guidebook *Pythagorean Tarot* (2001, 2023). Recent books include his illustrated translation of *The Tablet of Cebes: With Illustrations Adapted from Hans Holbein the Younger*, *Cebes' Path to Enlightenment: A Translation of the Tablet of Cebes with an Extensive Commentary on Its Meaning with Color Illustrations*, *Pythagorean Theology and the Esoteric Elements*, *The Oracles of Homer and the Bones: Divination with the Ancient Homeromanteion and Astragalomanteion*, *Fruit from Wisdom's Tree: Divination with* the Wilkins Noemamanteia Through the Arts Gnostice, *The Orphic Holodemiurgia: A Contemplative Practice Drawn from the Orphic and Pythagorean Traditions*, and *Plethon's Laws and Other Works (Translated): a Bilingual Edition of Georgios Gemistos Plethon's Book of Laws and Other Works*. Opsopaus's award-winning Biblioteca Arcana website (http://opsopaus.com) has been a resource for Pagans and magicians for more than twenty-five years.

Brandy Williams

Brandy Williams is a Georgian Wicca high priestess, a Pagan magician, and a Tantric yogini. Her books include *Cord Magic: Tapping into the Power of String, Yearn, Twists & Knots*, *Practical Magic for Beginners: Techniques & Rituals to Focus Magical Energy*, *The Woman Magician: Revisioning Western Metaphysics from a Woman's Perspective and Experience*, and *For the Love of the Gods: The History and Modern Practice of Theurgy*. She teaches at magical conferences in person and online. She lives in Washington State surrounded by a living forest.

To Write to the Authors

If you wish to contact the authors or would like more information about this book, please write to the authors in care of Llewellyn Worldwide Ltd. and we will forward your request. The authors and the publisher appreciate hearing from you and learning of your enjoyment of this book and how it has helped you. Llewellyn Worldwide Ltd. cannot guarantee that every letter written to the authors can be answered, but all will be forwarded. Please write to:

Clio Ajana, Jean-Louis de Biasi, Patrick Dunn, Hercules Invictus,
Tony Mierzwicki, John Opsopaus, PhD, Brandy Williams
c/o Llewellyn Worldwide
2143 Wooddale Drive
Woodbury, MN 55125-2989

Please enclose a self-addressed stamped envelope for reply,
or $1.00 to cover costs. If outside the U.S.A., enclose
an international postal reply coupon.

Many of Llewellyn's authors have websites with additional information and resources. For more information, please visit our website at https://www.llewellyn.com.